BICENTENNIAL

1807

⊕WILEY

2007

BICENTENNIAL

THE WILEY BICENTENNIAL—KNOWLEDGE FOR GENERATIONS

$\mathcal{E}$ach generation has its unique needs and aspirations. When Charles Wiley first opened his small printing shop in lower Manhattan in 1807, it was a generation of boundless potential searching for an identity. And we were there, helping to define a new American literary tradition. Over half a century later, in the midst of the Second Industrial Revolution, it was a generation focused on building the future. Once again, we were there, supplying the critical scientific, technical, and engineering knowledge that helped frame the world. Throughout the 20th Century, and into the new millennium, nations began to reach out beyond their own borders and a new international community was born. Wiley was there, expanding its operations around the world to enable a global exchange of ideas, opinions, and know-how.

For 200 years, Wiley has been an integral part of each generation's journey, enabling the flow of information and understanding necessary to meet their needs and fulfill their aspirations. Today, bold new technologies are changing the way we live and learn. Wiley will be there, providing you the must-have knowledge you need to imagine new worlds, new possibilities, and new opportunities.

Generations come and go, but you can always count on Wiley to provide you the knowledge you need, when and where you need it!

WILLIAM J. PESCE
PRESIDENT AND CHIEF EXECUTIVE OFFICER

PETER BOOTH WILEY
CHAIRMAN OF THE BOARD

Microsoft Certified Application Specialist (MCAS)

Approved Courseware

■ What does this logo mean?

It means this courseware has been approved by the Microsoft® Certified Application Specialist program to be among the finest available for learning Microsoft® Office Word 2007, Microsoft® Office Excel 2007, Microsoft® Office PowerPoint 2007, Microsoft® Office Access 2007, or Microsoft® Office Outlook 2007. It also means that upon completion of this courseware, you may be prepared to take an exam for Microsoft Certified Application Specialist qualification.

■ What is a Microsoft Certified Application Specialist?

A Microsoft Certified Application Specialist is an individual who has passed exams for certifying his or her skills in one or more of the Microsoft Office desktop applications such as Microsoft Word, Microsoft Excel, Microsoft PowerPoint, Microsoft Outlook, or Microsoft Access. The Microsoft Certified Application Specialist program is the only program approved by Microsoft for testing proficiency in Microsoft Office desktop applications. This testing program can be a valuable asset in any job search or career development.

■ More Information

To learn more about becoming a Microsoft Certified Application Specialist and exam availability, visit www.microsoft.com/learning/msbc.

Microsoft, the Microsoft Office Logo, PowerPoint, and Outlook are trademarks or registered trademarks of Microsoft Corporation in the United States and/or other countries, and the Microsoft Certified Application Specialist logo is used under license from the owner.

Microsoft® Official Academic Course

Microsoft® Office Outlook® 2007

BICENTENNIAL
1807
WILEY
2007
BICENTENNIAL

Credits

EXECUTIVE EDITOR	John Kane
SENIOR EDITOR	Gary Schwartz
DIRECTOR OF MARKETING AND SALES	Mitchell Beaton
EDITORIAL ASSISTANT	Jennifer Lartz
DEVELOPMENT AND PRODUCTION	Custom Editorial Productions, Inc
PRODUCTION MANAGER	Kelly Tavares
CREATIVE DIRECTOR	Harry Nolan
COVER DESIGNER	Hope Miller
COVER PHOTO	Corbis
TECHNOLOGY AND MEDIA	Phyllis Bregman

Wiley 200th Anniversary logo designed by: Richard J. Pacifico

This book was set in Garamond by Aptara, Inc. and printed and bound by Bind Rite Graphics. The cover was also printed by Bite Rite Graphics.

ISBN-13 978-0-47006952-3 (U.S.)
ISBN-13 978-0-47016387-0 (International)

Printed in the United States of America

10 9 8 7 6 5

Foreword from the Publisher

Wiley's publishing vision for the Microsoft Official Academic Course series is to provide students and instructors with the skills and knowledge they need to use Microsoft technology effectively in all aspects of their personal and professional lives. Quality instruction is required to help both educators and students get the most from Microsoft's software tools and to become more productive. Thus our mission is to make our instructional programs trusted educational companions for life.

To accomplish this mission, Wiley and Microsoft have partnered to develop the highest quality educational programs for Information Workers, IT Professionals, and Developers. Materials created by this partnership carry the brand name "Microsoft Official Academic Course," assuring instructors and students alike that the content of these textbooks is fully endorsed by Microsoft, and that they provide the highest quality information and instruction on Microsoft products. The Microsoft Official Academic Course textbooks are "Official" in still one more way—they are the officially sanctioned courseware for Microsoft IT Academy members.

The Microsoft Official Academic Course series focuses on *workforce development*. These programs are aimed at those students seeking to enter the workforce, change jobs, or embark on new careers as information workers, IT professionals, and developers. Microsoft Official Academic Course programs address their needs by emphasizing authentic workplace scenarios with an abundance of projects, exercises, cases, and assessments.

The Microsoft Official Academic Courses are mapped to Microsoft's extensive research and job-task analysis, the same research and analysis used to create the Microsoft Certified Application Specialist (MCAS) and Microsoft Certified Application Professional (MCAP) exams. The textbooks focus on real skills for real jobs. As students work through the projects and exercises in the textbooks they enhance their level of knowledge and their ability to apply the latest Microsoft technology to everyday tasks. These students also gain resume-building credentials that can assist them in finding a job, keeping their current job, or in furthering their education.

The concept of life-long learning is today an utmost necessity. Job roles, and even whole job categories, are changing so quickly that none of us can stay competitive and productive without continuously updating our skills and capabilities. The Microsoft Official Academic Course offerings, and their focus on Microsoft certification exam preparation, provide a means for people to acquire and effectively update their skills and knowledge. Wiley supports students in this endeavor through the development and distribution of these courses as Microsoft's official academic publisher.

Today educational publishing requires attention to providing quality print and robust electronic content. By integrating Microsoft Official Academic Course products, *WileyPLUS*, and Microsoft certifications, we are better able to deliver efficient learning solutions for students and teachers alike.

Bonnie Lieberman
General Manager and Senior Vice President

Preface

Welcome to the Microsoft Official Academic Course (MOAC) program for the 2007 Microsoft Office system. MOAC represents the collaboration between Microsoft Learning and John Wiley & Sons, Inc. publishing company. Microsoft and Wiley teamed up to produce a series of textbooks that deliver compelling and innovative teaching solutions to instructors and superior learning experiences for students. Infused and informed by in-depth knowledge from the creators of Microsoft Office and Windows Vista™, and crafted by a publisher known worldwide for the pedagogical quality of its products, these textbooks maximize skills transfer in minimum time. With MOAC, students are hands on right away—there are no superfluous text passages to get in the way of learning and using the software. Students are challenged to reach their potential by using their new technical skills as highly productive members of the workforce.

Because this knowledgebase comes directly from Microsoft, architect of the 2007 Office system and creator of the Microsoft Certified Application Specialist (MCAS) exams, you are sure to receive the topical coverage that is most relevant to students' personal and professional success. Microsoft's direct participation not only assures you that MOAC textbook content is accurate and current; it also means that students will receive the best instruction possible to enable their success on certification exams and in the workplace.

■ The Microsoft Official Academic Course Program

The *Microsoft Official Academic Course* series is a complete program for instructors and institutions to prepare and deliver great courses on Microsoft software technologies. With MOAC, we recognize that, because of the rapid pace of change in the technology and curriculum developed by Microsoft, there is an ongoing set of needs beyond classroom instruction tools for an instructor to be ready to teach the course. The MOAC program endeavors to provide solutions for all these needs in a systematic manner in order to ensure a successful and rewarding course experience for both instructor and student—technical and curriculum training for instructor readiness with new software releases; the software itself for student use at home for building hands-on skills, assessment, and validation of skill development; and a great set of tools for delivering instruction in the classroom and lab. All are important to the smooth delivery of an interesting course on Microsoft software, and all are provided with the MOAC program. We think about the model below as a gauge for ensuring that we completely support you in your goal of teaching a great course. As you evaluate your instructional materials options, you may wish to use the model for comparison purposes with available products.

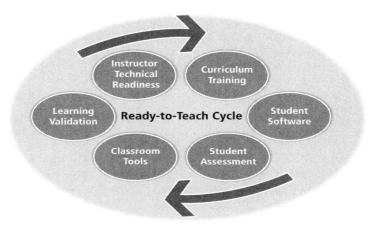

■ Organization

MOAC for 2007 Microsoft Office system is designed to cover all the learning objectives in the MCAS exams, referred to as "objective domains." The Microsoft Certified Application Specialist (MCAS) exam objectives are highlighted throughout the textbooks. Unique features of our task-based approach include a Lesson Skills Matrix that correlates skills taught in each lesson to the MCAS objectives; Certification, Workplace, and Internet Ready exercises; and three levels of increasingly rigorous lesson-ending activities: Competency, Proficiency, and Mastery Assessment.

Following is a list of key features in each lesson designed to prepare your students for success on these exams and in the workplace:

- Each lesson begins with a **Lesson Skill Matrix.** More than a standard list of learning objectives, the Skill Matrix correlates each software skill covered in the lesson to the specific MCAS "objective domain."
- Every lesson features a real-world **Business Case** scenario that places the software skills and knowledge to be acquired in a real-world setting.
- Every lesson opens with a **Software Orientation.** This feature provides an overview of the software features students will be working with in the lesson. The orientation includes a large, labeled screen image.
- Engaging point-of-use **Reading Aids** provide students with hints, introduce alternative methods for producing results, alert them to pitfalls, provide learning cross-references, and tell them the names of files found on the Student CD.
- **Certification Ready?** features throughout the text signal students where a specific certification objective is covered. It provides students with a chance to check their understanding of that particular MCAS objective and, if necessary, review the section of the lesson where it is covered. MOAC offers complete preparation for MCAS certification.
- Concise and frequent **Step-by-Step** instructions teach students new features and provide an opportunity for hands-on practice.
- **Circling Back.** These integrated projects provide students with an opportunity to review and practice skills learned in previous lessons.
- **Competency, Proficiency, and Mastery Assessment** provide three progressively more challenging lesson-ending activities.
- **Internet Ready.** Projects combine the knowledge students acquire in a lesson with a Web-based research task.
- **Workplace Ready.** These features preview how 2007 Microsoft Office system applications are used in real-world situations.

■ Pedagogical Features

Many pedagogical features have been developed specifically for *Microsoft Official Academic Course* programs. Presenting the extensive procedural information and technical concepts woven throughout the textbook raises challenges for the student and instructor alike. The Illustrated Book Tour that follows provides a guide to the rich features contributing to *Microsoft Official Academic Course* program's pedagogical plan.

Each book within the *Microsoft Official Academic Course* series features:

- **Lesson Skill Matrix:** The skill matrix lists the instructional goals for the lesson so that you know what skills you will be asked to master. The Matrix previews the lesson structure, helping you grasp key concepts and prepares you for learning software skills. These skills are also linked directly to the Microsoft Certified Application Specialist (MCAS) certification skill, when appropriate.

- **Key Terms:** Important technical vocabulary is listed at the beginning of the lesson. When these terms are used later in the lesson, they appear in bold italic type and are defined. The Glossary contains all of the key terms and their definitions.

- **Software Orientation:** This feature provides an overview of the software you will be using in the lesson. The orientation will detail the general properties of the software or specific features, such as a ribbon or dialog box.

- **The Bottom Line:** Each main topic within the lesson has a summary of why this topic is relevant.

- **Hands-on practice:** Numbered steps give detailed, step-by-step instructions to help you learn software skills. The steps also show results and screen images to match what you should see on your computer screen.

- **Student CD:** The companion CD contains the data files needed for each lesson. These files are indicated by the CD icon in the margin of the textbook.

- **Informational text for each topic:** Easy-to-read, technique-focused information can be found following each exercise.

- **Illustrations:** Screen images provide visual feedback as you work through the exercises. The images reinforce key concepts, provide visual clues about the steps, and allow you to check your progress.

- **Reader aids:** Helpful hints, such as *Take Note,* and alternate ways to accomplish tasks (*Another Way*) are located throughout the lessons. Reader aids provide additional relevant or background information that adds value to the lesson. Reader aids, such as *Troubleshooting,* also point out things to watch out for or things to avoid.

- **Button images:** When the text instructs you to click a particular toolbar button, an image of the button is shown in the margin.

- **Certification Ready?:** This feature signals the point in the text where a specific certification objective is covered. It provides you with a chance to check your understanding of that particular MCAS objective and, if necessary, review the section of the lesson where it is covered.

- **New Feature:** The New Feature icon appears in the margin next to any software feature that is new to Office 2007.

xii | **Illustrated Book Tour**

- **Workplace Ready:** These special features provide a glimpse of how the software application can be put into practice in a real-world situation.
- **Circling Back:** This feature provides you with an opportunity to review and practice skills learned in previous lessons.
- **Knowledge Assessment:** True/false, multiple choice, matching, or fill-in-the-blank questions test or reinforce your understanding of key lesson topics.
- **Competency Assessment:** These projects are similar to the exercises you completed within the lesson. Specific steps for completion are provided so that you can practice what you have learned.
- **Proficiency Assessment:** These projects give you additional opportunity to practice skills that you learned in the lesson. Not all the steps for completion are provided. Completing these exercises helps you verify whether you understand the lesson and reinforces your learning.
- **Mastery Assessment:** These projects require you to work independently—as you would in the workplace. Steps needed to complete the problems are not supplied. You must apply the knowledge you have acquired in the lesson to complete the problems successfully.
- **Internet Ready:** These projects combine what you have learned with research on the Internet.
- **Glossary:** Technical vocabulary is defined in the Glossary. Terms in the Glossary also appear in boldface italic type and are defined within the lessons.
- **Index:** All Glossary terms and application features appear in the Index.

www.wiley.com/college/microsoft *or call the* **MOAC Toll-Free Number: 1+(888) 764-7001 (North America only)**

■ Lesson Features

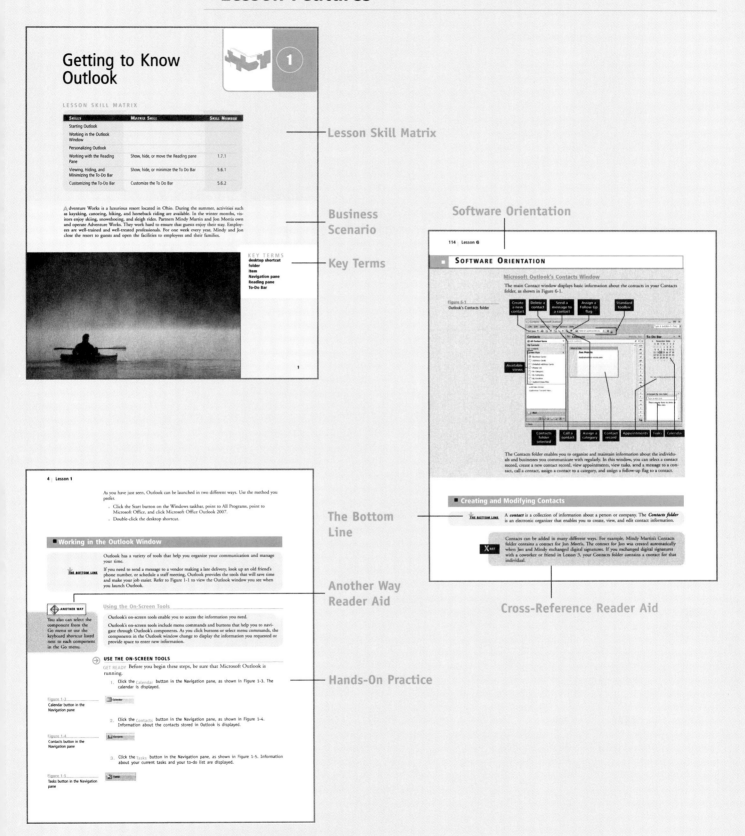

Lesson Skill Matrix

Business Scenario

Key Terms

Software Orientation

The Bottom Line

Another Way Reader Aid

Cross-Reference Reader Aid

Hands-On Practice

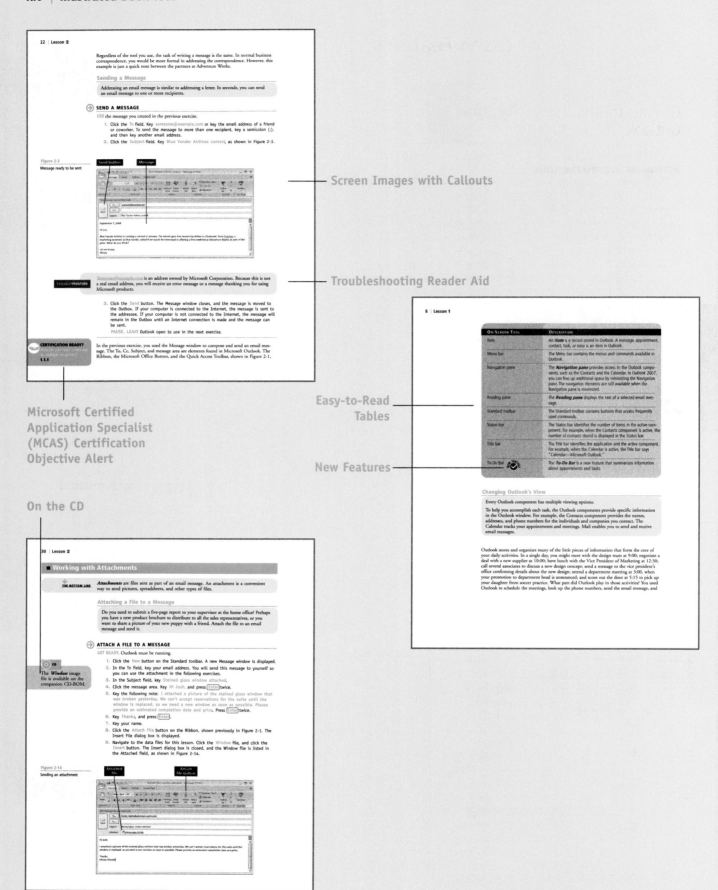

Screen Images with Callouts

Troubleshooting Reader Aid

Microsoft Certified
Application Specialist
(MCAS) Certification
Objective Alert

Easy-to-Read
Tables

New Features

On the CD

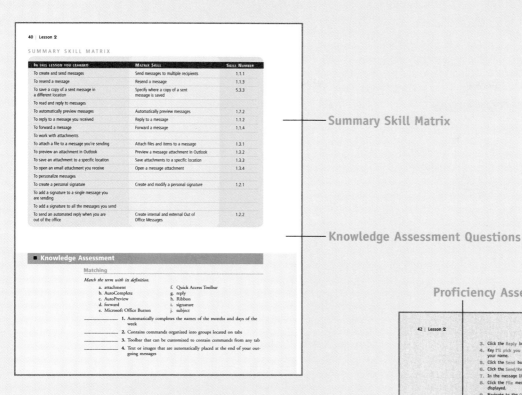

Summary Skill Matrix

40 | Lesson 2

SUMMARY SKILL MATRIX

IN THIS LESSON YOU LEARNED	MATRIX SKILL	SKILL NUMBER
To create and send messages	Send messages to multiple recipients	1.1.1
To resend a message	Resend a message	1.1.3
To save a copy of a sent message in a different location	Specify where a copy of a sent message is saved	5.3.3
To read and reply to messages		
To automatically preview messages	Automatically preview messages	1.7.2
To reply to a message you received	Reply to a message	1.1.2
To forward a message	Forward a message	1.1.4
To work with attachments		
To attach a file to a message you're sending	Attach files and items to a message	1.3.1
To preview an attachment in Outlook	Preview a message attachment in Outlook	1.3.2
To save an attachment to a specific location	Save attachments to a specific location	1.3.3
To open an email attachment you receive	Open a message attachment	1.3.4
To personalize messages		
To create a personal signature	Create and modify a personal signature	1.2.1
To add a signature to a single message you are sending		
To add a signature to all the messages you send		
To send an automated reply when you are out of the office	Create internal and external Out of Office Messages	1.2.2

Knowledge Assessment Questions

■ Knowledge Assessment

Matching

Match the term with its definition.

a. attachment   f. Quick Access Toolbar
b. AutoComplete   g. reply
c. AutoPreview   h. Ribbon
d. forward   i. signature
e. Microsoft Office Button   j. subject

_____ 1. Automatically completes the names of the months and days of the week

_____ 2. Contains commands organized into groups located on tabs

_____ 3. Toolbar that can be customized to contain commands from any tab

_____ 4. Text or images that are automatically placed at the end of your outgoing messages

Proficiency Assessment Projects

42 | Lesson 2

3. Click the Reply button on the Standard toolbar.v
4. Key I'll pick you up at 1:00 PM. Don't be late! Press Enter twice. Key your name.
5. Click the Send button.
6. Click the Send/Receive button on the Standard toolbar.
7. In the message list, click the reply message.
8. Click the File menu and select the Save As option. The Save As dialog box is displayed.
9. Navigate to the Outlook Solutions Lesson 02 folder. Click the Save button. The message is saved as RE Lunch tomorrow.htm.
LEAVE Outlook open for the next project.

■ Proficiency Assessment

Project 2-3: **Send an Attachment**

The last guest in the best suite at Adventure Works accidently broke the stained glass window in the suite. You must replace the window before you can accept any reservations for the suite.

TROUBLESHOOTING The email addresses provided in these projects belong to unused domains owned by Microsoft. When you send a message to these addresses, you will receive an error message stating that the message could not be delivered. Delete the error messages when they arrive.

CD
The *Window* image file is available on the companion CD-ROM.

1. Create a new email message to Nancy Anderson at the Graphic Design Institute. Nancy's email address is Nancy@graphicdesigninstitute.com. Ask Nancy if she can design a window similar to the stained glass window that was broken. Ask Nancy how long the project will take and how much it will cost.
2. Attach the *Window.jpg* file located in the data files for this lesson.
3. Send the message.
LEAVE Outlook open for the next project.

Project 2-4: **Resend a Message**

Complete Project 2-3 before starting this project.

1. You need more than one estimate, but you don't want to key all the information again. In the Sent Items folder, open the message you sent in Project 2-3.
2. Use the Resend function to create a new message.
3. Change the message so it can be sent to Michael Entin at the School of Fine Art. His email address is Michael@fineartschool.net.
4. Send the message.
LEAVE Outlook open for the next project.

■ Mastery Assessment

Project 2-5: **Send a Message Using Stationery**

You work for the Adventure Works resort. Mindy Martin, one of the owners, asked you to select stationery to be used when messages are sent to guests from resort employees.

Competency Assessment Projects

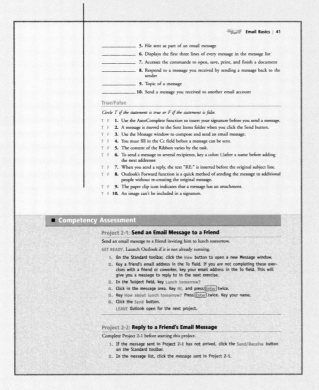

Email Basics | 41

_____ 5. File sent as part of an email message

_____ 6. Displays the first three lines of every message in the message list

_____ 7. Accesses the commands to open, save, print, and finish a document

_____ 8. Respond to a message you received by sending a message back to the sender

_____ 9. Topic of a message

_____ 10. Send a message you received to another email account

True/False

Circle T if the statement is true or F if the statement is false.

T F 1. Use the AutoComplete function to insert your signature before you send a message.
T F 2. A message is moved to the Sent Items folder when you click the Send button.
T F 3. Use the Message window to compose and send an email message.
T F 4. You must fill in the Cc field before a message can be sent.
T F 5. The content of the Ribbon varies by the task.
T F 6. To send a message to several recipients, key a colon (:) after a name before adding the next addressee
T F 7. When you send a reply, the text "RE:" is inserted before the original subject line.
T F 8. Outlook's Forward function is a quick method of sending the message to additional people without re-creating the original message.
T F 9. The paper clip icon indicates that a message has an attachment.
T F 10. An image can't be included in a signature.

■ Competency Assessment

Project 2-1: **Send an Email Message to a Friend**

Send an email message to a friend inviting him to lunch tomorrow.

GET READY. Launch Outlook if it is not already running.

1. On the Standard toolbar, click the New button to open a new Message window.
2. Key a friend's email address in the To field. If you are not completing these exercises with a friend or coworker, key your email address in the To field. This will give you a message to reply to in the next exercise.
3. In the Subject field, key Lunch tomorrow?
4. Click in the message area. Key Hi, and press Enter twice.
5. Key How about lunch tomorrow? Press Enter twice. Key your name.
6. Click the Send button.
LEAVE Outlook open for the next project.

Project 2-2: **Reply to a Friend's Email Message**

Complete Project 2-1 before starting this project.

1. If the message sent in Project 2-1 has not arrived, click the Send/Receive button on the Standard toolbar.
2. In the message list, click the message sent in Project 2-1.

154 | Lesson 7

7. Create a new message. In the To field, key your email address. In the Subject field, key 007. In the message body, key Testing Search Folder. Click the Send button.
8. Click the Send/Receive button if the 007 message has not arrived. After the message arrives, click the Project 007 folder to view its content. It should contain the 007 message in the Sent Items folder and the 007 message in the Inbox.
LEAVE Outlook open for the next project.

■ Mastery Assessment ———————————— Mastery Assessment Projects

Project 7-5: Create a Secondary Address Book

Diane works for a new company, but she wants to stay in touch with friends she made at Wingtip Toys. Diane decided to create a secondary address book before she imports personal contacts for her friends.

1. If necessary, click the Folder List button in the Navigation pane to display the Folder List.
2. Click the Contacts folder in the Folder List.
3. Click the New arrow to display the dropdown menu and click Folder. The Create New Folder window is displayed.
4. In the Name field, key Diane's Contacts. Because you selected the Contacts folder before creating a new folder, Contact Items is already displayed in the *Folder contains* field and the Contacts folder is selected in the *Select where to place the folder* list. Click OK. The Diane's Contacts folder is created in the Contacts folder.
LEAVE Outlook open for the next project.

Project 7-6: Import a Secondary Address Book from a File

After creating the Diane's Contacts folder, Diane can import contact records for her friends at Wingtip Toys.

1. Click the Diane's Contacts folder in the Folder List, if necessary.
2. Click the File menu and then click the Import and Export option to display the Import and Export Wizard.
3. Click Import from another program or file in the list of available actions. Click the Next button.
4. Click Microsoft Excel 97-2003 in the list of available import file types. Click the Next button.
5. Click the Browse button. Navigate to the data files for this lesson and click the Source Diane's Contacts file. Click OK to close the Browse window and return to the Import a File window. Click the Next button.
6. Verify that Diane's Contacts is selected as the destination folder. Click the Next button.
7. Click the Finish button. The contacts are imported and displayed in the Diane's Contacts folder.
CLOSE Outlook.

The *Source Diane's Contacts* file is available on the companion CD-ROM.

INTERNET READY ———————————— Internet Ready Project

Microsoft provides templates for a wide variety of electronic business cards. Sophisticated, casual, fun, and serious designs are available. Go to www.Microsoft.com. Search for electronic business cards. Download a style that appeals to you. Modify the card and use it as your electronic business card.

Workplace Ready ————

Managing Tasks | 245

★ Workplace Ready

Break It Down

Earning a degree, managing a project, and training new workers seem like unrelated activities. What do they have in common? All three activities are complicated processes that seem daunting when you look at the whole. However, each activity is made up of smaller steps. Enroll in a series of specific classes to earn a degree. Perform specific actions when you manage a project. Teach workers to follow specific steps.

Break down a large goal into smaller tasks that you can perform yourself or assign to others for completion. Start with the ultimate goal. Break it down into a list of steps to be completed. Convert the steps into tasks. Match the tasks with the people available to perform the tasks.

When you assign tasks to other people, make sure that the task owner has all the tools needed to complete the task. The task owner needs the ability and authority to perform the task. Ability includes skill and equipment. Authority ensures that the task owner can obtain any necessary information or assistance from other workers.

When you create tasks, remember these important tips.

- Break down large jobs into manageable tasks.
- Match tasks to people.
- Ensure that the task owner has the ability and authority to succeed.

Circling Back Exercises ————

156 | Circling Back

↻ Circling Back

Kim Ralls was promoted to Shift Supervisor and transferred to the downtown office at City Power & Light. Although Kim was transferred, her computer and other equipment did not move with her. She needs to set up Outlook 2007 with new rules and contacts to help her manage her new responsibilities. She also needs to update her electronic business card to display her new title and contact information.

➔ Project 1: Create Mail and Contacts Folders

Kim starts the process of customizing Outlook 2007 to meet her needs by creating new folders. One mail folder will contain messages about requests for new service. Another folder will contain contact information for the CP&L service technicians responsible for establishing service at new homes and businesses.

GET READY. Launch Outlook if it is not already running.

1. Click the Folder List button in the bottom of the Navigation pane to display the Folder List.
2. Click the arrow next to New in the standard toolbar. Click Folder. The Create New Folder dialog box is displayed.
3. In the Name field, key New Service to identify the new folder. Verify that Mail and Post Items is selected in the *Folder contains* field. If necessary, click Personal Folders in the *Select where to place the folder* list. Click OK to create the folder.
4. Click the arrow next to New in the standard toolbar. Click Folder. The Create New Folder dialog box is displayed.
5. In the Name field, key New Service Techs to identify the new folder. Select Contact Items in the *Folder contains* field. If necessary, click Contacts in the *Select where to place the folder* list. Click OK to create the folder.
LEAVE Outlook open for the next project.

➔ Project 2: Create a Rule

Kim receives messages requesting new service from the Customer Service department. Messages could come from a dozen different Customer Service representatives. However, the Subject field for every message contains the words "New Service Request." Kim decided to create a rule moving all of the requests to the New Service folder.

USE the New Service folder created in the previous project. Your computer must be connected to the Internet to test the rule at the end of this project.

1. If necessary, click the Mail button in the Navigation pane to display the Mail folder.
2. Click the Tools menu, and click the Rules and Alerts option. The Rules and Alerts window is displayed. Turn off all rules except the *Clear categories on mail* rule.
3. Click the New Rule button. The Rules Wizard window is displayed.
4. In the *Stay Organized* category, click Move messages with specific words in the subject to a folder.
5. In the *Step 2* area, click specific words. The Search Text window is displayed.
6. In the *Specify words or phrases to search for in the subject* field, key New Service Request. Click the Add button. Click OK to close the Search Text window. The Rules Wizard window is displayed.
7. In the *Step 2* area of the Rules Wizard window, click specified to identify the destination folder. The Folder List is displayed in the Rules and Alerts window.

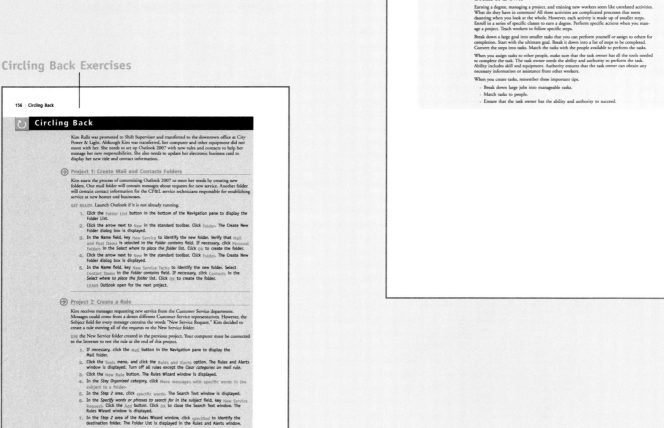

Conventions and Features Used in This Book

This book uses particular fonts, symbols, and heading conventions to highlight important information or to call your attention to special steps. For more information about the features in each lesson, refer to the Illustrated Book Tour section.

CONVENTION	MEANING
NEW FEATURE	This icon indicates a new or greatly improved Office 2007 feature in this version of the software.
THE BOTTOM LINE	This feature provides a brief summary of the material to be covered in the section that follows.
CLOSE	Words in all capital letters and in a different font color than the rest of the text indicate instructions for opening, saving, or closing files or programs. They also point out items you should check or actions you should take.
CERTIFICATION READY?	This feature signals the point in the text where a specific certification objective is covered. It provides you with a chance to check your understanding of that particular MCAS objective and, if necessary, review the section of the lesson where it is covered.
CD	This indicates a file that is available on the student CD.
TAKE NOTE *	Reader aids appear in shaded boxes found in your text. *Take Note* provides helpful hints related to particular tasks or topics.
ANOTHER WAY	*Another Way* provides an alternative procedure for accomplishing a particular task.
TROUBLESHOOTING	*Troubleshooting* covers common problems and pitfalls.
X REF	These notes provide pointers to information discussed elsewhere in the textbook or describe interesting features of Office 2007 that are not directly addressed in the current topic or exercise.
SAVE	When a toolbar button is referenced in an exercise, the button's picture is shown in the margin.
Alt + Tab	A plus sign (+) between two key names means that you must press both keys at the same time. Keys that you are instructed to press in an exercise will appear in the font shown here.
A *cell* is the area where data is entered.	Key terms appear in bold italic.
Key My Name is.	Any text you are asked to key appears in color.
Click OK.	Any button on the screen you are supposed to click on or select will also appear in color.
OPEN *FitnessClasses*.	The names of data files will appear in bold, italic, and color for easy identification.

Instructor Support Program

The *Microsoft Official Academic Course* programs are accompanied by a rich array of resources that incorporate the extensive textbook visuals to form a pedagogically cohesive package. These resources provide all the materials instructors need to deploy and deliver their courses. Resources available online for download include:

- **6-Month Office 2007 Trial Edition (available in North America only).** Students receive 6-months' access to Microsoft Office Professional 2007 when you adopt a MOAC 2007 Microsoft Office system textbook. The textbook includes the trial CD and a product key that allows students to activate the CD for a 6-month period.

- The **Instructor's Guide** contains Solutions to all the textbook exercises, Syllabi for various term lengths, Data Files for all the documents students need to work the exercises. The Instructor's Guide also includes chapter summaries and lecture notes. The Instructor's Guide is available from the Book Companion site (http://www.wiley.com/college/microsoft) and from *WileyPLUS*.

- The **Test Bank** contains hundreds of multiple-choice, true-false, and short answer questions and is available to download from the Instructor's Book Companion site (http://www.wiley.com/college/microsoft) and from *WileyPLUS*. A complete answer key is provided. It is available as a computerized test bank and in Microsoft Word format. The easy-to-use test-generation program fully supports graphics, print tests, student answer sheets, and answer keys. The software's advanced features allow you to create an exam to meet your exact specifications. The computerized test bank provides:

  - Varied question types to test a variety of comprehension levels—multiple-choice, true-false, and short answer.

  - Allows instructors to edit, randomize, and create questions freely.

  - Allows instructors to create and print different versions of a quiz or exam.

- **PowerPoint Presentations and Images.** A complete set of PowerPoint presentations is available on the Instructor's Book Companion site (http://www.wiley.com/college/microsoft) and in *WileyPLUS* to enhance classroom presentations. Approximately 50 PowerPoint slides are provided for each lesson. Tailored to the text's topical coverage and Skills Matrix, these presentations are designed to convey key Office 2007 concepts addressed in the text.

  All figures from the text are on the Instructor's Book Companion site (http://www.wiley.com/college/microsoft) and in *WileyPLUS*. You can incorporate them into your PowerPoint presentations, or create your own overhead transparencies and handouts.

  By using these visuals in class discussions, you can help focus students' attention on key elements of Office 2007 and help them understand how to use it effectively in the workplace.

- **Microsoft Business Certification Pre-Test and Exams**. With each MOAC textbook, students receive information allowing them to access a Pre-Test, Score Report, and Learning Plan, either directly from Certiport, one of Microsoft's exam delivery partners, or through links from *WileyPLUS* Premium. They also receive a code and information for taking the certification exams.

- The **MSDN Academic Alliance** is designed to provide the easiest and most inexpensive way for university departments to make the latest Microsoft software available to faculty and students in labs, classrooms, and on student PCs. A free 1-year membership is available to qualified MOAC adopters.

MSDN ACADEMIC ALLIANCE—FREE 1-YEAR MEMBERSHIP
AVAILABLE TO QUALIFIED ADOPTERS!

MSDN Academic Alliance (MSDN AA) is designed to provide the easiest and most inexpensive way for universities to make the latest Microsoft software available in labs, classrooms, and on student PCs. MSDN AA is an annual membership program for departments teaching Science, Technology, Engineering, and Mathematics (STEM) courses. The membership provides a complete solution to keep academic labs, faculty, and students on the leading edge of technology.

As a bonus to this free offer, faculty will be introduced to Microsoft's Faculty Connection and Academic Resource Center. It takes time and preparation to keep students engaged while giving them a fundamental understanding of theory, and the Microsoft Faculty Connection is designed to help STEM professors with this preparation by providing articles, curriculum, and tools that professors can use to engage and inspire today's technology students.

Software provided in the MSDN AA program carries a high retail value but is being provided here through the Wiley and Microsoft publishing partnership and is made available to your department free of charge with the adoption of any Wiley qualified textbook.*

* Contact your Wiley rep for details.

For more information about the MSDN Academic Alliance program, go to:

http://msdn.microsoft.com/academic/

- **The Wiley Faculty Network** lets you tap into a large community of your peers effortlessly. Wiley Faculty Network mentors are faculty like you, from educational institutions around the country, who are passionate about enhancing instructional efficiency and effectiveness through best practices. Faculty Network activities include technology training and tutorials, virtual seminars, peer-to-peer exchanges of experience and ideas, personal consulting, and sharing of resources. To register for a seminar, go to www.wherefacultyconnect.com or phone 1-866-4FACULTY.

WileyPLUS

Broad developments in education over the past decade have influenced the instructional approach taken in the Microsoft Official Academic Course programs. The way that students learn, especially about new technologies, has changed dramatically in the Internet era. Electronic learning materials and Internet-based instruction is now as much a part of classroom instruction as printed textbooks. *WileyPLUS* provides the technology to create an environment where students reach their full potential and experience academic success that will last them a lifetime!

WileyPLUS is a powerful and highly-integrated suite of teaching and learning resources designed to bridge the gap between what happens in the classroom and what happens at home and on the job. *WileyPLUS* provides Instructors with the resources to teach their students new technologies and guide them to reach their goals of getting ahead in the job market by having the skills to become certified and advance in the workforce. For students, *WileyPLUS* provides the tools for study and practice that are available to them 24/7, wherever and whenever they want to study. *WileyPLUS* includes a complete online version of the student textbook; PowerPoint presentations; homework and practice assignments and quizzes; links to Microsoft's Pre-Test, Learning Plan, and a code for taking the certification exam (in *WileyPLUS* Premium); image galleries; testbank questions; gradebook; and all the instructor resources in one easy-to-use website.

WileyPLUS Premium (available in North America only) includes all of the above features as well as links to Microsoft's Pre-Tests, Learning Plan, and a code for taking the corresponding certification exam.

MICROSOFT BUSINESS CERTIFICATION PRE-TEST AND EXAMS AVAILABLE THROUGH *WILEYPLUS* PREMIUM

Enhance your students' knowledge and skills and increase their performance on Microsoft Business Certification exams with adoption of the Microsoft Official Academic Course program for Office 2007.

With the majority of the workforce classified as *information workers*, certification on the 2007 Microsoft Office system is a critical tool in terms of validating the desktop computing knowledge and skills required to be more productive in the workplace. Certification is the primary tool companies use to validate the proficiency of desktop computing skills among employees. It gives organizations the ability to help assess employees' actual computer skills and select job candidates based on verifiable skills applying the latest productivity tools and technology.

Microsoft Pre-tests, delivered by Certiport, provide a simple, low-cost way for individuals to identify their desktop computing skill level. Pre-Tests are taken online, making the first step towards certification easy and convenient. Through the Pre-Tests, individuals can receive a custom learning path with recommended training.

To help students to study for and pass the Microsoft Certified Application Specialist, or MCAS exam, each MOAC textbook includes information allowing students to access a Pre-Test, Score Report, and Learning Plan, either directly from Certiport or through links from the *WileyPLUS* Premium course. Students also receive a code and information for taking the certification exams. Students who do not have access to *WileyPLUS* Premium can find information on how to purchase access to the Pre-Test and a code for taking the certification exams by clicking on their textbook at:

http://www.wiley.com/college/microsoft.

The Pre-Test can only be taken once. It provides a simple, low-cost way for students to evaluate and identify their skill level. Through the Pre-Test, students receive a recommended study plan that they can print out to help them prepare for the live certification exams. The Pre-Test is comprised of a variety of selected response questions, including matching, sequencing exercises, "hot spots" where students must identify an item or function, and traditional multiple-choice questions. After students have mastered all the certification objectives, they can use their code to take the actual Microsoft Certified Application Specialist (MCAS) exams for Office 2007.

WileyPLUS Premium includes a complete online version of the student textbook, PowerPoint® presentations, homework and practice assignments and quizzes, links to Microsoft's Pre-Test, Learning Plan and a certification voucher, image galleries, test bank questions, gradebook, and all the instructor resources in one, easy-to-use website. Together, with *WileyPLUS* and the MCAS Pre-Test and exams delivered by Certiport, we are creating the best of both worlds in academic learning and performance based validation in preparation for a great career and a globally recognized Microsoft certification—the higher education learning management system that accesses the industry-leading certification pre-test.

Contact your Wiley rep today about this special offer.

Organized around the everyday activities you and your students perform in the class, *WileyPLUS* helps you:

- **Prepare & Present** outstanding class presentations using relevant PowerPoint slides and other *WileyPLUS* materials—and you can easily upload and add your own.
- **Create Assignments** by choosing from questions organized by lesson, level of difficulty, and source—and add your own questions. Students' homework and quizzes are automatically graded, and the results are recorded in your gradebook.
- **Offer context-sensitive help to students, 24/7.** When you assign homework or quizzes, you decide if and when students get access to hints, solutions, or answers where appropriate—or they can be linked to relevant sections of their complete, online text for additional help whenever—and wherever they need it most.
- **Track Student Progress:** Analyze students' results and assess their level of understanding on an individual and class level using the *WileyPLUS* gradebook, or export data to your own personal gradebook.
- **Administer Your Course:** *WileyPLUS* can easily be integrated with another course management system, gradebook, or other resources you are using in your class, providing you with the flexibility to build your course, your way.
- **Seamlessly integrate all of the rich *WileyPLUS* content and resources with WebCT and Blackboard**—with a single sign-on.

Please view our online demo at **www.wiley.com/college/wileyplus.** Here you will find additional information about the features and benefits of *WileyPLUS,* how to request a "test drive" of *WileyPLUS* for this title, and how to adopt it for class use.

Adoption Options

To provide you and your students with the right choices for learning, studying, and passing the MCAS certification exams, we have put together various options for your adoption requirements.

All selections include the student CD. Please contact your Wiley rep for more information:
- Textbook with 6-month Microsoft Office Trial
- Textbook, 6-month Microsoft Office Trial, *WileyPLUS*
- Textbook, 6-month Microsoft Office Trial, *WileyPLUS* Premium (includes access to Certiport)
- *WileyPLUS* (includes full e-book)
- *WileyPLUS* Premium (includes full e-book and access to Certiport)

Important Web Addresses and Phone Numbers

To locate the Wiley Higher Education Rep in your area, go to the following Web address and click on the "*Who's My Rep?*" link at the top of the page.

http://www.wiley.com/college

Or Call the MOAC Toll Free Number: 1 + (888) 764-7001

To learn more about becoming a Microsoft Certified Application Specialist and exam availability, visit www.microsoft.com/learning/msbc.

http://www.wiley.com/college/microsoft *or* call the MOAC Toll-Free Number: 1+(888) 764-7001

Student Support Program

Book Companion Website (www.wiley.com/college/microsoft)

The book companion site for the MOAC series includes the Instructor Resources and Web links to important information for students and instructors.

WileyPLUS

WileyPLUS is a powerful and highly-integrated suite of teaching and learning resources designed to bridge the gap between what happens in the classroom and what happens at home and on the job. For students, *WileyPLUS* provides the tools for study and practice that are available 24/7, wherever and whenever they want to study. *WileyPLUS* includes a complete online version of the student textbook; PowerPoint presentations; homework and practice assignments and quizzes; links to Microsoft's Pre-Test, Learning Plan, and a code for taking the certification exam (in *WileyPLUS* Premium); image galleries; test bank questions; gradebook; and all the instructor resources in one easy-to-use website.

WileyPLUS provides immediate feedback on student assignments and a wealth of support materials. This powerful study tool will help your students develop their conceptual understanding of the class material and increase their ability to answer questions.

- A **Study and Practice** area links directly to text content, allowing students to review the text while they study and answer. Access to Microsoft's Pre-Test, Learning Plan, and a code for taking the MCAS certification exam is available in Study and Practice. Additional Practice Questions tied to the MCAS certification that can be re-taken as many times as necessary, are also available.

- An **Assignment** area keeps all the work you want your students to complete in one location, making it easy for them to stay on task. Students have access to a variety of interactive self-assessment tools, as well as other resources for building their confidence and understanding. In addition, all of the assignments and quizzes contain a link to the relevant section of the multimedia book, providing students with context-sensitive help that allows them to conquer obstacles as they arise.

- A **Personal Gradebook** for each student allows students to view their results from past assignments at any time.

Please view our online demo at www.wiley.com/college/wileyplus. Here you will find additional information about the features and benefits of *WileyPLUS,* how to request a "test drive" of *WileyPLUS* for this title, and how to adopt it for class use.

6-MONTH MICROSOFT OFFICE 2007 TRIAL EDITION

MOAC textbooks provide an unparalleled value to students in today's performance-based courses. All MOAC 2007 Microsoft Office system textbooks sold in North America are packaged with a 6-month trial CD of Microsoft Office Professional 2007. The textbook includes the CD and a product key that allows students to activate Microsoft Office Professional 2007 for the 6-month trial period. After purchasing the textbook containing the Microsoft Office Professional 2007 Trial CD, students must install the CD onto their computer and, when prompted, enter the Office Trial product key that allows them to activate the software.

Installing the Microsoft Office Professional 2007 Trial CD provides students with the state-of-the-art 2007 Microsoft Office system software, allowing them to use the practice files on the Student CD and in *WileyPLUS* to learn and study by doing, which is the best and most effective way to acquire and remember new computing skills.

TAKE NOTE*

For the best performance, the default selection during Setup is to uninstall previous versions of Office. There is also an option to remove previous versions of Office. With all trial software, Microsoft recommends that you have your original CDs available to reinstall if necessary. If you want to return to your previous version of Office, you need to uninstall the trial software. This should be done through the Add or Remove Programs icon in Microsoft Windows Control Panel (or Uninstall a program in the Control Panel of Windows Vista).

Installation of Microsoft Office Professional 2007 6-Month Trial software will remove your existing version of Microsoft Outlook. However, your contacts, calendar, and other personal information will not be deleted. At the end of the trial, if you choose to upgrade or to reinstall your previous version of Outlook, your personal settings and information will be retained.

Installing the 2007 Microsoft Office System 6-Month Trial

1. Insert the trial software CD-ROM into the CD drive on your computer. The CD will be detected, and the Setup.exe file should automatically begin to run on your computer.
2. When prompted for the Office Product Key, enter the Product Key provided with the software, and then click **Next.**
3. Enter your name and organization user name, and then click **Next.**
4. Read the End-User License Agreement, select the *I Accept the Terms in the License Agreement* check box, and then click **Next.**
5. Select the install option, verify the installation location or click **Browse** to change the installation location, and then click **Next.**
6. Verify the program installation preferences, and then click **Next.**
7. Click **Finish** to complete the setup.

Upgrading Microsoft Office Professional 2007 6-Month Trial Software to the Full Product

You can convert the software into full use without removing or reinstalling software on your computer. When you complete your trial, you can purchase a product license from any Microsoft reseller and enter a valid Product Key when prompted during Setup.

Uninstalling the Trial Software and Returning to Your Previous Office Version

If you want to return to your previous version of Office, you need to uninstall the trial software. This should be done through the Add or Remove Programs icon in Control Panel (or Uninstall a program in the Control Panel of Windows Vista).

Uninstall Trial Software

1. Quit any programs that are running.
2. In Control Panel, click **Add or Remove Programs** (or **Uninstall a program** in Windows Vista).
3. Click **Microsoft Office Professional 2007,** and then click **Remove** (or **Uninstall** in Windows Vista).

TAKE NOTE If you selected the option to remove a previous version of Office during installation of the trial software, you need to reinstall your previous version of Office. If you did not remove your previous version of Office, you can start each of your Office programs either through the Start menu or by opening files for each program. In some cases, you may have to recreate some of your shortcuts and default settings.

Student CD

The CD-ROM included with this book contains the practice files that you will use as you perform the exercises in the book. By using the practice files, you will not waste time creating the samples used in the lessons, and you can concentrate on learning how to use Microsoft Office 2007. With the files and the step-by-step instructions in the lessons, you will learn by doing, which is an easy and effective way to acquire and remember new skills.

IMPORTANT This course assumes that the 2007 Microsoft Office system has already been installed on the PC you are using. Note that Microsoft Product Support does not support this trial version.

Copying the Practice Files

Your instructor might already have copied the practice files before you arrive in class. However, your instructor might ask you to copy the practice files on your own at the start of class. Also, if you want to work through any of the exercises in this book on your own at home or at your place of business after class, you may want to copy the practice files. Note that you can also open the files directly from the CD-ROM, but you should be cautious about carrying the CD-ROM around with you as it could become damaged.

ANOTHER WAY If you only want to copy the files for one lesson, you can open the Data folder and right-click the desired Lesson folder within the Data folder.

1. Insert the CD-ROM in the CD-ROM drive of your computer.
2. Start Windows Explorer.
3. In the left pane of Explorer, locate the icon for your CD-ROM and click on this icon. The folders and files contained on the CD will appear listed on the right.
4. Locate and select the **Data** folder. This is the folder which contains all of the practice files, separated by Lesson folders.
5. Right-click on the **Data** folder and choose **Copy** from the menu.
6. In the left pane of Windows Explorer, locate the location to which you would like to copy the practice files. This can be a drive on your local PC or an external drive.
7. Right-click on the drive/location to which you want to copy the practice files and choose **Paste.** This will copy the entire Data folder to your chosen location.
8. Close Windows Explorer.

Deleting the Practice Files

Use the following steps when you want to delete the practice files from your hard disk or other drive. Your instructor might ask you to perform these steps at the end of class. Also, you should perform these steps if you have worked through the exercises at home or at your place of business and want to work through the exercises again. Deleting the practice files and then reinstalling them ensures that all files and folders are in their original condition if you decide to work through the exercises again.

1. Start Windows Explorer.
2. Browse through the drives and folders to locate the practice files.
3. Select the **Data** folder.
4. Right-click on the **Data** folder and choose **Delete** from the menu.
5. Close Windows Explorer.

Locating and Opening Practice Files

If you only want to delete only the files for one lesson, you can open the Data folder and right-click the desired Lesson folder within the Data folder.

After you (or your instructor) have copied the practice files, all the files you need for this course will be stored in a folder named Data located on the disk you choose.

1. Click the **Office Button** in the top left corner of your application.
2. Choose **Open** from the menu.
3. In the Open dialog box, browse through the Folders panel to locate the drive and folder where you copied the files.
4. Double-click on the **Data** folder.
5. Double-click on the **Lesson** folder for the lesson in which you are working.
6. Select the file that you want and click **Open** or double-click on the file that you want.

Wiley Desktop Editions

You can use the Search function in the Open dialog box to quickly find the specific file for which you are looking.

Wiley MOAC Desktop Editions are innovative, electronic versions of printed textbooks. Students buy the desktop version for 60% off the price of the printed text, and get the added value of permanence and portability. Wiley Desktop Editions provide students with numerous additional benefits that are not available with other e-text solutions:

Wiley Desktop Editions are NOT subscriptions; students download the Wiley Desktop Edition to their computer desktops. Students own the content they buy to keep for as long as they want. Once a Wiley Desktop Edition is downloaded to the computer desktop, students have instant access to all of the content without being online. Students can also print out the sections they prefer to read in hard copy. Students also have access to fully integrated resources within their Wiley Desktop Edition. From highlighting their e-text to taking and sharing notes, students can easily personalize their Wiley Desktop Edition as they are reading or following along in class.

Please visit Microsoft Office Online for help using Office 2007, Clip Art, Templates, and other valuable information:
http://office.microsoft.com/

Preparing to Take the Microsoft Certified Application Specialist (MCAS) Exam

The Microsoft Certified Application Specialist program is part of the new and enhanced Microsoft Business Certifications. It is easily attainable through a series of verifications that provide a simple and convenient framework for skills assessment and validation.

For organizations, the new certification program provides better skills verification tools that help with assessing not only in-demand skills on the 2007 Microsoft Office system, but also the ability to quickly complete on-the-job tasks. Individuals will find it easier to identify and work towards the certification credential that meets their personal and professional goals.

To learn more about becoming a Microsoft Certified Application Specialist and exam availability, visit www.microsoft.com/learning/msbc.

Microsoft Certified Application Specialist (MCAS) Program

The core Microsoft Office Specialist credential has been upgraded to validate skills with the 2007 Microsoft Office system as well as the new Windows Vista operating system. The Application Specialist certifications target information workers and cover the most popular business applications such as Word 2007, PowerPoint 2007, Excel 2007, Access 2007, and Outlook 2007.

By becoming certified, you demonstrate to employers that you have achieved a predictable level of skill in the use of a particular Office application. Employers often require certification either as a condition of employment or as a condition of advancement within the company or other organization. The certification examinations are sponsored by Microsoft but administered through exam delivery partners like Certiport.

Preparing to Take an Exam

Unless you are a very experienced user, you will need to use a test preparation course to prepare to complete the test correctly and within the time allowed. The *Microsoft Official Academic Course* series is designed to prepare you with a strong knowledge of all exam topics, and with some additional review and practice on your own. You should feel confident in your ability to pass the appropriate exam.

After you decide which exam to take, review the list of objectives for the exam. This list can be found in the MCAS Objectives Appendix at the back of this book. You can also easily identify tasks that are included in the objective list by locating the Lesson Skill Matrix at the start of each lesson and the Certification Ready sidebars in the margin of the lessons in this book.

To take the MCAS test, visit *www.microsoft.com/learning/msbc* to locate your nearest testing center. Then call the testing center directly to schedule your test. The amount of advance notice you should provide will vary for different testing centers, and it typically depends on the number of computers available at the testing center, the number of other testers who have already been scheduled for the day on which you want to take the test, and the number of times per week that the testing center offers MCAS testing. In general, you should call to schedule your test at least two weeks prior to the date on which you want to take the test.

When you arrive at the testing center, you might be asked for proof of identity. A driver's license or passport is an acceptable form of identification. If you do not have either of these items of documentation, call your testing center and ask what alternative forms of identification will be accepted. If you are retaking a test, bring your MCAS identification number, which will have been given to you when you previously took the test. If you have not prepaid or if your organization has not already arranged to make payment for you, you will need to pay the test-taking fee when you arrive.

Test Format

All MCAS certification tests are live, performance-based tests. There are no true/false or short-answer questions. Instructions are general: you are told the basic tasks to perform on the computer, but you aren't given any help in figuring out how to perform them. You are not permitted to use reference material.

As you complete the tasks stated in a particular test question, the testing software monitors your actions. An example question might be:

Open the file named *Wiley Guests* and select the word *Welcome* in the first paragraph. Change the font to 12 point, and apply bold formatting. Select the words *at your convenience* in the second paragraph, move them to the end of the first paragraph using drag and drop, and then center the first paragraph.

When the test administrator seats you at a computer, you will see an online form that you use to enter information about yourself (name, address, and other information required to process your exam results). While you complete the form, the software will generate the test from a master test bank and then prompt you to continue. The first test question will appear in a window. Read the question carefully, and then perform all the tasks stated in the test question. When you have finished completing all tasks for a question, click the Next Question button.

You have 45 to 50 minutes to complete all questions, depending on the test that you are taking. The testing software assesses your results as soon as you complete the test, and the test administrator can print the results of the test so that you will have a record of any tasks that you performed incorrectly. If you pass, you will receive a certificate in the mail within two to four weeks. If you do not pass, you can study and practice the skills that you missed and then schedule to retake the test at a later date.

Tips for Successfully Completing the Test

The following tips and suggestions are the result of feedback received from many individuals who have taken one or more MCAS tests:

- Make sure that you are thoroughly prepared. If you have extensively used the application for which you are being tested, you might feel confident that you are prepared for the test. However, the test might include questions that involve tasks that you rarely or never perform when you use the application at your place of business, at school, or at home. You must be knowledgeable in all the MCAS objectives for the test that you will take.

- Read each exam question carefully. An exam question might include several tasks that you are to perform. A partially correct response to a test question is counted as an incorrect response. In the example question on the previous page, you might apply bold formatting and move the words *at your convenience* to the correct location, but forget to center the first paragraph. This would count as an incorrect response and would result in a lower test score.

- You are not allowed to use the application's Help system. The Help function is always disabled for all exams.

- The test does display the amount of time that you have left. The test program also displays the number of items that you have completed along with the total number of test items (for example, "35 of 40 items have been completed"). Use this information to gauge your pace.

- If you skip a question, you can return to it later.

If You Do Not Pass the Test

If you do not pass, you can use the assessment printout as a guide to practice the items that you missed. There is no limit to the number of times that you can retake a test; however, you must pay the fee each time that you take the test. When you retake the test, expect to see some of the same test items on the subsequent test; the test software randomly generates the test items from a master test bank before you begin the test. Also expect to see several questions that did not appear on the previous test.

Acknowledgments

MOAC Instructor Advisory Board

We would like to thank our Instructor Advisory Board, an elite group of educators who has assisted us every step of the way in building these products. Advisory Board members have acted as our sounding board on key pedagogical and design decisions leading to the development of these compelling and innovative textbooks for future Information Workers. Their dedication to technology education is truly appreciated.

Catherine Binder, Strayer University & Katharine Gibbs School–Philadelphia

Catherine currently works at both Katharine Gibbs School in Norristown, PA and Strayer University in King of Prussia, PA. Catherine has been at Katharine Gibbs School for 4 years. Catherine is currently the Department Chair/Lead instructor for PC Networking at Gibbs and the founder/advisor of the TEK Masters Society. Since joining Strayer University a year and a half ago she has risen in the ranks from adjunct to DIT/Assistant Campus Dean.

Catherine has brought her 10+ year's industry experience as Network Administrator, Network Supervisor, Professor, Bench Tech, Manager and CTO from such places as Foster Wheeler Corp, KidsPeace Inc., Victoria Vogue, TESST College, AMC Theatres, Blue Mountain Publishing and many more to her teaching venue.

Catherine began as an adjunct in the PC Networking department and quickly became a full-time instructor. At both schools she is in charge of scheduling, curricula and departmental duties. She happily advises about 80+ students and is committed to Gibbs/Strayer life, her students, and continuing technology education every day.

Penny Gudgeon, CDI College

Penny is the Program Manager for IT curriculum at Corinthian Colleges, Inc. Until January 2006, Penny was responsible for all Canadian programming and web curriculum for five years. During that time, Corinthian Colleges, Inc. acquired CDI College of Business and Technology in 2004. Before 2000 she spent four years as IT instructor at one of the campuses. Penny joined CDI College in 1997 after her working for 10 years first in programming and later in software productivity education. Penny previously has worked in the fields of advertising, sales, engineering technology and programming. When not working from her home office or indulging her passion for life long learning, and the possibilities of what might be, Penny likes to read mysteries, garden and relax at home in Hamilton, Ontario, with her Shih-Tzu, Gracie, and husband, Al.

Jana Hambruch, School District of Lee County

Ms. Hambruch currently serves as Director for the Information Technology Magnet Programs at The School District of Lee County in Ft Myers, Florida. She is responsible for the implementation and direction of three schools that fall under this grant program. This program has been recognized as one of the top 15 most innovative technology programs in the nation. She is also co-author of the grant proposal for the IT Magnet Grant prior to taking on the role of Director.

Ms. Hambruch has over ten years experience directing the technical certification training programs at many Colleges and Universities, including Barry University, the University of

South Florida, Broward Community College, and at Florida Gulf Coast University, where she served as the Director for the Center for Technology Education. She excels at developing alternative training models that focus on the tie between the education provider and the community in which it serves.

Ms. Hambruch is a past board member and treasurer of the Human Resources Management Association of SW Florida, graduate of Leadership Lee County Class of 2002, Steering Committee Member for Leadership Lee County Class of 2004 and a former board member of the Career Coalition of Southwest Florida. She has frequently lectured for organizations such as Microsoft, American Society of Training and Development, Florida Gulf Coast University, Florida State University, University of Nevada at Las Vegas, University of Wisconsin at Milwaukee, Canada's McGill University, and Florida's State Workforce Summit.

Dee Hobson, **Richland College**

Dee Hobson is currently a faculty member of the Business Office Systems and Support Division at Richland College. Richland is one of seven colleges in the Dallas County Community College District and has the distinction of being the first community college to receive the Malcolm Baldrige National Quality Award in 2005. Richland also received the Texas Award for Performance Excellence in 2005.

The Business Office Systems and Support Division at Richland is also a Certiport Authorized Microsoft Office testing center. All students enrolling in one of Microsoft's application software courses (Word, Excel, PowerPoint, and Access) are required to take the respective Microsoft certification exam at the end of the semester.

Dee has taught computer and business courses in K-12 public schools and at a proprietary career college in Dallas. She has also been involved with several corporate training companies and with adult education programs in the Dallas area. She began her computer career as an employee of IBM Corporation in St. Louis, Missouri. During her ten-year IBM employment, she moved to Memphis, Tennessee, to accept a managerial position and to Dallas, Texas, to work in a national sales and marketing technical support center.

Keith Hoell, **Katharine Gibbs School–New York**

Keith has worked in both non-profit and proprietary education for over 10 years, initially at St. John's University in New York, and then as full-time faculty, Chairperson and currently Dean of Information Systems at the Katharine Gibbs School in New York City. He also worked for General Electric in the late 80's and early 90's as the Sysop of a popular bulletin board dedicated to ASCII-Art on GE's pioneering GEnie on-line service before the advent of the World Wide Web. He has taught courses and workshops dealing with many mainstream IT issues and varied technology, especially those related to computer hardware and operating system software, networking, software applications, IT project management and ethics, and relational database technology. An avid runner and a member of The New York Road Runners, he won the Footlocker Five Borough Challenge representing Queens at the 2005 ING New York City Marathon while competing against the 4 other borough reps. He currently resides in Queens, New York.

Michael Taylor, **Seattle Central Community College**

Michael worked in education and training for the last 20 years in both the public and private sector. He currently teaches and coordinates the applications support program at Seattle Central Community College and also administers the Microsoft IT Academy. His experience outside the educational world is in Travel and Tourism with wholesale tour operations and cruise lines.

Interests outside of work include greyhound rescue. (He adopted 3 x-racers who bring him great joy.) He also enjoys the arts and is fortunate to live in downtown Seattle where there is much to see and do.

MOAC Office 2007 Reviewers

We also thank the many reviewers who pored over the manuscript providing invaluable feedback in the service of quality instructional materials.

Access

Susan Fry, Boise State University
Leslie Jernberg, Eastern Idaho Technical College
Dr. Deborah Jones, South Georgia Technical College
Suzanne Marks, Bellevue Community College
Kim Styles, Tri-County Technical College & Anderson School District 5

Excel

Christie Hovey, Lincoln Land Community College
Barbara Lave, Portland Community College
Donna Madsen, Kirkwood Community College
James M. Veneziano, Davenport University—Caro
Dorothy Weiner, Manchester Community College

PowerPoint

Barbara Gillespie, Cuyamaca College
Tatyana Pashnyak, Bainbridge College
Michelle Poertner, Northwestern Michigan College
Janet Sebesy, Cuyahoga Community College

Outlook

Julie Boyles, Portland Community College
Joe LaMontagne, Davenport University—Grand Rapids
Randy Nordell, American River College
Echo Rantanen, Spokane Community College

Project

Janis DeHaven, Central Community College
Dr. Susan Jennings, Stephen F. Austin State University
Diane D. Mickey, Northern Virginia Community College
Linda Nutter, Peninsula College
Marika Reinke, Bellevue Community College

Word

Diana Anderson, Big Sandy Community & Technical College
Donna Hendricks, South Arkansas Community College
Dr. Donna McGill-Cameron, Yuba Community College—Woodland Campus
Patricia McMahon, South Suburban College
Nancy Noe, Linn-Benton Community College
Teresa Roberts, Wilson Technical Community College

Focus Group and Survey Participants

Finally we thank the hundreds of instructors who participated in our focus groups and surveys to ensure that the Microsoft Official Academic Courses best met the needs of our customers.

Jean Aguilar, Mt. Hood Community College
Konrad Akens, Zane State College
Michael Albers, University of Memphis
Diana Anderson, Big Sandy Community & Technical College
Phyllis Anderson, Delaware County Community College

Judith Andrews, Feather River College
Damon Antos, American River College
Bridget Archer, Oakton Community College
Linda Arnold, Harrisburg Area Community College–
  Lebanon Campus

Neha Arya, Fullerton College

Mohammad Bajwa, Katharine Gibbs School–New York

Virginia Baker, University of Alaska Fairbanks

Carla Bannick, Pima Community College

Rita Barkley, Northeast Alabama Community College

Elsa Barr, Central Community College – Hastings

Ronald W. Barry, Ventura County Community College District

Elizabeth Bastedo, Central Carolina Technical College

Karen Baston, Waubonsee Community College

Karen Bean, Blinn College

Scott Beckstrand, Community College of Southern Nevada

Paulette Bell, Santa Rosa Junior College

Liz Bennett, Southeast Technical Institute

Nancy Bermea, Olympic College

Lucy Betz, Milwaukee Area Technical College

Meral Binbasioglu, Hofstra University

Catherine Binder, Strayer University & Katharine Gibbs School–Philadelphia

Terrel Blair, El Centro College

Ruth Blalock, Alamance Community College

Beverly Bohner, Reading Area Community College

Henry Bojack, Farmingdale State University

Matthew Bowie, Luna Community College

Julie Boyles, Portland Community College

Karen Brandt, College of the Albemarle

Stephen Brown, College of San Mateo

Jared Bruckner, Southern Adventist University

Pam Brune, Chattanooga State Technical Community College

Sue Buchholz, Georgia Perimeter College

Roberta Buczyna, Edison College

Angela Butler, Mississippi Gulf Coast Community College

Rebecca Byrd, Augusta Technical College

Kristen Callahan, Mercer County Community College

Judy Cameron, Spokane Community College

Dianne Campbell, Athens Technical College

Gena Casas, Florida Community College at Jacksonville

Jesus Castrejon, Latin Technologies

Gail Chambers, Southwest Tennessee Community College

Jacques Chansavang, Indiana University–Purdue University Fort Wayne

Nancy Chapko, Milwaukee Area Technical College

Rebecca Chavez, Yavapai College

Sanjiv Chopra, Thomas Nelson Community College

Greg Clements, Midland Lutheran College

Dayna Coker, Southwestern Oklahoma State University– Sayre Campus

Tamra Collins, Otero Junior College

Janet Conrey, Gavilan Community College

Carol Cornforth, West Virginia Northern Community College

Gary Cotton, American River College

Edie Cox, Chattahoochee Technical College

Rollie Cox, Madison Area Technical College

David Crawford, Northwestern Michigan College

J.K. Crowley, Victor Valley College

Rosalyn Culver, Washtenaw Community College

Sharon Custer, Huntington University

Sandra Daniels, New River Community College

Anila Das, Cedar Valley College

Brad Davis, Santa Rosa Junior College

Susan Davis, Green River Community College

Mark Dawdy, Lincoln Land Community College

Jennifer Day, Sinclair Community College

Carol Deane, Eastern Idaho Technical College

Julie DeBuhr, Lewis-Clark State College

Janis DeHaven, Central Community College

Drew Dekreon, University of Alaska–Anchorage

Joy DePover, Central Lakes College

Salli DiBartolo, Brevard Community College

Melissa Diegnau, Riverland Community College

Al Dillard, Lansdale School of Business

Marjorie Duffy, Cosumnes River College

Sarah Dunn, Southwest Tennessee Community College

Shahla Durany, Tarrant County College–South Campus

Kay Durden, University of Tennessee at Martin

Dineen Ebert, St. Louis Community College–Meramec

Donna Ehrhart, State University of New York–Brockport

Larry Elias, Montgomery County Community College

Glenda Elser, New Mexico State University at Alamogordo

Angela Evangelinos, Monroe County Community College

Angie Evans, Ivy Tech Community College of Indiana

Linda Farrington, Indian Hills Community College

Dana Fladhammer, Phoenix College

Richard Flores, Citrus College

Connie Fox, Community and Technical College at Institute of Technology West Virginia University

Wanda Freeman, Okefenokee Technical College

Brenda Freeman, Augusta Technical College

Susan Fry, Boise State University

Roger Fulk, Wright State University–Lake Campus

Sue Furnas, Collin County Community College District

Sandy Gabel, Vernon College

Laura Galvan, Fayetteville Technical Community College

Candace Garrod, Red Rocks Community College

Sherrie Geitgey, Northwest State Community College

Chris Gerig, Chattahoochee Technical College

Barb Gillespie, Cuyamaca College

Jessica Gilmore, Highline Community College

Pamela Gilmore, Reedley College

Debbie Glinert, Queensborough Community College

Steven Goldman, Polk Community College

Bettie Goodman, C.S. Mott Community College

Mike Grabill, Katharine Gibbs School–Philadelphia

Francis Green, Penn State University

Walter Griffin, Blinn College

Fillmore Guinn, Odessa College

Helen Haasch, Milwaukee Area Technical College

John Habal, Ventura College

Joy Haerens, Chaffey College
Norman Hahn, Thomas Nelson Community College
Kathy Hall, Alamance Community College
Teri Harbacheck, Boise State University
Linda Harper, Richland Community College
Maureen Harper, Indian Hills Community College
Steve Harris, Katharine Gibbs School–New York
Robyn Hart, Fresno City College
Darien Hartman, Boise State University
Gina Hatcher, Tacoma Community College
Winona T. Hatcher, Aiken Technical College
BJ Hathaway, Northeast Wisconsin Tech College
Cynthia Hauki, West Hills College – Coalinga
Mary L. Haynes, Wayne County Community College
Marcie Hawkins, Zane State College
Steve Hebrock, Ohio State University Agricultural
    Technical Institute
Sue Heistand, Iowa Central Community College
Heith Hennel, Valencia Community College
Donna Hendricks, South Arkansas Community College
Judy Hendrix, Dyersburg State Community College
Gloria Hensel, Matanuska-Susitna College University
    of Alaska Anchorage
Gwendolyn Hester, Richland College
Tammarra Holmes, Laramie County Community College
Dee Hobson, Richland College
Keith Hoell, Katharine Gibbs School–New York
Pashia Hogan, Northeast State Technical
    Community College
Susan Hoggard, Tulsa Community College
Kathleen Holliman, Wallace Community College Selma
Chastity Honchul, Brown Mackie College/Wright
    State University
Christie Hovey, Lincoln Land Community College
Peggy Hughes, Allegany College of Maryland
Sandra Hume, Chippewa Valley Technical College
John Hutson, Aims Community College
Celia Ing, Sacramento City College
Joan Ivey, Lanier Technical College
Barbara Jaffari, College of the Redwoods
Penny Jakes, University of Montana College of Technology
Eduardo Jaramillo, Peninsula College
Barbara Jauken, Southeast Community College
Susan Jennings, Stephen F. Austin State University
Leslie Jernberg, Eastern Idaho Technical College
Linda Johns, Georgia Perimeter College
Brent Johnson, Okefenokee Technical College
Mary Johnson, Mt. San Antonio College
Shirley Johnson, Trinidad State Junior College–
    Valley Campus
Sandra M. Jolley, Tarrant County College
Teresa Jolly, South Georgia Technical College
Dr. Deborah Jones, South Georgia Technical College
Margie Jones, Central Virginia Community College
Randall Jones, Marshall Community and Technical College

Diane Karlsbraaten, Lake Region State College
Teresa Keller, Ivy Tech Community College of Indiana
Charles Kemnitz, Pennsylvania College of Technology
Sandra Kinghorn, Ventura College
Bill Klein, Katharine Gibbs School–Philadelphia
Bea Knaapen, Fresno City College
Kit Kofoed, Western Wyoming Community College
Maria Kolatis, County College of Morris
Barry Kolb, Ocean County College
Karen Kuralt, University of Arkansas at Little Rock
Belva-Carole Lamb, Rogue Community College
Betty Lambert, Des Moines Area Community College
Anita Lande, Cabrillo College
Junnae Landry, Pratt Community College
Karen Lankisch, UC Clermont
David Lanzilla, Central Florida Community College
Nora Laredo, Cerritos Community College
Jennifer Larrabee, Chippewa Valley Technical College
Debra Larson, Idaho State University
Barb Lave, Portland Community College
Audrey Lawrence, Tidewater Community College
Deborah Layton, Eastern Oklahoma State College
Larry LeBlanc, Owen Graduate School–
    Vanderbilt University
Philip Lee, Nashville State Community College
Michael Lehrfeld, Brevard Community College
Vasant Limaye, Southwest Collegiate Institute for the
    Deaf – Howard College
Anne C. Lewis, Edgecombe Community College
Stephen Linkin, Houston Community College
Peggy Linston, Athens Technical College
Hugh Lofton, Moultrie Technical College
Donna Lohn, Lakeland Community College
Jackie Lou, Lake Tahoe Community College
Donna Love, Gaston College
Curt Lynch, Ozarks Technical Community College
Sheilah Lynn, Florida Community College–Jacksonville
Pat R. Lyon, Tomball College
Bill Madden, Bergen Community College
Heather Madden, Delaware Technical &
    Community College
Donna Madsen, Kirkwood Community College
Jane Maringer-Cantu, Gavilan College
Suzanne Marks, Bellevue Community College
Carol Martin, Louisiana State University–Alexandria
Cheryl Martucci, Diablo Valley College
Roberta Marvel, Eastern Wyoming College
Tom Mason, Brookdale Community College
Mindy Mass, Santa Barbara City College
Dixie Massaro, Irvine Valley College
Rebekah May, Ashland Community & Technical College
Emma Mays-Reynolds, Dyersburg State
    Community College
Timothy Mayes, Metropolitan State College of Denver
Reggie McCarthy, Central Lakes College

Matt McCaskill, Brevard Community College
Kevin McFarlane, Front Range Community College
Donna McGill, Yuba Community College
Terri McKeever, Ozarks Technical Community College
Patricia McMahon, South Suburban College
Sally McMillin, Katharine Gibbs School–Philadelphia
Charles McNerney, Bergen Community College
Lisa Mears, Palm Beach Community College
Imran Mehmood, ITT Technical Institute–King of
    Prussia Campus
Virginia Melvin, Southwest Tennessee Community College
Jeanne Mercer, Texas State Technical College
Denise Merrell, Jefferson Community & Technical College
Catherine Merrikin, Pearl River Community College
Diane D. Mickey, Northern Virginia Community College
Darrelyn Miller, Grays Harbor College
Sue Mitchell, Calhoun Community College
Jacquie Moldenhauer, Front Range Community College
Linda Motonaga, Los Angeles City College
Sam Mryyan, Allen County Community College
Cindy Murphy, Southeastern Community College
Ryan Murphy, Sinclair Community College
Sharon E. Nastav, Johnson County Community College
Christine Naylor, Kent State University Ashtabula
Haji Nazarian, Seattle Central Community College
Nancy Noe, Linn-Benton Community College
Jennie Noriega, San Joaquin Delta College
Linda Nutter, Peninsula College
Thomas Omerza, Middle Bucks Institute of Technology
Edith Orozco, St. Philip's College
Dona Orr, Boise State University
Joanne Osgood, Chaffey College
Janice Owens, Kishwaukee College
Tatyana Pashnyak, Bainbridge College
John Partacz, College of DuPage
Tim Paul, Montana State University–Great Falls
Joseph Perez, South Texas College
Mike Peterson, Chemeketa Community College
Dr. Karen R. Petitto, West Virginia Wesleyan College
Terry Pierce, Onandaga Community College
Ashlee Pieris, Raritan Valley Community College
Jamie Pinchot, Thiel College
Michelle Poertner, Northwestern Michigan College
Betty Posta, University of Toledo
Deborah Powell, West Central Technical College
Mark Pranger, Rogers State University
Carolyn Rainey, Southeast Missouri State University
Linda Raskovich, Hibbing Community College
Leslie Ratliff, Griffin Technical College
Mar-Sue Ratzke, Rio Hondo Community College
Roxy Reissen, Southeastern Community College
Silvio Reyes, Technical Career Institutes
Patricia Rishavy, Anoka Technical College
Jean Robbins, Southeast Technical Institute

Carol Roberts, Eastern Maine Community College
    and University of Maine
Teresa Roberts, Wilson Technical Community College
Vicki Robertson, Southwest Tennessee Community College
Betty Rogge, Ohio State Agricultural Technical Institute
Lynne Rusley, Missouri Southern State University
Claude Russo, Brevard Community College
Ginger Sabine, Northwestern Technical College
Steven Sachs, Los Angeles Valley College
Joanne Salas, Olympic College
Lloyd Sandmann, Pima Community College–Desert
    Vista Campus
Beverly Santillo, Georgia Perimeter College
Theresa Savarese, San Diego City College
Sharolyn Sayers, Milwaukee Area Technical College
Judith Scheeren, Westmoreland County
    Community College
Adolph Scheiwe, Joliet Junior College
Marilyn Schmid, Asheville-Buncombe Technical
    Community College
Janet Sebesy, Cuyahoga Community College
Phyllis T. Shafer, Brookdale Community College
Ralph Shafer, Truckee Meadows Community College
Anne Marie Shanley, County College of Morris
Shelia Shelton, Surry Community College
Merilyn Shepherd, Danville Area Community College
Susan Sinele, Aims Community College
Beth Sindt, Hawkeye Community College
Andrew Smith, Marian College
Brenda Smith, Southwest Tennessee Community College
Lynne Smith, State University of New York–Delhi
Rob Smith, Katharine Gibbs School–Philadelphia
Tonya Smith, Arkansas State University–Mountain Home
Del Spencer – Trinity Valley Community College
Jeri Spinner, Idaho State University
Eric Stadnik, Santa Rosa Junior College
Karen Stanton, Los Medanos College
Meg Stoner, Santa Rosa Junior College
Beverly Stowers, Ivy Tech Community College of Indiana
Marcia Stranix, Yuba College
Kim Styles, Tri-County Technical College
Sylvia Summers, Tacoma Community College
Beverly Swann, Delaware Technical & Community College
Ann Taff, Tulsa Community College
Mike Theiss, University of Wisconsin–Marathon Campus
Romy Thiele, Cañada College
Sharron Thompson, Portland Community College
Ingrid Thompson-Sellers, Georgia Perimeter College
Barbara Tietsort, University of Cincinnati–Raymond
    Walters College
Janine Tiffany, Reading Area Community College
Denise Tillery, University of Nevada Las Vegas
Susan Trebelhorn, Normandale Community College
Noel Trout, Santiago Canyon College

Cheryl Turgeon, Asnuntuck Community College
Steve Turner, Ventura College
Sylvia Unwin, Bellevue Community College
Lilly Vigil, Colorado Mountain College
Sabrina Vincent, College of the Mainland
Mary Vitrano, Palm Beach Community College
Brad Vogt, Northeast Community College
Cozell Wagner, Southeastern Community College
Carolyn Walker, Tri-County Technical College
Sherry Walker, Tulsa Community College
Qi Wang, Tacoma Community College
Betty Wanielista, Valencia Community College
Marge Warber, Lanier Technical College–Forsyth Campus
Marjorie Webster, Bergen Community College
Linda Wenn, Central Community College
Mark Westlund, Olympic College
Carolyn Whited, Roane State Community College
Winona Whited, Richland College
Jerry Wilkerson, Scott Community College
Joel Willenbring, Fullerton College

Barbara Williams, WITC Superior
Charlotte Williams, Jones County Junior College
Bonnie Willy, Ivy Tech Community College of Indiana
Diane Wilson, J. Sargeant Reynolds Community College
James Wolfe, Metropolitan Community College
Marjory Wooten, Lanier Technical College
Mark Yanko, Hocking College
Alexis Yusov, Pace University
Naeem Zaman, San Joaquin Delta College
Kathleen Zimmerman, Des Moines Area
    Community College

We would also like to thank Lutz Ziob, Sanjay Advani, Jim DiIanni, Merrick Van Dongen, Jim LeValley, Bruce Curling, Joe Wilson, and Naman Kahn at Microsoft for their encouragement and support in making the Microsoft Official Academic Course programs the finest instructional materials for mastering the newest Microsoft technologies for both students and instructors.

Brief Contents

Contents

Lesson 8: Calendar Basics   159

Lesson 9: Managing Meetings   172

Lesson 10: Advanced Calendar Management   196

FOR INSTRUCTORS

WileyPLUS is built around the activities you perform in your class each day. With WileyPLUS you can:

Prepare & Present
Create outstanding class presentations using a wealth of resources such as PowerPoint™ slides, image galleries, interactive simulations, and more. You can even add materials you have created yourself.

Create Assignments
Automate the assigning and grading of homework or quizzes by using the provided question banks, or by writing your own.

Track Student Progress
Keep track of your students' progress and analyze individual and overall class results.

Now Available with WebCT and Blackboard!

"It has been a great help, and I believe it has helped me to achieve a better grade."

Michael Morris,
Columbia Basin College

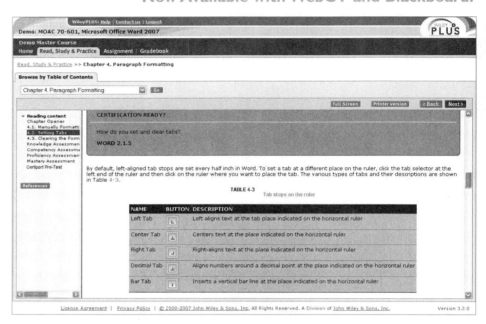

FOR STUDENTS

You have the potential to make a difference!

WileyPLUS is a powerful online system packed with features to help you make the most of your potential and get the best grade you can!

With WileyPLUS you get:

A complete online version of your text and other study resources.

Problem-solving help, instant grading, and feedback on your homework and quizzes.

The ability to track your progress and grades throughout the term.

Access to Microsoft's Assessment, Learning Plan, and MCAS examination voucher.

For more information on what *WileyPLUS* can do to help you and your students reach their potential, please visit www.wiley.com/college/*wileyplus*.

76% of students surveyed said it made them better prepared for tests.*

*Based on a survey of 972 student users of *WileyPLUS*

Getting to Know Outlook

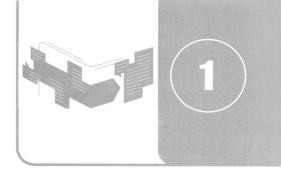

LESSON SKILL MATRIX

SKILLS	MATRIX SKILL	SKILL NUMBER
Starting Outlook		
Working in the Outlook Window		
Personalizing Outlook		
Working with the Reading Pane	Show, hide, or move the Reading pane	1.7.1
Viewing, Hiding, and Minimizing the To-Do Bar	Show, hide, or minimize the To Do Bar	5.6.1
Customizing the To-Do Bar	Customize the To Do Bar	5.6.2

Adventure Works is a luxurious resort located in Ohio. During the summer, activities such as kayaking, canoeing, hiking, and horseback riding are available. In the winter months, visitors enjoy skiing, snowshoeing, and sleigh rides. Partners Mindy Martin and Jon Morris own and operate Adventure Works. They work hard to ensure that guests enjoy their stay. Employees are well-trained and well-treated professionals. For one week every year, Mindy and Jon close the resort to guests and open the facilities to employees and their families.

KEY TERMS
desktop shortcut
folder
item
Navigation pane
Reading pane
To-Do Bar

■ SOFTWARE ORIENTATION

Microsoft Outlook's Opening Screen

Before you begin working in Microsoft Outlook, you need to be familiar with the primary user interface. When you first launch Microsoft Outlook, you will see a screen similar to that shown in Figure 1-1.

Figure 1-1

Outlook opening screen

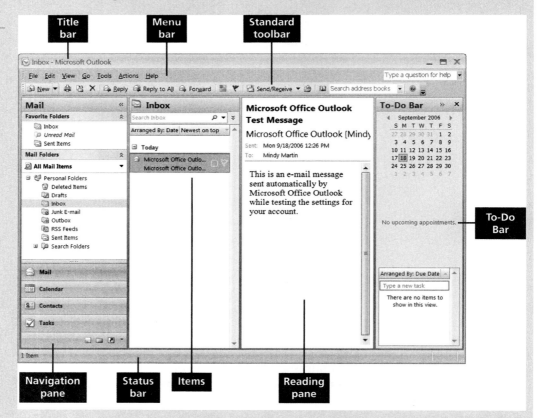

The elements and features of this screen are typical for Microsoft Outlook. Your screen may vary if default settings have been changed or if other preferences have been set. Use this figure as a reference throughout this lesson as well as the rest of this book.

■ Starting Outlook

THE BOTTOM LINE

Microsoft Outlook 2007 can be launched in two different ways.

Starting Microsoft Outlook is similar to starting any other Microsoft Office application. You can launch Outlook from the Start button on the Windows taskbar at the bottom of your screen. You can also launch Outlook by double-clicking a shortcut created on the Windows desktop.

Launching Outlook from the Start Menu

Like all Microsoft Office applications, Microsoft Outlook can be launched from the Start button. In fact, using the Start button might be the most common method of launching Outlook. After Outlook is installed, click the Start button on the Windows taskbar, point to All Programs, point to Microsoft Office, and click Microsoft Office Outlook 2007.

LAUNCH OUTLOOK FROM THE START MENU

GET READY. Before you begin these steps, be sure to turn on or log on to your computer.

1. Click the Start button.
2. Point to All Programs. Point to Microsoft Office. Click Microsoft Office Outlook 2007. Microsoft Outlook 2007 is launched.
3. Compare your screen to Figure 1-1 and identify the labeled items.
4. Click the Close button in the upper-right corner.

   PAUSE. You will launch Outlook again in the next exercise.

You have just launched Outlook from the Start menu and familiarized yourself with the locations of the elements on the main Outlook window. In the next exercise, you will launch Outlook from a shortcut on your desktop.

Launching Outlook from a Desktop Shortcut

You can also launch Microsoft Outlook 2007 from a desktop shortcut.
As you saw in the previous exercise, you can launch Outlook from the Start menu. However, some people prefer to use a desktop shortcut. A ***desktop shortcut*** is an icon placed on the Windows desktop that launches an application, opens a folder, or opens a file. Simply double-click the desktop shortcut to perform the specified action.

LAUNCH OUTLOOK FROM A DESKTOP SHORTCUT

GET READY. Before you begin these steps, be sure that Microsoft Outlook is not running.

1. Click the Start button.
2. Point to All Programs. Point to Microsoft Office. Right-click Microsoft Office Outlook 2007. Point to Send To. Click the Desktop (create shortcut) option. The desktop shortcut shown in Figure 1-2 is created.

Figure 1-2

Desktop shortcut for Microsoft Office Outlook 2007

3. Minimize any applications so you can see your desktop.
4. Double-click the Microsoft Office Outlook 2007 desktop shortcut. Microsoft Outlook 2007 is launched.

   PAUSE. LEAVE Outlook open to use in the next exercise.

As you have just seen, Outlook can be launched in two different ways. Use the method you prefer.

- Click the Start button on the Windows taskbar, point to All Programs, point to Microsoft Office, and click Microsoft Office Outlook 2007.
- Double-click the desktop shortcut.

■ Working in the Outlook Window

THE BOTTOM LINE

Outlook has a variety of tools that help you organize your communication and manage your time.

If you need to send a message to a vendor making a late delivery, look up an old friend's phone number, or schedule a staff meeting, Outlook provides the tools that will save time and make your job easier. Refer to Figure 1-1 to view the Outlook window you see when you launch Outlook.

ANOTHER WAY

You also can select the component from the Go menu or use the keyboard shortcut listed next to each component in the Go menu.

Using the On-Screen Tools

Outlook's on-screen tools enable you to access the information you need.

Outlook's on-screen tools include menu commands and buttons that help you to navigate through Outlook's components. As you click buttons or select menu commands, the components in the Outlook window change to display the information you requested or provide space to enter new information.

⊖ USE THE ON-SCREEN TOOLS

GET READY Before you begin these steps, be sure that Microsoft Outlook is running.

1. Click the Calendar button in the Navigation pane, as shown in Figure 1-3. The calendar is displayed.

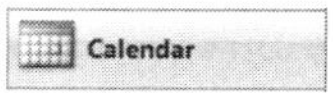

Figure 1-3

Calendar button in the Navigation pane

2. Click the Contacts button in the Navigation pane, as shown in Figure 1-4. Information about the contacts stored in Outlook is displayed.

Figure 1-4

Contacts button in the Navigation pane

3. Click the Tasks button in the Navigation pane, as shown in Figure 1-5. Information about your current tasks and your to-do list are displayed.

Figure 1-5

Tasks button in the Navigation pane

4. Click the Notes button in the Navigation pane, as shown in Figure 1-6. Any notes already entered are displayed.

Figure 1-6

Notes, Folder List, and Shortcuts buttons in the Navigation pane

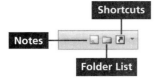

5. Click the Folder List button in the Navigation pane, as shown in Figure 1-6. The list of folders is displayed in the upper area of the Navigation pane.

6. Click the Shortcuts button in the Navigation pane, as shown in Figure 1-6. Any shortcuts already created are displayed in the upper area of the Navigation pane.

7. Click the Minimize button at the top of the Navigation pane, as shown in Figure 1-7. The Navigation pane is displayed as a vertical strip on the left side of the Outlook window.

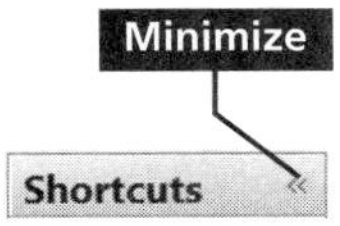

Figure 1-7

Minimize the Navigation pane

8. Click the Expand button at the top of the minimized Navigation pane, as shown in Figure 1-8. The Navigation pane is restored to its previous size and location.

Figure 1-8

Expand the Navigation pane

9. Click the Mail button in the Navigation pane, as shown in Figure 1-9. The window should return to the default view displayed when you launched Outlook.

Figure 1-9

Mail button in the Navigation pane

PAUSE. LEAVE Outlook open to use in the next exercise.

In the previous exercise, you took a quick look at the Outlook components by using the Navigation pane. The following table describes the basic function of each on-screen tool used to access Outlook's components. More detailed information about using the components is available in the following sections of this lesson and the remaining lessons.

On-Screen Tool	Description
Item	An *item* is a record stored in Outlook. A message, appointment, contact, task, or note is an item in Outlook.
Menu bar	The Menu bar contains the menus and commands available in Outlook.
Navigation pane	The *Navigation pane* provides access to the Outlook components, such as the Contacts and the Calendar. In Outlook 2007, you can free up additional space by minimizing the Navigation pane. The navigation elements are still available when the Navigation pane is minimized.
Reading pane	The *Reading pane* displays the text of a selected email message.
Standard toolbar	The Standard toolbar contains buttons that access frequently used commands.
Status bar	The Status bar identifies the number of items in the active component. For example, when the Contacts component is active, the number of contacts stored is displayed in the Status bar.
Title bar	The Title bar identifies the application and the active component. For example, when the Calendar is active, the Title bar says "Calendar—Microsoft Outlook."
To-Do Bar NEW FEATURE	The *To-Do Bar* is a new feature that summarizes information about appointments and tasks.

Changing Outlook's View

Every Outlook component has multiple viewing options.

To help you accomplish each task, the Outlook components provide specific information in the Outlook window. For example, the Contacts component provides the names, addresses, and phone numbers for the individuals and companies you contact. The Calendar tracks your appointments and meetings. Mail enables you to send and receive email messages.

Outlook stores and organizes many of the little pieces of information that form the core of your daily activities. In a single day, you might meet with the design team at 9:00; negotiate a deal with a new supplier at 10:00; have lunch with the Vice President of Marketing at 12:30; call several associates to discuss a new design concept; send a message to the vice president's office confirming details about the new design; attend a department meeting at 3:00, when your promotion to department head is announced; and scoot out the door at 5:15 to pick up your daughter from soccer practice. What part did Outlook play in those activities? You used Outlook to schedule the meetings, look up the phone numbers, send the email message, and set up the reminders that helped you arrive on time for every meeting. You used Outlook's Calendar, Mail, and Contacts components to keep you on top of everything. That promotion was well deserved!

In the previous exercise, you used the on-screen tools to move through the Outlook components. In this exercise, you will access the Outlook components again and see some of the viewing options available in each one. Don't worry about using the components yet. The components you use most frequently are covered in more detail in the following lessons. Shortcuts and the Journal are not frequently used, and they are not covered in this book.

CHANGE OUTLOOK'S VIEW

GET READY. Before you begin these steps, be sure that Microsoft Outlook is running.

1. If necessary, click the Mail button in the Navigation pane to display the Mail folder, as shown in Figure 1-10.

Figure 1-10

Mail folder

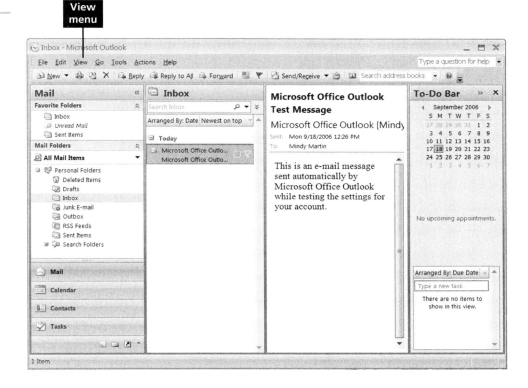

2. Open the View menu. Point to Arrange By to see the basic viewing options for the Mail folder. Point to Current View to see additional viewing options. The options currently active are identified by a checkmark.

3. Click the Calendar button in the Navigation pane to display the Calendar folder, and click the Day button above the calendar as shown in Figure 1-11. The view showing today's date is displayed.

Figure 1-11

Calendar folder

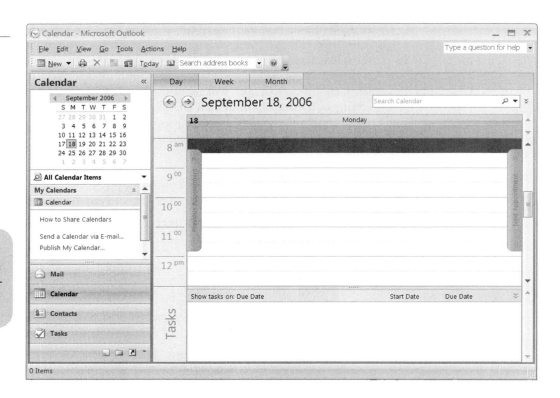

 ANOTHER WAY

You can also click the Day, Week, and Month buttons below the Standard toolbar to change the view.

4. Open the View menu. The Day option is currently selected. In the View menu, click the Work Week, Week, and Month options. Note the changes in the Outlook window as you change views. Open the View menu again and click the Day option to return to the day view. Open the View menu again and point to Current View to see additional viewing options for the Calendar. The options currently active are identified by a checkmark.

5. Click the Contacts button in the Navigation pane to display the Contacts folder, as shown in Figure 1-12.

Figure 1-12

Contacts folder

Viewing options

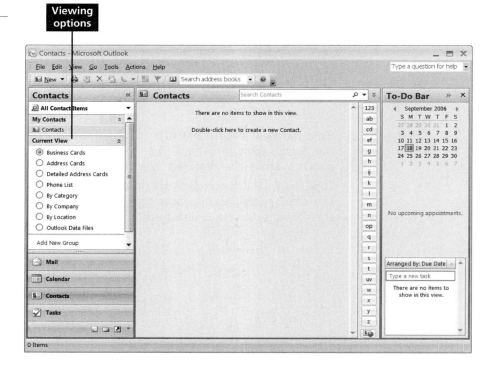

6. Open the View menu. Point to Current View to see the viewing options. The options currently active are identified by a checkmark. Note that the same options listed in the Current View menu are displayed in the Navigation pane.

7. Click the Tasks button in the Navigation pane to display the Tasks folder, as shown in Figure 1-13.

Figure 1-13

Tasks folder

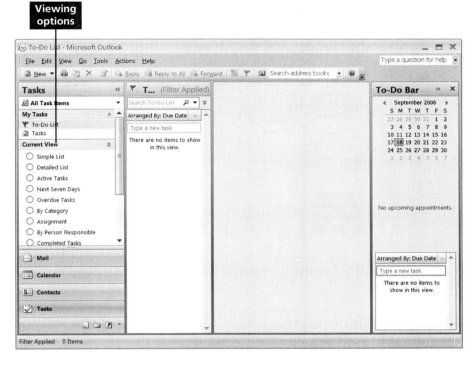

8. Open the View menu. Point to Current View to see the viewing options. The options currently active are identified by a checkmark. Note that the same options listed in the Current View menu are displayed in the Navigation pane.

9. Click the Notes button in the Navigation pane to display the Notes folder, as shown in Figure 1-14.

Figure 1-14

Notes folder

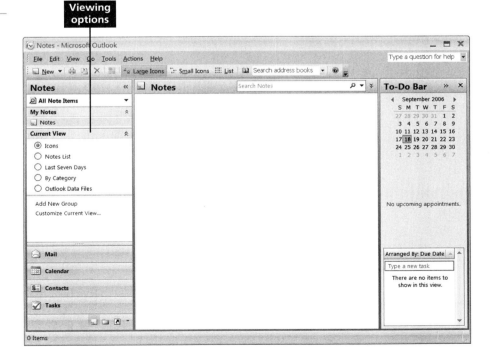

10. Open the View menu. Point to Current View to see the viewing options. The options currently active are identified by a checkmark. Note that the same options listed in the Current View menu are displayed in the Navigation pane.

11. Click the Folder List button in the Navigation pane to display the Folder List in the upper area of the Navigation pane, as shown in Figure 1-15. Note that the Notes folder is highlighted in the Folder List and the main portion of the Outlook window still displays the Notes folder. Clicking the Folder List button only affects the information displayed in the Navigation pane.

Figure 1-15

Folder List and Notes folder displayed

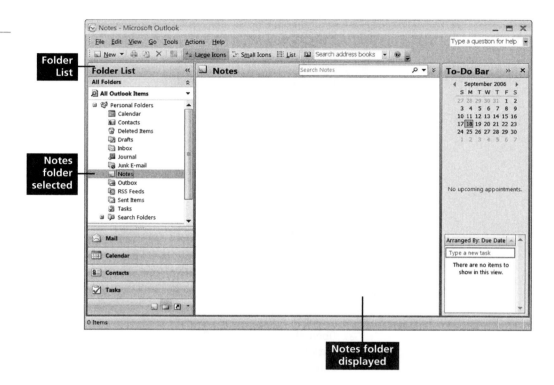

12. Click the Mail button in the Navigation pane to return to the default view displayed when Outlook is launched.

PAUSE. LEAVE Outlook open to use in the next exercise.

Outlook components are commonly called *folders,* because the items are organized into folders. For example, when you click the Mail button, Outlook's Mail component, or Mail folder, is displayed. This becomes more obvious when you display the Folder List, as shown in Figure 1-15. Every Outlook component is a folder in the Folder List. If you create folders in the future to further organize your Outlook items, the folders you create will also be displayed in the Folder List.

In the previous exercise, you displayed each of the commonly used Outlook folders. The following table briefly describes how these Outlook folders are used.

FOLDER	DESCRIPTION
Calendar	The Calendar folder contains a calendar and appointment book to help you keep track of your schedule.
Contacts	The Contacts folder stores contact information about individuals, groups, and companies.
Folder List	The Folder List identifies all of your Outlook folders. If your company or organization uses Microsoft Exchange Server, public folders you can access also are listed.
Mail	The Mail folder contains your email messages. Folders in the Mail folder include your Inbox (messages received), Sent Items (messages sent), Outbox (messages waiting to be sent), and Junk E-mail (unwanted messages you received that were not directed to another folder).
Notes	The Notes folder stores small pieces of information on electronic sticky notes. Notes can be forwarded as email messages.
Tasks	The Tasks folder displays tasks assigned to you.

■ Personalizing Outlook

You can arrange the elements on the Outlook window to fit your needs.

Resize, rearrange, hide, or display Outlook components to create an environment that meets your requirements. Reposition the Reading pane. Hide components you don't use. Expand panes that contain critical information you need to see.

Working with the Reading Pane

Show, hide, or move the Reading pane.

Arrange the Reading pane to fit your needs. Do you get a lot of long email messages? Display the Reading pane vertically on the right to display the most text possible. Perhaps the messages you receive contain a lot of information in the item listing area. Display the Reading pane horizontally.

⟶ WORK WITH THE READING PANE

GET READY. Before you begin these steps, be sure that Microsoft Outlook is running.

1. If necessary, click the Mail button in the Navigation pane to display the Mail folder.

2. Click the View menu, point to Reading Pane, and select the Bottom option. The Reading pane is displayed horizontally, across the bottom of the message viewing area, as shown in Figure 1-16.

Figure 1-16

Reading pane displayed in the bottom position

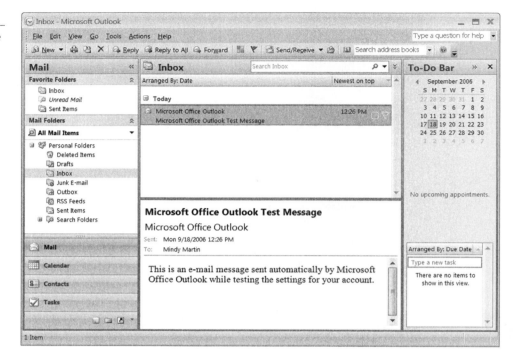

3. Click the View menu, point to Reading Pane, and select the Off option. The Reading pane is hidden, as shown in Figure 1-17.

Figure 1-17

Reading pane is hidden

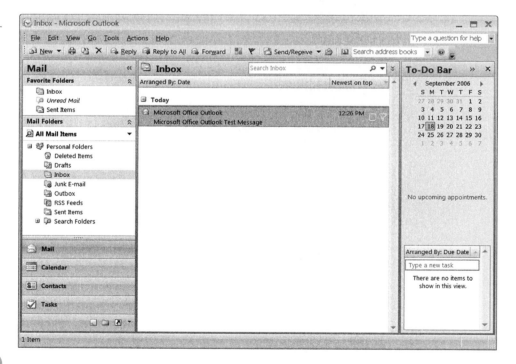

CERTIFICATION READY?
How do you show, hide, or move the Reading pane?
1.7.1

4. Click the View menu, point to Reading Pane, and select the Right option. The Reading pane is displayed in its default position on the right.
   PAUSE. LEAVE Outlook open to use in the next exercise.

Viewing, Hiding, and Minimizing the To-Do Bar

Show, hide, or minimize the new To-Do Bar.
The To-Do Bar is a new feature in Outlook 2007. It summarizes the current items that need your attention. You can show, hide, or minimize the To-Do Bar.

VIEW, HIDE, AND MINIMIZE THE TO-DO BAR

GET READY. Before you begin these steps, be sure that Microsoft Outlook is running.

1. If necessary, click the Mail button in the Navigation pane to display the Mail folder.

2. Click the View menu, point to To-Do Bar, and select the Minimized option. The To-Do Bar is minimized to a slim pane on the right side of the Outlook window, as shown in Figure 1-18.

Figure 1-18

Minimized To-Do Bar

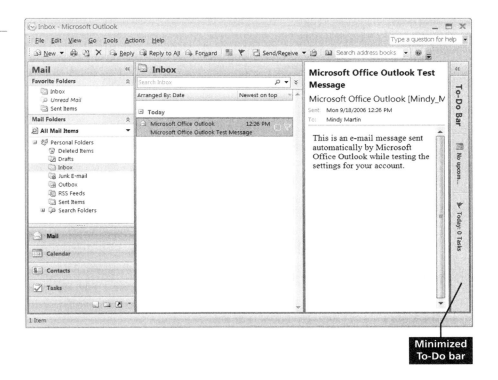

Minimized
To-Do bar

3. Click the View menu, point to To-Do Bar, and select the Off option. The To-Do Bar is hidden.

4. Click the View menu, point to To-Do Bar, and select the Normal option. The To-Do Bar is restored to its original size and position.

   PAUSE. LEAVE Outlook open to use in the next exercise.

CERTIFICATION READY?
How do you show, hide, or minimize the To-Do Bar?
5.6.1

In the previous exercise, you hid, minimized, and expanded the To-Do Bar. In the next exercise, you will customize the To-Do Bar for your use.

Customizing the To-Do Bar NEW FEATURE

You can select the elements to include on the new To-Do Bar.
The To-Do Bar summarizes the current Outlook items that need some follow-up. With a single glance, you can see your appointments, tasks, and email messages that require some action.

CUSTOMIZE THE TO-DO BAR

GET READY. Before you begin these steps, be sure that Microsoft Outlook is running.

1. If necessary, click the Mail button in the Navigation pane to display the Mail folder and verify that the To-Do Bar is displayed.
2. Click the View menu, point to To-Do Bar, and select Options. The To-Do Bar Options dialog box is displayed, as shown in Figure 1-19.

Figure 1-19

To-Do Bar Options dialog box

 ANOTHER WAY

You can also show or hide the To-Do Bar by opening the View menu and selecting the To-Do Bar.

3. Examine the options. The checkmark indicates that the element is currently displayed. The numbers indicate the number of months you want to display in the Date Navigator and the number of appointments to be displayed.
4. Click the Show Task List checkbox and click the OK button. The dialog box closes and the Task List is removed from the To-Do Bar.
5. Click the View menu, point to To-Do Bar, and select the Task List option. The Task List is displayed on the To-Do Bar.

PAUSE. CLOSE outlook.

CERTIFICATION READY?
How do you customize the To-Do Bar?
5.6.2

In the previous exercise, you customized the To-Do Bar by selecting the elements to be displayed. The following table describes the elements in the To-Do Bar so you can decide which elements you want to use.

TO-DO BAR ELEMENT	DESCRIPTION
Appointments	The Appointments element displays appointments scheduled in Outlook. You can select the number of appointments to be displayed.
Date Navigator	The Date Navigator displays a small calendar. You can select the number of months to be displayed.
Task Input Panel	Key new tasks into the Task Input Panel.
Task list	The task list displays the tasks that have been assigned to you.

SUMMARY SKILL MATRIX

IN THIS LESSON YOU LEARNED	MATRIX SKILL	SKILL NUMBER
To start Outlook from the Start button or a desktop shortcut		
To work in the Outlook window		
To use the on-screen tools		
To change the view in Outlook		
To personalize Outlook		
To work with the Reading pane	Show, hide, or move the Reading pane	1.7.1
To view, hide, and minimize the To-Do Bar	Show, hide, or minimize the To Do Bar	5.6.1
To customize the To-Do Bar	Customize the To Do Bar	5.6.2

■ Knowledge Assessment

Matching

Match the term with its definition.

a. desktop shortcut   f. maximize
b. folder   g. minimize
c. item   h. Navigation pane
d. launch   i. Title bar
e. Reading pane   j. To-Do Bar

_____ 1. A record stored in Outlook

_____ 2. Reduce the size of a pane or window

_____ 3. New feature that summarizes information about appointments and tasks

_____ 4. Start running an application

_____ 5. Common name for Outlook components

_____ 6. Restore a minimized pane or window

_____ 7. Provides access to the Outlook components, such as the Contacts and Calendar

_____ 8. Displays the text of a selected email message

_____ 9. Identifies the application and the active component

_____ 10. An icon placed on the Windows desktop that launches an application, opens a folder, or opens a file

True/False

Circle T if the statement is true or F if the statement is false.

(T) F **1.** Like all Microsoft Office applications, Microsoft Outlook can be launched from the Start button.

(T) F **2.** A desktop shortcut is an icon placed on the Windows desktop that launches an application, opens a folder, or opens a file.

T (F) **3.** Select a component from the Go menu to minimize the component.

T (F) **4.** The Status bar identifies the application and the active component.

(T) F **5.** In Outlook, messages, appointments, contacts, tasks, and notes are called items.

T (F) **6.** The Viewing pane displays the text of a selected email message.

(T) F **7.** The Calendar folder contains an appointment book.

(T) F **8.** The Reading pane can be hidden.

(T) F **9.** In the To-Do Bar, you can see your appointments, tasks, and email messages that require some action.

T (F) **10.** The Date Navigator in the To-Do Bar can only display one month.

■ Competency Assessment

Project 1-1: View the Outlook Menus

Become familiar with the Outlook menus.

GET READY. Before you begin these steps, be sure that Microsoft Outlook is running.

1. If necessary, click the Mail button in the Navigation pane to display the Mail folder and verify that the To-Do Bar is displayed.
2. Click the File menu. Point to each option in the File menu.
3. Click the Edit menu. Point to each option in the Edit menu.
4. Click the View menu. Point to each option in the View menu.
5. Click the Go menu. Point to each option in the Go menu.
6. Click the Tools menu. Point to each option in the Tools menu.
7. Click the Actions menu. Point to each option in the Actions menu.
8. Click the Help menu. Point to each option in the Help menu.

   LEAVE Outlook open for the next project.

Project 1-2: Use the Folder List

Use the Folder List to display the Outlook folders.

1. Click the Folder List button in the Navigation pane. The Folder List is displayed in the upper area of the Navigation pane.
2. Click the Calendar folder in the Folder List. The Calendar is displayed.
3. Click the Contacts folder in the Folder List. The Contacts folder is displayed.
4. Click the Folder List button again. Click the Deleted Items folder in the Folder List. The Deleted Items folder is displayed. Any deleted Outlook items are stored here until this folder is emptied.

5. Right-click the Deleted Items folder in the Folder List. Note the Empty "Deleted Items" Folder option. Selecting this option permanently deletes these items.
6. Click the Inbox folder in the Folder List. By default, the Inbox folder contains any email messages you have received.
7. Click the Notes folder in the Folder List. The Notes folder is displayed.
8. Click the Tasks folder in the Folder List. The Tasks folder is displayed.
9. Click the Mail button in the Navigation pane to return to Outlook's default view.

   LEAVE Outlook open for the next project.

■ Proficiency Assessment

Project 1-3: Use Keyboard Shortcuts to View Outlook Folders

The main Outlook folders can be accessed by keyboard shortcuts. Use the shortcuts to display the folders.

1. Identify the keyboard shortcuts used to display the Mail, Calendar, Contacts, Tasks, Notes, and Folder List components.
2. Use the keyboard shortcuts to display the Outlook components.

   LEAVE Outlook open for the next project.

Project 1-4: Customize the To-Do Bar

Change the number of months and appointments displayed in the To-Do Bar.

1. If necessary, click the Mail button in the Navigation pane to display the Mail folder and verify that the To-Do Bar is displayed.
2. Display the options for Outlook's To-Do Bar.
3. Change the options to display two months and five appointments.
4. Return to the main Outlook window to see the changes in the To-Do Bar.
5. Display the options for Outlook's To-Do Bar again.
6. Change the options to the default values to display one month and three appointments.
7. Return to the main Outlook window to see the changes in the To-Do Bar.

   LEAVE Outlook open for the next project.

■ Mastery Assessment

Project 1-5: Identify the New Features in Outlook 2007

The To-Do Bar discussed in this lesson is only one of many new features in Outlook 2007.

1. Use Microsoft Office Outlook Help to investigate the new features in Outlook 2007.
2. Identify the new features that could affect how you use Outlook 2007.

   LEAVE Outlook open for the next project.

Project 1-6: **Customize the Outlook Window**

The panes inside the Outlook window can be resized like the panes in most Microsoft Office products.

1. If necessary, click the Mail button in the Navigation pane to display the Mail folder and verify that the To-Do Bar is displayed.

2. Using the mouse, hover over a border between two panes. When the pointer icon changes, drag the border to resize the pane.

3. Adjust the size of all the panes.

4. Close Outlook. Launch Outlook. The resized panes should be displayed.

   CLOSE Outlook.

INTERNET READY

Unfortunately, you might not be the only user on your computer. You might share your computer with a coworker at the office or a family member at home. How can you keep your email private without requiring passwords or a series of arcane gestures and dance steps? Create an email profile. Use the Internet or Microsoft Office Outlook Help to investigate the benefits and limitations of an email profile.

Email Basics

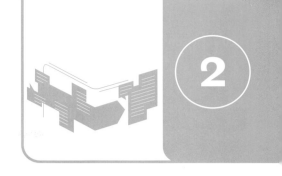

2

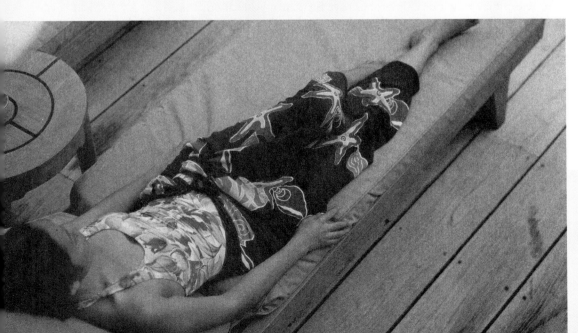

KEY TERMS
attachment
AutoComplete
AutoPreview
Microsoft Office Button
Quick Access Toolbar
Ribbon
signature
subject

indy Martin and Jon Morris own and operate Adventure Works, a luxury resort in Ohio. They stay busy throughout the day. Frequently, they work different shifts to stay on top of the activities that occur at different times of the day. Sometimes, they rely on email to keep each other informed.

■ SOFTWARE ORIENTATION

Microsoft Outlook's Message Window

Email is the most frequently used Outlook component. The message window, shown in Figure 2-1, is familiar to every Outlook user.

Figure 2-1

Outlook's Message window

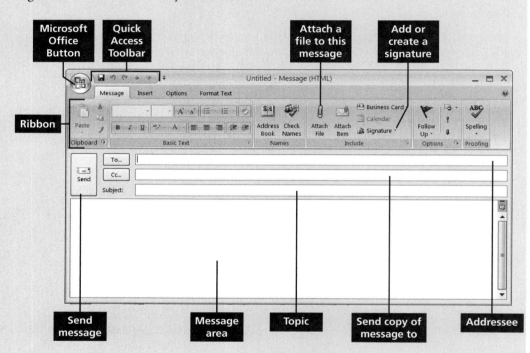

Many of the elements in the Message window are familiar to you if you use Microsoft Word 2007. The editor used to create messages in Outlook is based on Microsoft Word 2007. Your screen may vary if default settings have been changed or if other preferences have been set. Use this figure as a reference throughout this lesson as well as the rest of this book.

■ Creating and Sending Messages

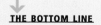
THE BOTTOM LINE

Creating and sending messages are the most common user activities in Outlook. Sending an email message is easier than addressing and mailing a letter. An email message can be sent to one or more recipients, resent if necessary, and saved for future reference.

Composing a Message

Microsoft Outlook's email component is a full-featured composition tool that provides many of the same functions found in Microsoft Word.

Keying, copying, cutting, and deleting text in an Outlook message are identical to these same functions in Microsoft Word 2007. Formatting and spellchecking text also are similar.

→ **COMPOSE A MESSAGE**

GET READY. Before you begin these steps, be sure to launch Microsoft Outlook.

1. If necessary, click the Mail button in the Navigation pane to display the Mail folder, as shown in Figure 2-2.

Figure 2-2

Outlook's opening screen

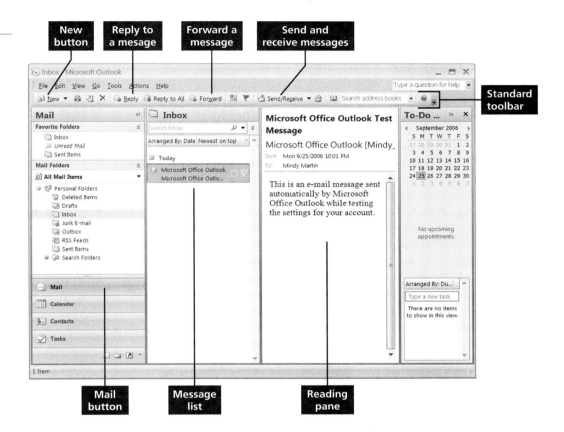

2. Click the New button in the Standard toolbar. The Message window is displayed.
3. Click the message area.
4. Key today's date in month–day–year format. For example, key September 7, 2006. As you begin to key the name of the month, Outlook will display the name of the month. Press Enter to accept the suggested month or continue keying the letters to ignore the suggestion. This is the **AutoComplete** function. It helps you quickly enter the names of the months and days of the week. AutoComplete cannot be turned off.
5. Press Enter twice to move to the next line and add a blank line.
6. Key Hi Jon, and press Enter. Press Enter again to add a blank line.
7. Key Blue Yonder Airlines is running a contest in January. The winner gets free round-trip airfare to Cincinnati. Terry Crayton, a marketing assistant at Blue Yonder, asked if we would be interested in offering a free weekend at Adventure Works as part of the prize. What do you think?
8. Press Enter twice to end the paragraph and insert a blank line.
9. Key Let me know, and press Enter.
10. Key your name, and press Enter.

PAUSE. LEAVE the message open to use in the next exercise.

Regardless of the tool you use, the task of writing a message is the same. In normal business correspondence, you would be more formal in addressing the correspondence. However, this example is just a quick note between the partners at Adventure Works.

Sending a Message

Addressing an email message is similar to addressing a letter. In seconds, you can send an email message to one or more recipients.

→ SEND A MESSAGE

USE the message you created in the previous exercise.

1. Click the To field. Key someone@example.com or key the email address of a friend or coworker. To send the message to more than one recipient, key a semicolon (;), and then key another email address.
2. Click the Subject field. Key Blue Yonder Airlines contest, as shown in Figure 2-3.

Figure 2-3

Message ready to be sent

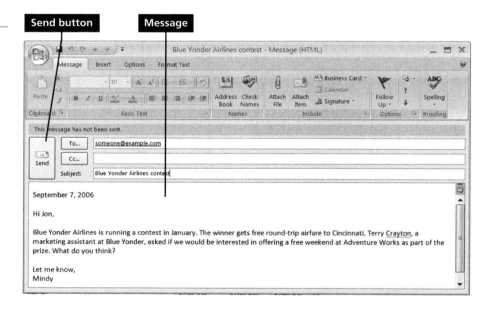

TROUBLESHOOTING

Someone@example.com is an address owned by Microsoft Corporation. Because this is not a real email address, you will receive an error message or a message thanking you for using Microsoft products.

3. Click the Send button. The Message window closes, and the message is moved to the Outbox. If your computer is connected to the Internet, the message is sent to the addressee. If your computer is not connected to the Internet, the message will remain in the Outbox until an Internet connection is made and the message can be sent.

   PAUSE. LEAVE Outlook open to use in the next exercise.

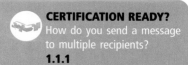

CERTIFICATION READY?
How do you send a message to multiple recipients?
1.1.1

In the previous exercise, you used the Message window to compose and send an email message. The To, Cc, Subject, and message area are elements found in Microsoft Outlook. The Ribbon, the Microsoft Office Button, and the Quick Access Toolbar, shown in Figure 2-1, are new in Microsoft Outlook 2007. The following table describes the function of each element in the Message window.

ELEMENT	DESCRIPTION
Cc	The Cc field is optional. You can send a message without entering anything in the Cc field. Generally, you would use this to send a copy of the message to individuals who you think should be informed about the message content, but you don't expect the person receiving a copy to take any action.
Message area	Key the content of the message in the message area.
Microsoft Office Button	Use the new **Microsoft Office Button** to access common Outlook tasks, such as creating a new Outlook item and saving, deleting, printing, or changing permissions for the current message.
Quick Access Toolbar	Use the new **Quick Access Toolbar** to save, print, or undo your recent actions and redo your recent actions. The position and content of the Quick Access Toolbar can be customized.
Ribbon	The new **Ribbon** organizes commands into logical groups. The groups are placed under tabs that focus on a particular activity. In the Message window, the tabs include Message, Insert, Options, and Format Text. The content of the Ribbon varies by the task. The Ribbon in the Message window contains different options than the Ribbon in the Contact window.
Subject	Key a brief description of the information in the message. The **Subject** tells the recipient what the message is about and makes it easier to find the message later.
To	Key the name or email address of the person or people who will receive the message you are sending. To send the message to several addressees, key a semicolon after a name before adding the next addressee.

Resending a Message

Occasionally, you may want to resend a message. Perhaps you want to send the same message to additional recipients or the recipient has accidentally deleted the message and needs another copy.

→ RESEND A MESSAGE

USE the message you sent in the previous exercise.

1. In the Navigation pane, click the Sent Items folder. The email messages you sent will be listed as items in the Sent Items folder, as shown in Figure 2-4.

Figure 2-4

Sent Items folder

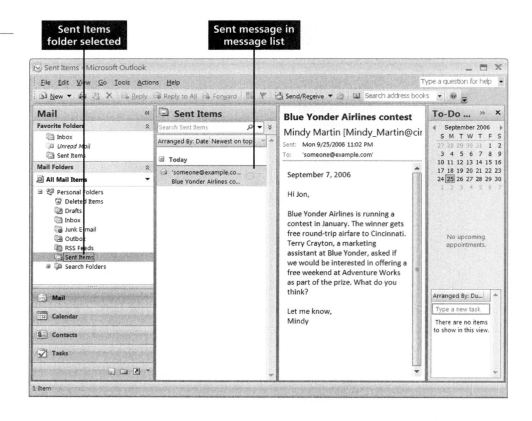

TROUBLESHOOTING

If your computer has not been connected to the Internet since you started this lesson, the messages you sent will still be in the Outbox. Outgoing messages are moved to the Outbox when you click the Send button. They are moved to the Sent Items folder when you connect to the Internet and the messages are sent.

2. In the list of items that have been sent, double-click the message you sent in the last exercise. The message is displayed in a new window, as shown in Figure 2-5. The title bar of the new window is the subject of the message.

Figure 2-5

Sent message

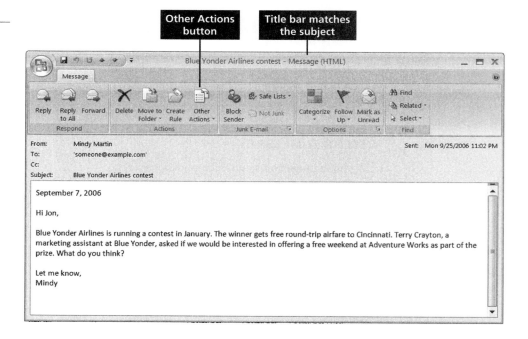

3. Click the Other Actions button in the Actions group on the Ribbon. Select the Resend This Message option. This opens the message in a new window. It enables you to key additional addresses and edit the content of the message.

4. Click after the addressee in the To field. Key a semicolon (;) and an additional email address, as shown in Figure 2-6. For this exercise, use your email address as the addressee.

Figure 2-6

Message ready to be resent

5. Click the Send button. The Message window closes, and the message is moved to the Outbox. The message is sent when your computer is connected to the Internet.

6. Close the Message window that was displayed when you double-clicked the sent item.

7. In the Navigation pane, click the Inbox folder. The Inbox is displayed.
   PAUSE. LEAVE Outlook open to use in the next exercise.

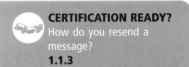

CERTIFICATION READY?
How do you resend a message?
1.1.3

In the previous exercise, you resent a message. When you resend a message, you can delete the original addressee, add new addressees, and edit the message content.

Saving a Copy of a Sent Message in a Different Location

By default, sent messages are saved in the Sent Items folder. You might want to save a copy of a message in a different location. For example, you can keep messages about a specific project in a different folder. Or, you can keep correspondence with a specific individual in a separate folder. Organizing your messages can help you stay on top of a hectic day.

SAVE A COPY OF A SENT MESSAGE IN A DIFFERENT LOCATION

GET READY. Before you begin these steps, be sure to launch Microsoft Outlook.

1. Click the New button in the Standard toolbar. The Message window is displayed.
2. Click the To field. Key the email address of a friend or coworker.
3. Click the Subject field. Key Different Save Location.
4. Click the Options tab on the Ribbon, as shown in Figure 2-7.

Figure 2-7

New message to be saved in a different location

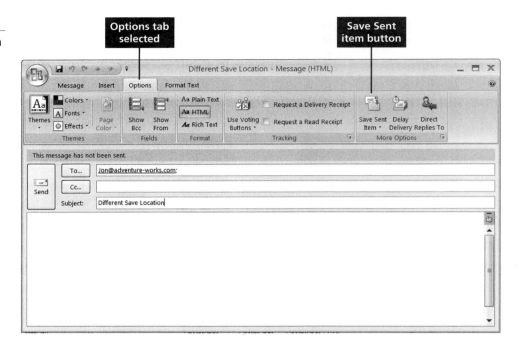

5. Click the Save Sent Item button and select the Other Folder option. The Select Folder dialog box is displayed, as shown in Figure 2-8.

Figure 2-8

Select Folder dialog box

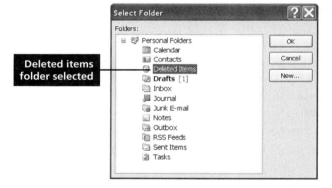

6. Select the Deleted Items folder, and click OK to close the dialog box.

 TROUBLESHOOTING Normally, you will create a new folder or save the message to a folder you created earlier. That isn't necessary for this exercise.

X REF

You will learn more about creating and using folders in Lesson 4.

7. Click the Send button. The Message window closes, and the message is moved to the Outbox. The message is sent when your computer is connected to the Internet.
8. In the main Outlook window, click the Deleted Items folder in the Navigation pane. The message will be displayed in the Deleted Items folder when it has been sent.
9. Click the Inbox in the Navigation pane.

PAUSE. LEAVE Outlook open to use in the next exercise.

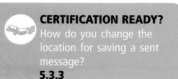

CERTIFICATION READY?
How do you change the location for saving a sent message?
5.3.3

Save sent messages in different folders determined by the message content or addressee. Later, you will learn to create rules that automatically move messages to different folders.

■ Reading and Replying to Messages

↓
THE BOTTOM LINE When you receive an email message, you naturally want to read it and send a reply. Outlook enables you to preview and reply to a message with a few mouse clicks.

Automatically Previewing Messages

If you return to your desk after a meeting to find 20 messages in your Inbox and another meeting to attend in 5 minutes, it's impossible to read all the messages and still get to the meeting on time. Use *AutoPreview* to view the first three lines of every message in the message list.

➔ AUTOMATICALLY PREVIEW MESSAGES

GET READY. Outlook must be running to turn on the AutoPreview option.

1. Click the View menu. Select the AutoPreview option. The first three lines of text in each message are displayed, as shown in Figure 2-9.

Figure 2-9

AutoPreview messages

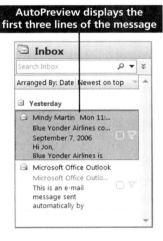

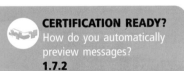
CERTIFICATION READY?
How do you automatically preview messages?
1.7.2

2. Click the View menu. Select the AutoPreview option. This turns off the AutoPreview function.

PAUSE. LEAVE Outlook open to use in the next exercise.

AutoPreview requires more space in the message list. Therefore, you probably want to turn off the feature most of the time.

Sending a Reply to a Message

Every message doesn't require a reply, but many messages need a response of some type. When you use the Reply function, your response is automatically addressed to the person who sent the message to you.

➔ SEND A REPLY TO A MESSAGE

USE the message you received when you sent a message to yourself in a previous exercise.

1. In the Inbox, click the message with the subject "Blue Yonder Airlines contest." The message is selected.

If you click the Reply to All button on the Standard toolbar, the reply will be sent to the sender and everyone who received the original message.

2. Click the Reply button on the Standard toolbar. The message is displayed in a new window, as shown in Figure 2-10. Note that the To and Subject fields are already filled. In the Subject field, the text "RE:" was inserted before the original subject line. "RE:" tells the recipient that the message is a reply about the Blue Yonder Airlines contest topic. The original message is included at the bottom of the window. It is sent as part of the reply.

Figure 2-10

Reply to a message you received

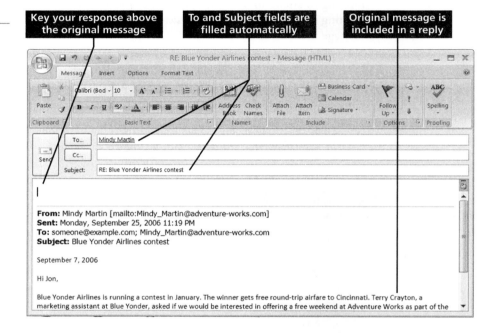

3. Key The contest could be a good idea. Let's set up a meeting.

4. Press Enter. Click the Send button. The Message window closes, and the reply is moved to the Outbox. The message is sent when your computer is connected to the Internet.

PAUSE. LEAVE Outlook open to use in the next exercise.

CERTIFICATION READY?
How do you send a reply to a message?
1.1.2

When a reply has been sent, the icon next to the original message is changed. An arrow pointing left, as shown in Figure 2-11, indicates that you replied to the message. When you view the main Outlook window, this icon tells you which messages you have answered.

Figure 2-11

Icon indicates a reply was sent

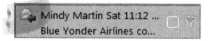

■ Forwarding a Message

Outlook enables you to forward a message you received to another person or several people.

THE BOTTOM LINE

Occasionally, you receive a message that should be sent to additional people. Outlook's Forward function is a quick method of sending the message to additional people without re-creating the original message.

→ FORWARD A MESSAGE

USE the message you received when you sent a message to yourself in a previous exercise.

1. In the Inbox, click the message with the subject "Blue Yonder Airlines contest." The message is selected.

2. Click the Forward button on the Standard toolbar. The message is displayed in a new window, as shown in Figure 2-12. Note that the Subject field is already filled. In the Subject field, the text "FW:" has been inserted before the original subject line. "FW:" tells the recipient that the message has been forwarded by the sender. The original message is included at the bottom of the window.

Figure 2-12

Forward a message you received

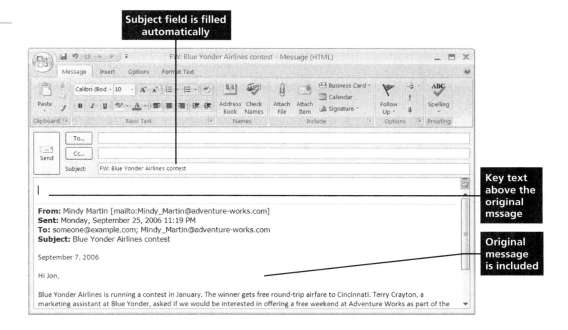

3. In the To field, key someone@example.com.

4. Click the message area above the original message. Key What is the value of the airfare and weekend at Adventure Works?

5. Press Enter. Key your name.

6. Click the Send button. The Message window closes, and the message is moved to the Outbox. The message is sent when your computer is connected to the Internet.

PAUSE. LEAVE Outlook open to use in the next exercise.

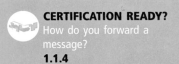

CERTIFICATION READY?
How do you forward a message?
1.1.4

When a message has been forwarded, the icon next to the original message is changed. An arrow pointing right, as shown in Figure 2-13, indicates that you forwarded the message.

Figure 2-13

Icon indicates the message was forwarded

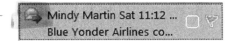

■ Working with Attachments

THE BOTTOM LINE
Attachments are files sent as part of an email message. An attachment is a convenient way to send pictures, spreadsheets, and other types of files.

Attaching a File to a Message

Do you need to submit a five-page report to your supervisor at the home office? Perhaps you have a new product brochure to distribute to all the sales representatives, or you want to share a picture of your new puppy with a friend. Attach the file to an email message and send it.

⊕ ATTACH A FILE TO A MESSAGE

GET READY. Outlook must be running.

CD

The *Window* image file is available on the companion CD-ROM.

1. Click the New button on the Standard toolbar. A new Message window is displayed.
2. In the To field, key your email address. You will send this message to yourself so you can use the attachment in the following exercises.
3. In the Subject field, key Stained glass window attached.
4. Click the message area. Key Hi Josh, and press ⌷Enter⌷ twice.
5. Key the following note: I attached a picture of the stained glass window that was broken yesterday. We can't accept reservations for the suite until the window is replaced, so we need a new window as soon as possible. Please provide an estimated completion date and price. Press ⌷Enter⌷ twice.
6. Key Thanks, and press ⌷Enter⌋.
7. Key your name.
8. Click the Attach File button on the Ribbon, shown previously in Figure 2-1. The Insert File dialog box is displayed.
9. Navigate to the data files for this lesson. Click the Window file, and click the Insert button. The Insert dialog box is closed, and the Window file is listed in the Attached field, as shown in Figure 2-14.

Figure 2-14

Sending an attachment

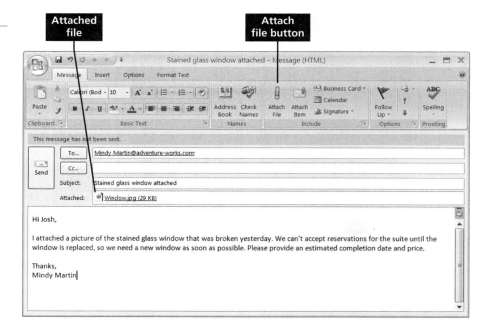

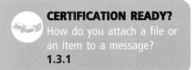

10. Click the Send button. The Message window closes, and the message is moved to the Outbox. The message is sent when your computer is connected to the Internet. PAUSE. LEAVE Outlook open to use in the next exercise.

An attachment can be a file or an Outlook item, such as a contact, a note, or a task. When you attach a file to a message, the filename, size, and an icon representing the file are displayed in the Attached field. If you attach more than one file, the files are listed separately in the Attached field.

To attach an Outlook item, click the arrow next to the Attach File button on the Ribbon. Select Item. The Insert Item dialog box is displayed. In the Look In list, select the Outlook folder containing the item. In the Items list, click the Outlook item to be attached and click OK. The Insert Item dialog box is closed, and the item is listed in the Attached field of the email message.

Previewing an Attachment in Outlook

Outlook's new Attachment Previewer enables you to view attachments in the Reading pane. Without the need to save and open an attachment, you can make critical decisions quickly and efficiently.

Note: For some types of files, you may be asked if you want to preview the file before the attachment is displayed.

(→) PREVIEW AN ATTACHMENT

USE the message with the attachment you received when you sent a message to yourself in the previous exercise.

1. If the message with the Window attachment has not arrived yet, click the Send/Receive button on the Standard toolbar to check for new messages. The paper clip icon with the message, as shown in Figure 2-15, indicates that the message has an attachment.

Figure 2-15

Message with attachment
received

2. Click the message. The message is displayed in the Reading pane, as shown in Figure 2-16.

Figure 2-16

Reading pane containing the
message with an attachment

3. In the Reading pane, click the attachment's filename. The attachment is displayed in the Reading pane, as shown in Figure 2-17. For some types of files, you may be asked if you want to preview the file before the attachment is displayed.

Figure 2-17

Attachment displayed in the Reading pane

Window.jpg
Size: 30 KB
Image dimensions: 411 x 406

Click to return to the message

TROUBLESHOOTING For your protection, all scripts, macros, and ActiveX controls are disabled in a previewed document.

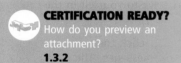

CERTIFICATION READY?
How do you preview an attachment?
1.3.2

4. In the Reading pane, click the Message icon to close the preview and display the message.

PAUSE. LEAVE Outlook open to use in the next exercise.

Outlook comes with several previewers. Additional previewers are available through Microsoft's Web site.

Saving an Attachment to a Specific Location

Attachments can be saved before or after previewing the attachment. Attachments can be saved from the message list, from the Reading pane, and from an open message. In the following three exercises, you will save an attachment from each location.

⊕ SAVE AN ATTACHMENT FROM THE MESSAGE LIST

USE the message with the attachment you received when you sent a message to yourself in a previous exercise.

1. In the message list, click the message with the subject "Stained glass window attached," if necessary.
2. Click the File menu, point to Save Attachments, and select Window.jpg. The Save Attachment dialog box is displayed. By default, the My Documents folder is displayed.
3. Create a new folder named Outlook Solutions Lesson 02 in the My Documents folder.
4. In the File name field, change the name of the file to *Window from message list*. Click the Save button.

PAUSE. LEAVE Outlook open to use in the next exercise.

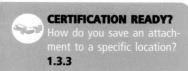

CERTIFICATION READY?
How do you save an attachment to a specific location?
1.3.3

In the previous exercise, you created a folder and saved an attachment from the message list. In the next exercise, you will not create a new folder. You will save the attachment from the Reading pane.

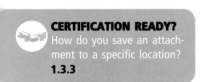 **SAVE AN ATTACHMENT FROM THE READING PANE**

USE the message with the attachment you received when you sent a message to yourself in a previous exercise.

1. In the message list, click the message with the subject "Stained glass window attached," if necessary.
2. In the Reading pane, right-click the Window.jpg attachment.
3. Select Save As on the shortcut menu. The Save Attachments dialog box is displayed.
4. If necessary, navigate to the Outlook Solutions Lesson 02 folder you created in the previous exercise.
5. In the File name field, change the name of the file to *Window from Reading pane*. Click the Save button.

   PAUSE. LEAVE Outlook open to use in the next exercise.

In the previous exercise, you saved an attachment from the Reading pane to a folder you created earlier. In the next exercise, you will save an attachment from an open message.

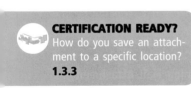 **SAVE AN ATTACHMENT FROM AN OPEN MESSAGE**

USE the message with the attachment you received when you sent a message to yourself in a previous exercise.

1. In the message list, double-click the message with the subject "Stained glass window attached." The message is opened in a new window.
2. In the new window, right-click the Window.jpg attachment.
3. Select Save As on the shortcut menu. The Save Attachments dialog box is displayed.
4. If necessary, navigate to the Outlook Solutions Lesson 02 folder you created in the previous exercise.
5. In the File name field, change the name of the file to *Window from open message*. Click the Save button.
6. Click the Close button in the upper-right corner of the open message window. The message is closed.

   PAUSE. LEAVE Outlook open to use in the next exercise.

In the previous exercise, you saved an attachment from an open message. Now you have saved an attachment from the message list, from the Reading pane, and from an open message.

Opening an Attachment

Just as you can save an attachment from the message list, the Reading pane, and an open message, you can also open an attachment from these locations. In the following three exercises, you will open an attachment from each location.

⊙ OPEN AN ATTACHMENT FROM THE MESSAGE LIST

USE the message with the attachment you received when you sent a message to yourself in a previous exercise.

1. In the message list, right-click the message with the subject "Stained glass window attached," if necessary.

2. In the shortcut menu, click View Attachments and select Window.jpg. The Opening Mail Attachment dialog box is displayed, as shown in Figure 2-18.

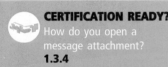 **TROUBLESHOOTING**   If you opened this type of attachment in the past, the Opening Mail Attachment dialog box may not be displayed.

Figure 2-18

Opening Mail Attachment dialog box

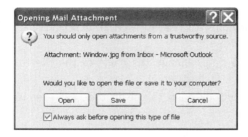

 **TROUBLESHOOTING**   It is safer to save an attachment and scan the file with an antivirus software program before opening an attachment. Do not open attachments from unknown sources.

CERTIFICATION READY?
How do you open a message attachment?
1.3.4

3. Click Open. The application designated to open .jpg files on your computer is used to open the application.

4. Close the Window file and exit the application used to open the file, if necessary.
   PAUSE. LEAVE Outlook open to use in the next exercise.

In the previous exercise, you opened an attachment from the message list. In the next exercise, you will open the attachment from the Reading pane.

⊙ OPEN AN ATTACHMENT FROM THE READING PANE

USE the message with the attachment you received when you sent a message to yourself in a previous exercise.

1. In the message list, click the message with the subject "Stained glass window attached," if necessary.

2. In the Reading pane, double-click the attachment. The Opening Mail Attachment dialog box is displayed. Refer to Figure 2-18.

3. Click Open. The application designated to open .jpg files on your computer is used to open the application.

CERTIFICATION READY?
How do you open a message attachment?
1.3.4

4. Close the Window file and exit the application used to open the file, if necessary.
   PAUSE. LEAVE Outlook open to use in the next exercise.

In the previous exercise, you opened an attachment from the Reading pane. In the next exercise, you will open the attachment from an open message.

⊙ OPEN AN ATTACHMENT FROM AN OPEN MESSAGE

USE the message with the attachment you received when you sent a message to yourself in a previous exercise.

1. In the message list, double-click the message with the subject "Stained glass window attached." The message is opened in a new window.

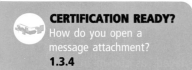

CERTIFICATION READY?
How do you open a message attachment?
1.3.4

2. In the new window, right-click the Window.jpg attachment. Click Open on the shortcut menu. The Opening Mail Attachment dialog box is displayed. Refer to Figure 2-18.

3. Click Open. The application designated to open .jpg files on your computer is used to open the application.

4. Close the Window file and exit the application used to open the file, if necessary.
PAUSE. LEAVE Outlook open to use in the next exercise.

In the previous exercise, you opened an attachment from an open message. Now you have opened an attachment from the message list, from the Reading pane, and from an open message.

■ Personalizing Messages

THE BOTTOM LINE
You can personalize your messages in many ways. Formatting, colors, and images probably come to mind first. However, the signature is one of the most useful places to personalize your messages.

Creating a Personal Signature

A *signature* is text or images that are automatically placed at the end of your outgoing messages. A signature can be as fancy or as plain as you like.

 **CREATE A PERSONAL SIGNATURE**

GET READY. Outlook must be running to create a signature.

1. Click New on the Standard toolbar. A new message window is displayed. By default, the Message tab of the Ribbon is displayed.

2. In the Include group on the Ribbon, click Signature and select Signatures. The Signatures and Stationery dialog box is displayed, as shown in Figure 2-19.

Figure 2-19

Signatures and Stationery dialog box

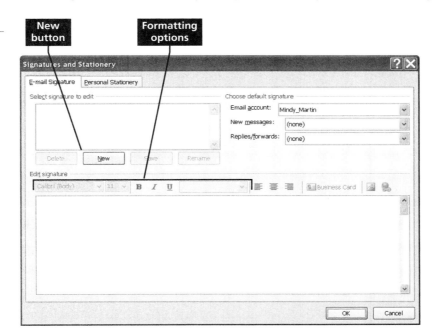

TAKE NOTE *

If you share your email account with other users or additional Outlook profiles have been created, signatures created by other users may be listed in the Signatures and Stationery dialog box.

3. Click the New button. The New Signature dialog box is displayed, as shown in Figure 2-20.

Figure 2-20

New Signature dialog box

4. Key Lesson 2 in the *Type a name for this signature* field and click OK. The New Signature dialog box is closed, and Lesson 2 is highlighted in the Select signature to edit list box.
5. Click in the empty Edit signature box. Any changes you make here are applied to the selected Lesson 2 signature. If additional signatures were listed, you could select a different signature and make changes to it.
6. Key your name and press Enter. Key your title and press Enter. Key your email address and press Enter twice. Key the name of your company and press Enter. Key the Web address of your company and press Enter. If you do not have a title, company, or company Web site, key the information that applies to you.

TROUBLESHOOTING

If formatting has been applied to your email messages or other signatures, the same formatting might be applied to the signature as you key the text. You can change the formatting after you key the signature.

7. Select all the text in the signature. Select the Ariel font. Select the font size 10. Select the color Blue.
8. Select your name. Click Bold and Italic. Change the font size to 12, as shown in Figure 2-21.

Figure 2-21

New signature

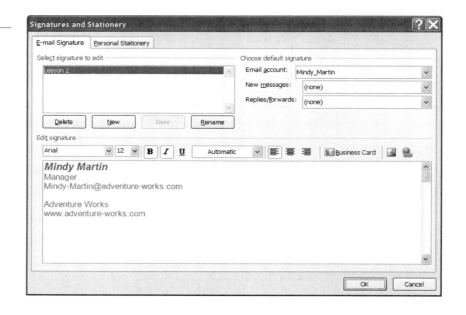

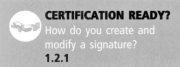

9. Verify that (none) is still selected in the New messages and Replies/forwards fields. Click OK. The dialog box is closed, and the signature is saved. Close the Message window.

PAUSE. LEAVE Outlook open to use in the next exercise.

In the previous exercise, you created a simple signature that provides valuable information. It contains your name, title, email address, company name, and the company's Web address. You also may want to include your phone number, your department, and your company's mailing address in your signature.

Although you can include images and more complicated formatting, the formatting you can do in the Signatures and Stationery dialog box is limited. For example, you can't resize an image in the Signatures and Stationery dialog box. However, you can open a new message, use the formatting tools in the new Message window to create a signature you like, cut the signature, and paste it into the Signatures and Stationery dialog box as a new signature.

Adding a Signature to a Single Message

You can choose to add a signature to an individual message. This enables you to create and use more than one signature.

 **ADD A SIGNATURE TO A SINGLE MESSAGE**

GET READY. Outlook must be running to create a new message.

1. Click New on the Standard toolbar. A new message window is displayed.
2. In the message area, key I'm testing my new signature. Press Enter twice.
3. In the Include group on the Ribbon, click Signature and select Lesson 2. The signature is inserted into the message, as shown in Figure 2-22.

Figure 2-22

Message using new signature

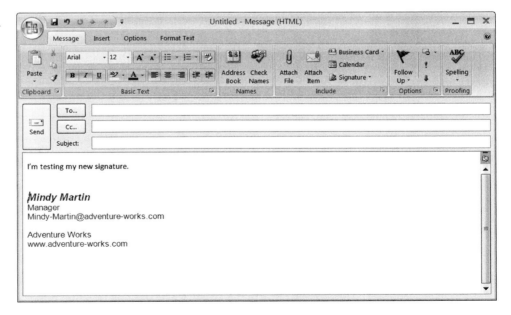

4. Click the To field and key your email address.

5. Click the Subject field and key Testing signature in a single message. Click the Send button.

6. If the message has not been received, click the Send/Receive button.

7. Click the message in the message list. Click the File menu and select the Save As option. The Save As dialog box is displayed.

8. Navigate to the Outlook Solutions Lesson 02 folder and click the Save button. The message is saved as Testing signature in a single message.htm.

   PAUSE. LEAVE Outlook open to use in the next exercise.

In the previous exercise, you inserted your new signature into a single message. Create several signatures. This enables you to select the signature to match the message. When you send a personal message, use a signature that includes a picture from your favorite sport or a photo of your new puppy. When you send a business message, use a signature that includes your business information.

Adding a Signature to All Outgoing Messages

If you primarily use your email account for the same type of email (business or personal), you can select a signature that is automatically inserted into every outgoing message. This gives you a quick consistent way to insert your signature.

⊕ ADD A SIGNATURE TO ALL OUTGOING MESSAGES

GET READY. Outlook must be running to create a new message.

1. Click New on the Standard toolbar. A new message window is displayed.

2. In the Include group on the Ribbon, click Signature and select Signatures. The Signatures and Stationery dialog box is displayed.

3. In the New Messages field, select Lesson 2, if necessary. Click OK. The Lesson 2 signature will automatically be added to every outgoing message. Close the message window.

   PAUSE. LEAVE Outlook open to use in the next exercise.

Even if you use your email account to send business and personal messages, you can save time by automatically adding a signature. Half of the time, the automatic signature will be the correct one. When it isn't correct, delete it from the message and insert the correct signature.

■ Working with Automated Replies

THE BOTTOM LINE

When you're out of the office, you will still receive email messages. You can automatically send a reply informing the addressee that you are out of the office.

Creating an Internal Out of Office Message

If you use a Microsoft Exchange Server email account, you can use the improved Out of Office Assistant to send an automated message informing coworkers that you are out of the office.

CREATE AN INTERNAL OUT OF OFFICE MESSAGE

GET READY. You must use a Microsoft Exchange Server account to complete this exercise.

1. Click the Tools menu and select the Out of Office Assistant option. The Out of Office Assistant dialog box is displayed.
2. Click the Send Out of Office auto-replies option.
3. Click the Only send during this time range option. Select 12:00 AM tomorrow as the Start time. Select 12:00 AM the following day as the End time.
4. Click the Inside My Organization tab, if necessary. Key I am out of the office today. I'll respond to your message tomorrow.
5. Click OK. The dialog box is closed. The Out of Office message will be sent when you receive messages from other email accounts in your organization.

   PAUSE. LEAVE Outlook open to use in the next exercise.

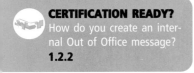

CERTIFICATION READY?
How do you create an internal Out of Office message?
1.2.2

Improvements to the Out of Office Assistant include additional formatting options, the ability to set the dates that you will be out of the office, and the ability to send an Out of Office message to correspondents outside of your organization.

In the previous exercise, you prepared a message to be sent as a reply to emails received from other members of your organization. In the next exercise, you will prepare an Out of Office message to be sent as a reply to messages sent by email accounts outside your organization.

Creating an External Out of Office Message

If you use a Microsoft Exchange Server email account, you can use the improved Out of Office Assistant to send an automated message informing people outside your organization that you are out of the office.

CREATE AN EXTERNAL OUT OF OFFICE MESSAGE

GET READY. You must use a Microsoft Exchange Server account to complete this exercise.

1. Click the Tools menu and select the Out of Office Assistant option. The Out of Office Assistant dialog box is displayed.
2. Click the Send Out of Office auto-replies option.
3. Click the Only send during this time range option. Select 12:00 AM tomorrow as the Start time. Select 12:00 AM the following day as the End time.
4. Click the Outside My Organization tab. In the text entry area, key I am out of the office today. I'll respond to your message tomorrow.
5. Click OK. The dialog box is closed. The Out of Office message will be sent when you receive messages from email accounts outside your organization.

   CLOSE Outlook.

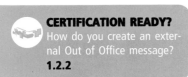

CERTIFICATION READY?
How do you create an external Out of Office message?
1.2.2

SUMMARY SKILL MATRIX

IN THIS LESSON YOU LEARNED	MATRIX SKILL	SKILL NUMBER
To create and send messages	Send messages to multiple recipients	1.1.1
To resend a message	Resend a message	1.1.3
To save a copy of a sent message in a different location	Specify where a copy of a sent message is saved	5.3.3
To read and reply to messages		
To automatically preview messages	Automatically preview messages	1.7.2
To reply to a message you received	Reply to a message	1.1.2
To forward a message	Forward a message	1.1.4
To work with attachments		
To attach a file to a message you're sending	Attach files and items to a message	1.3.1
To preview an attachment in Outlook	Preview a message attachment in Outlook	1.3.2
To save an attachment to a specific location	Save attachments to a specific location	1.3.3
To open an email attachment you receive	Open a message attachment	1.3.4
To personalize messages		
To create a personal signature	Create and modify a personal signature	1.2.1
To add a signature to a single message you are sending		
To add a signature to all the messages you send		
To send an automated reply when you are out of the office	Create internal and external Out of Office Messages	1.2.2

■ Knowledge Assessment

Matching

Match the term with its definition.

a. attachment
b. AutoComplete
c. AutoPreview
d. forward
e. Microsoft Office Button

f. Quick Access Toolbar
g. reply
h. Ribbon
i. signature
j. subject

B

_____ 1. Automatically completes the names of the months and days of the week

H

_____ 2. Contains commands organized into groups located on tabs

C

_____ 3. Toolbar that can be customized to contain commands from any tab

I

_____ 4. Text or images that are automatically placed at the end of your outgoing messages

_____ 5. File sent as part of an email message

_____ 6. Displays the first three lines of every message in the message list

_____ 7. Accesses the commands to open, save, print, and finish a document

_____ 8. Respond to a message you received by sending a message back to the sender

_____ 9. Topic of a message

_____ 10. Send a message you received to another email account

True/False

Circle T if the statement is true or F if the statement is false.

T (F) 1. Use the AutoComplete function to insert your signature before you send a message.

T (F) 2. A message is moved to the Sent Items folder when you click the Send button.

(T) F 3. Use the Message window to compose and send an email message.

T (F) 4. You must fill in the Cc field before a message can be sent.

(T) F 5. The content of the Ribbon varies by the task.

T (F) 6. To send a message to several recipients, key a colon (:)after a name before adding the next addressee

(T) F 7. When you send a reply, the text "RE:" is inserted before the original subject line.

(T) F 8. Outlook's Forward function is a quick method of sending the message to additional people without re-creating the original message.

(T) F 9. The paper clip icon indicates that a message has an attachment.

T (F) 10. An image can't be included in a signature.

■ Competency Assessment

Project 2-1: Send an Email Message to a Friend

Send an email message to a friend inviting him to lunch tomorrow.

GET READY. Launch Outlook if it is not already running.

1. On the Standard toolbar, click the New button to open a new Message window.

2. Key a friend's email address in the To field. If you are not completing these exercises with a friend or coworker, key your email address in the To field. This will give you a message to reply to in the next exercise.

3. In the Subject field, key Lunch tomorrow?

4. Click in the message area. Key Hi, and press Enter twice.

5. Key How about lunch tomorrow? Press Enter twice. Key your name.

6. Click the Send button.

LEAVE Outlook open for the next project.

Project 2-2: Reply to a Friend's Email Message

Complete Project 2-1 before starting this project.

1. If the message sent in Project 2-1 has not arrived, click the Send/Receive button on the Standard toolbar.

2. In the message list, click the message sent in Project 2-1.

3. Click the Reply button on the Standard toolbar.v
4. Key I'll pick you up at 1:00 PM. Don't be late! Press Enter twice. Key your name.
5. Click the Send button.
6. Click the Send/Receive button on the Standard toolbar.
7. In the message list, click the reply message.
8. Click the File menu and select the Save As option. The Save As dialog box is displayed.
9. Navigate to the Outlook Solutions Lesson 02 folder. Click the Save button. The message is saved as *RE Lunch tomorrow.htm*.

   LEAVE Outlook open for the next project.

■ Proficiency Assessment

Project 2-3: **Send an Attachment**

The last guest in the best suite at Adventure Works accidently broke the stained glass window in the suite. You must replace the window before you can accept any reservations for the suite.

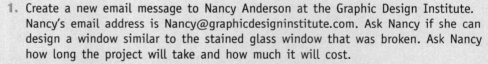

TROUBLE**SHOOTING** The email adddresses provided in these projects belong to unused domains owned by Microsoft. When you send a message to these addresses, you will receive an error message stating that the message could not be delivered. Delete the error messages when they arrive.

CD

The *Window* image file is available on the companion CD-ROM.

1. Create a new email message to Nancy Anderson at the Graphic Design Institute. Nancy's email address is Nancy@graphicdesigninstitute.com. Ask Nancy if she can design a window similar to the stained glass window that was broken. Ask Nancy how long the project will take and how much it will cost.
2. Attach the *Window.jpg* file located in the data files for this lesson.
3. Send the message.

   LEAVE Outlook open for the next project.

Project 2-4: **Resend a Message**

Complete Project 2-3 before starting this project.

1. You need more than one estimate, but you don't want to key all the information again. In the Sent Items folder, open the message you sent in Project 2-3.
2. Use the Resend function to create a new message.
3. Change the message so it can be sent to Michael Entin at the School of Fine Art. His email address is Michael@fineartschool.net.
4. Send the message.

   LEAVE Outlook open for the next project.

■ Mastery Assessment

Project 2-5: **Send a Message Using Stationery**

You work for the Adventure Works resort. Mindy Martin, one of the owners, asked you to select stationery to be used when messages are sent to guests from resort employees.

1. Open a new message.
2. Open the Signatures and Stationery dialog box. Click the Theme button on the Personal Stationery tab. Select the Clear day stationery theme.
3. Close the current message without saving a draft.
4. Open a new message. The stationery theme will be applied. If necessary, insert the Lesson 2 signature.
5. SAVE the unsent new message using the stationery as *Project 2-5.htm* in the Outlook Solutions Lesson 02 folder.
6. Close the message without completing or sending it.

   LEAVE Outlook open for the next project.

Project 2-6: **Create a Signature**

Mindy Martin, one of the owners of the Adventure Works resort, was pleased with the stationery you selected for outgoing email messages. She asked you to create a signature that uses the Window image.

The **Window** image file is available on the companion CD-ROM.

1. Open a new message.
2. Use the formatting tools in the New Message window to create an attractive signature using the Window image. Insert the *Window* image and resize it to fit in the signature. Use a table to position the elements in the message. Do not display the table's borders.
3. Cut the new signature from the message and paste it into a new signature in the Signatures and Stationery dialog box.
4. Create a new message using the new signature.
5. SAVE the unsent new message using the new signature as *Project 2-6.htm* in the Outlook Solutions Lesson 02 folder.

   CLOSE Excel.

INTERNET READY

Many people use images in their stationery or signature. It is tempting to download an image from a Web site to use in your email messages. However, the images used on the Internet are protected by copyright laws. If you don't have an image you created to use in your signature, visit www.microsoft.com. Microsoft provides a large library of clip art that can be downloaded and used in your documents.

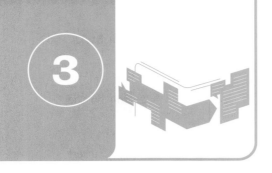

3 Advanced Email Tools

KEY TERMS
attribute
delivery receipt
digital ID
encryption
Hypertext Markup
** Language (HTML)**
InfoBar
plain text
read receipt
Rich Text Format (RTF)
sensitivity
spam

Business is booming. Mindy and Jon have accepted reservations for several major events to be held at the Adventure Works resort. Two weddings, a company retreat, and a confidential marketing meeting for a major toy company have been scheduled for next month. As the dates for the events get closer, email messages have been flying. The toy company insists on using security features, such as a digital ID, for all email communications.

■ SOFTWARE ORIENTATION

Microsoft Outlook's Message Options

The mail component in Microsoft Outlook can do more than send basic email messages. Many of the advanced email options in Microsoft Outlook are set in the Message Options dialog box shown in Figure 3-1.

Figure 3-1

Message Options dialog box

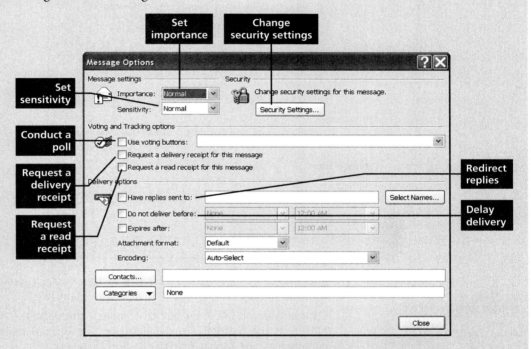

The advanced options in Microsoft Outlook enable you to change the message settings, address security issues, vote for selected items, set tracking options, and determine delivery options. In the Message Options dialog box, you can make decisions about these options for the message you are creating. These changes affect only the current message; they do not affect all messages you send.

 Automatically added stationery and signatures were turned off before capturing the screens in this lesson. Your screens will differ if you use stationery or a signature.

■ Selecting a Message Format

Microsoft Outlook can send messages in HTML, Rich Text Format (RTF), and plain text.

↓
THE BOTTOM LINE

The most attractive email messages contain formatted text. Formatting, including bullets, font sizes, font colors, and bold text can convey just the right impression. However, not all email applications can display these effects. Outlook enables you to send and receive messages in all three formats.

⊕ SELECT A MESSAGE FORMAT FOR ALL MESSAGES

GET READY. Before you begin these steps, be sure to launch Microsoft Outlook.

1. Click Tools in the menu and select Options. The Options dialog box is displayed. Click the Mail Format tab, as shown in Figure 3-2. Options selected in this dialog box apply to all outgoing messages.

Figure 3-2

Options dialog box

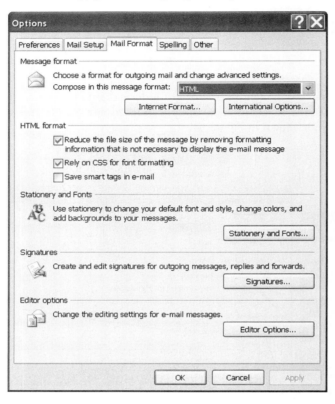

2. Click the arrow next to the *Compose in this message format* entry box. The three available formats are HTML, rich text, and plain text.
3. Click outside of the entry box to compress the options, then click the Cancel button at the bottom of the dialog box. The Options dialog box is closed. The default message format of HTML is not changed.

   PAUSE. LEAVE Outlook open to use in the next exercise.

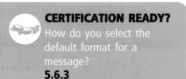

CERTIFICATION READY?
How do you select the default format for a message?
5.6.3

The default format for all messages is HTML. It provides the most flexibility. The following table provides information about the three available formats.

Table 3-1

Message formats

FORMAT	DESCRIPTION
HTML	*Hypertext Markup Language (HTML)* is used by Web browsers to display information. HTML enables you to format text and insert items such as horizontal lines, pictures, and animated graphics. Older and less robust email programs might not be able to display HTML.
RTF	*Rich Text Format (RTF)* uses tags to format text. It can be read by most word processors and newer email programs, but it can't display animated graphics and some Web page formatting.
Plain text	*Plain text* does not use any formatting. It can be read by all email programs. Without formatting though, the impression you can convey in your message is limited.

Because of the content and formatting options it provides, HTML is the best choice as the default format for the messages you compose and send. When you reply to a message, Outlook automatically uses the format of the received message as the format for your reply. If you receive a message in plain text, your reply will automatically be sent in plain text to ensure that the original sender can read your reply.

In the previous exercise, you saw that HTML is the default format for all messages you compose and send. However, you can choose to use RTF or plain text in an individual message.

→ SELECT A MESSAGE FORMAT FOR A SINGLE MESSAGE

GET READY. Before you begin these steps, be sure to launch Microsoft Outlook.

The **Picture Signature** document is available on the companion CD-ROM.

1. If necessary, click the Mail button in the Navigation pane to display the Mail folder.

2. Click the New button in the Standard toolbar. The Message window is displayed. By default, the Message tab is selected.

3. Open *Picture Signature* in the data files for this lesson. Select the table containing the picture and Mindy Martin's contact information. Right-click the table and click Copy on the shortcut menu. Close the *Picture Signature* document.

4. Click in the message area of the New Message window. Press Enter twice.

5. Right-click below the blank lines and click Paste on the shortcut menu. Mindy's signature, including the picture of the stained glass window, is pasted into the message.

6. In the To field, key the email address of a coworker or friend. In the Subject field, key Plain Text message.

7. In the message area above the signature, key This message will be sent in plain text. See Figure 3-3.

Figure 3-3

Formatted message

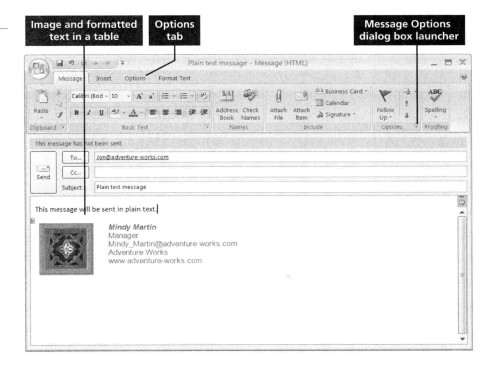

8. Click the Options tab. In the Format group, click Plain Text. The Microsoft Office Outlook Compatibility Checker dialog box in Figure 3-4 is displayed. The items listed in the dialog box identify the changes that will occur in this particular message.

Figure 3-4

Microsoft Office Outlook Compatibility Checker dialog box

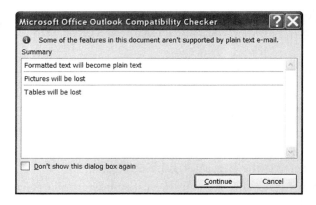

9. Click the Continue button. The picture and formatting are removed from the message, as shown in Figure 3-5.

Figure 3-5

Plain text message

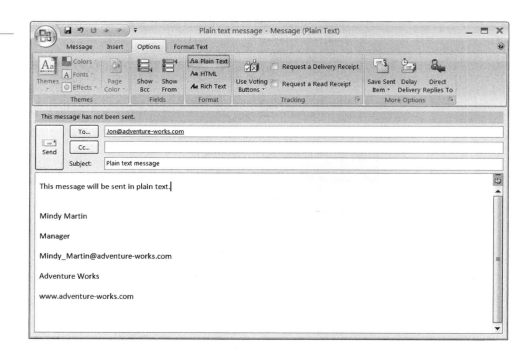

10. Click the Send button. The message is moved to the Outbox and it is sent when your computer is connected to the Internet.

PAUSE. LEAVE Outlook open to use in the next exercise.

In the previous exercise, you inserted a signature copied from an existing document. The signature contained a table, an image, and formatted text. When you changed the format of the message to plain text, the image, table, and text formatting were removed.

■ Using Advanced Message Options

THE BOTTOM LINE

Advanced message options enable you to specify settings that attract more attention to the messages you send. Many of these options are set in the Message Options dialog box shown in Figure 3-1 or the Ribbon on a message window.

Setting the Sensitivity Level

Set the sensitivity level in the Message Options dialog box shown in Figure 3-1. Although **sensitivity** does not affect how the message is sent or received, it does suggest how the recipient should treat the message and the type of information in the message. Sensitivity settings include Normal, Personal, Private, and Confidential.

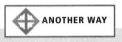
ANOTHER WAY

Select the sensitivity level in the Message Options dialog box.

SET THE SENSITIVITY LEVEL

GET READY. Before you begin these steps, be sure to launch Microsoft Outlook.

1. If necessary, click the Mail button in the Navigation pane to display the Mail folder.
2. Click the New button in the Standard toolbar. The Message window is displayed. By default, the Message tab is selected.
3. Click the Message Options dialog box launcher in the Ribbon shown in Figure 3-3. The Message Options dialog box shown in Figure 3-1 is displayed.
4. In the Message settings area, select Confidential from the Sensitivity list as shown in Figure 3-6.

Figure 3-6

Sensitivity level set to Confidential

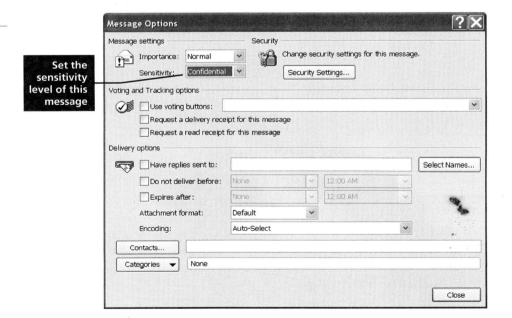

5. Click the Close button to accept the Confidential setting and return to the message window.
6. In the message area, key Sample confidential message.
7. In the To field, key your email address. In the Subject field, key Sample confidential message.
8. Click the Send button. The message is moved to the Outbox and it is sent when your computer is connected to the Internet.

9. Return to your Inbox if necessary. Click the Send/Receive button if the message has not arrived yet.

10. Click the received message to select it. The message has the text *Please treat this as Confidential* in the InfoBar at the top of the message. See Figure 3-7.

Figure 3-7

Confidential message received

Sample confidential message

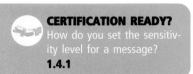

PAUSE. LEAVE Outlook open to use in the next exercise.

CERTIFICATION READY?
How do you set the sensitivity level for a message?
1.4.1

In the previous message, you saw that an InfoBar was added to the recipient's confidential message. An ***InfoBar*** is a banner containing information added automatically at the top of a message. An InfoBar is added for personal, private, and confidential messages. The messages are handled the same as any other message you send—the text in the InfoBar is the only difference.

The default sensitivity is normal. For normal messages, an InfoBar is not added to the recipient's message.

Setting the Importance Level

Some email messages are more important than others. Reminding a coworker to bring a critical part of your presentation to a meeting could spell the difference between a promotion and public embarrassment. Use the Importance setting to draw attention to a message.

⊕ SET THE IMPORTANCE LEVEL

GET READY. Before you begin these steps, be sure to launch Microsoft Outlook.

1. If necessary, click the Mail button in the Navigation pane to display the Mail folder.

2. Click the New button in the Standard toolbar. The Message window is displayed. By default, the Message tab is selected.

3. Click the High Importance button in the Options group on the Ribbon.

4. In the message area, key Sample important message.

5. In the To field, key your email address. In the Subject field, key Sample important message as shown in Figure 3-8.

ANOTHER WAY

Select the importance in the Message Options dialog box.

Figure 3-8

Creating an important message

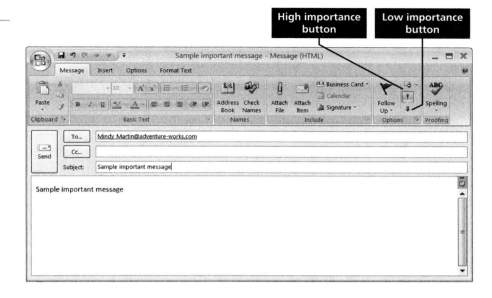

6. Click the Send button. The message is moved to the Outbox and it is sent when your computer is connected to the Internet.

7. Return to your Inbox if necessary. Click the Send/Receive button if the message has not arrived yet.

8. Select the new message. The message you receive has an exclamation point in the message list and the text *This message was sent with High importance* in the InfoBar at the top of the message. See Figure 3-9.

Figure 3-9

Important message received

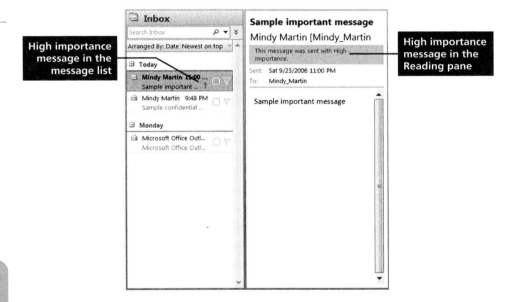

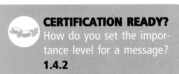
PAUSE. LEAVE Outlook open to use in the next exercise.

The importance level of a message can be set to High, Low, and Normal. High importance messages are identified for the recipient by a red exclamation point in the message list and the InfoBar at the top of the message in the Reading pane. Low importance messages are identified for the recipient by a blue down arrow in the message list and the InfoBar at the top of the message in the Reading pane. Normal importance messages are not marked.

If you set the importance level of a message to high or low, you can reset the importance level to normal before you send it. Simply click the High Importance button or the Low Importance button that is currently selected.

Adding a Follow-Up Flag for Recipients

When you send a message, you can add a flag that will be seen by the recipient. The follow-up flag tells the recipient that he is expected to take some action because he received the message.

⊕ ADD A FOLLOW-UP FLAG FOR RECIPIENTS

GET READY. Before you begin these steps, be sure to launch Microsoft Outlook.

1. If necessary, click the Mail button in the Navigation pane to display the Mail folder.

2. Click the New button in the Standard toolbar. The Message window is displayed. By default, the Message tab is selected.

3. In the To field, key the email address of a coworker or friend. In the Subject field, key Lunch tomorrow with Alan Brewer.

4. In the message area, key the following message. Don't forget lunch tomorrow with Alan Brewer from Fabrikam, Inc. He wants to discuss arrangements for the conference scheduled for our Blue Conference Room at the end of next month. Come prepared!

5. In the Options group, click the Follow-Up button and select the Flag For Recipients option. The Custom dialog box shown in Figure 3-10 is displayed.

Figure 3-10

Custom dialog box

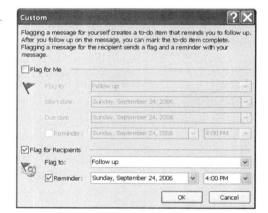

6. Click the Reminder checkbox so a reminder is not displayed. Click OK to flag the message without adding the reminder. The dialog box is closed. As shown in Figure 3-11, the InfoBar in the message you're creating indicates that the recipient will receive the Follow-Up flag. If you had kept the Reminder option selected, the date and time specified in the Custom dialog box would also be displayed in the InfoBar.

Figure 3-11

Creating a message with a
follow-up flag for the recipient

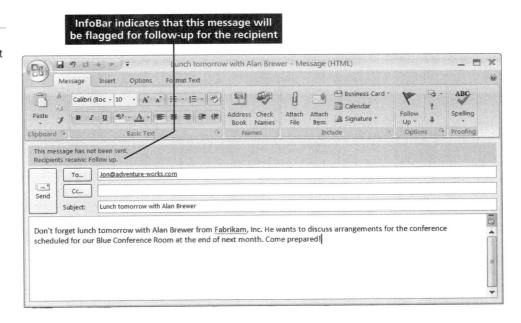

**InfoBar indicates that this message will
be flagged for follow-up for the recipient**

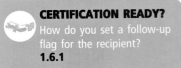

The text *This message has not been sent* is displayed in the InfoBar when it takes a few minutes to compose a message. This text is not displayed for the recipient.

CERTIFICATION READY?
How do you set a follow-up
flag for the recipient?
1.6.1

7. Click the Send button. The message is moved to the Outbox and it is sent when your computer is connected to the Internet.

PAUSE. LEAVE Outlook open to use in the next exercise.

X REF

You can find more
information about
tasks in Lesson 11.

When the message arrives in the recipient's Inbox, the message is marked by a flag, as shown in Figure 3-12. This draws attention to the message and indicates that some action might be required. A flag set by a sender contains a small silhouette, making it look different from a flag you set for yourself. If the recipient clicks the flag in the message list, it is added to the recipient's task list.

Figure 3-12

Received message with follow-
up flag set by the sender

**Follow-up
flag from
sender in the
message list**

**Follow-up
flag in the
Reading
pane**

Requesting Delivery and Read Receipts

Did she get the message? Requesting delivery and read receipts takes the mystery out of sending a message. You will know that the message was delivered to the recipient and opened for reading.

⊕ REQUEST DELIVERY AND READ RECEIPTS

GET READY. Before you begin these steps, be sure to launch Microsoft Outlook.

1. If necessary, click the Mail button in the Navigation pane to display the Mail folder.
2. Click the New button in the Standard toolbar. The Message window is displayed. By default, the Message tab is selected.
3. In the To field, key the email address of a coworker or friend. In the Subject field, key Sample delivery receipt and read receipt.
4. In the message area, key Sample delivery receipt and read receipt.
5. Click the Options tab on the Ribbon.
6. In the Tracking group, click the Request a Delivery Receipt and the Request a Read Receipt checkboxes as shown in Figure 3-13.

ANOTHER WAY

Click the *Request a delivery receipt for this message* checkbox and click the *Request a read receipt for this message* checkbox in the Message Options dialog box.

Figure 3-13

Creating a message requesting a delivery receipt and a read receipt

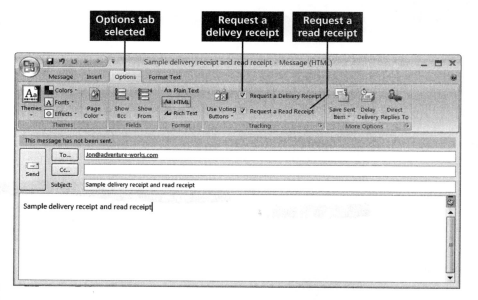

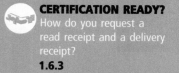

CERTIFICATION READY?

How do you request a read receipt and a delivery receipt?

1.6.3

7. Click the Send button. The message is moved to the Outbox and it is sent when your computer is connected to the Internet.

PAUSE. LEAVE Outlook open to use in the next exercise.

A ***delivery receipt*** tells you that the message has arrived in the recipient's mailbox; the message has been delivered. A delivery receipt does **not** guarantee that the recipient has opened or read the message.

A ***read receipt*** tells you that the message has been opened in the recipient's mailbox. However, the recipient can choose to send or not send a read receipt, as shown in Figure 3-14. This means that you might not receive a read receipt, even when the recipient has read the message.

Figure 3-14

Recipient can choose to send a
read receipt

If the recipient chooses to send the read receipt, it is sent to your mailbox by default as shown
in Figure 3-15. You can use additional settings that are not covered in this book to handle
read receipts you receive.

Figure 3-15

Read receipt received in
mailbox

Receiving Replies at a Specific Address

There are many reasons for directing replies to a different address. For example, your
company could set up a new email address that is used only for replies about a company
event or issue. If you send a message to your customers, you can direct the replies to a
different email address so your Inbox is not flooded with replies.

⊕ RECEIVE REPLIES AT A SPECIFIC ADDRESS

GET READY. Before you begin these steps, be sure to launch Microsoft Outlook.

1. If necessary, click the Mail button in the Navigation pane to display the Mail
folder.
2. Click the New button in the Standard toolbar. The Message window is displayed.
By default, the Message tab is selected.
3. Click the Options tab in the Ribbon as shown in Figure 3-16.

Figure 3-16

Options tab in a Message window

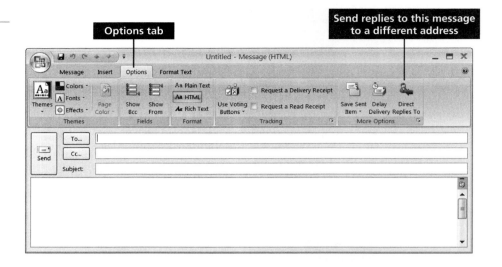

4. Click the Direct Replies To button in the More Options group. The Message Options dialog box is displayed as shown in Figure 3-17. In the Delivery Options area, the *Have replies sent* to checkbox is selected, and your email address is displayed.

Figure 3-17

Message Options dialog box

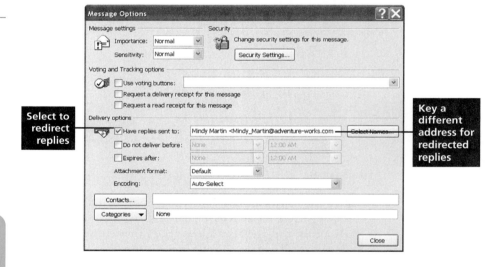

CERTIFICATION READY?

How do you request that replies be sent to a specific address?

1.6.5

5. Key the email address of a friend or coworker in the *Have replies sent* to field. Click the Close button at the bottom of the dialog box to return to the Message window.
6. Close the message window without saving or sending a message.

    PAUSE. LEAVE Outlook open to use in the next exercise.

 REF

You can find more information about contacts in Lesson 6.

If you have contacts entered in Outlook, you can choose a contact for the *Have replies sent to* field rather than keying an address. Using contact information in Outlook simplifies the process of directing replies to a different address.

Delaying a Message's Delivery

Occasionally, you might want to delay the delivery of a message. For example, a Human Resources specialist can write a message explaining a change in the benefits, but delay sending the message until the announcement is made later in the day. A delayed message is held in the Outbox until it is sent at the specified time. Even if you click the Send/Receive button, the message will remain in the Outbox until the specified time. Delay the delivery of a message in the Message Options dialog box shown in Figure 3-1.

DELAY A MESSAGE'S DELIVERY

ANOTHER WAY

Click the *Do not deliver before* checkbox and select the date and time in the Message Options dialog box.

GET READY. Before you begin these steps, be sure to launch Microsoft Outlook.

1. Click the New button in the Standard toolbar. The Message window is displayed. By default, the Message tab is selected.
2. Click the Options tab in the Ribbon. Click the Delay Delivery button on the Ribbon. The Message Options dialog box is displayed. The *Do not deliver before* checkbox is selected. Today's date and 5:00 PM are selected, as shown in Figure 3-18.

Figure 3-18

Message Options dialog box with delayed delivery selected

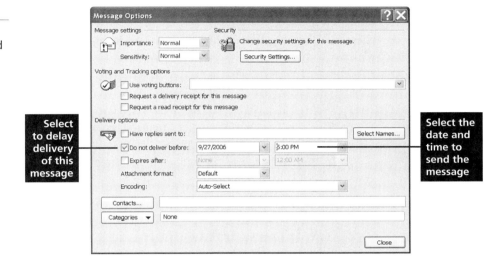

3. Select the next available time from the drop-down list. Do not change the date. Click the Close button at the bottom of the dialog box. Note that the Delay Delivery button is highlighted.
4. In the To field, key the email address of a coworker or friend. In the Subject field, key Delayed delivery.

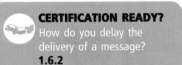

If you are using a POP3 email account rather than an internal company network, you must keep Outlook open until the message is sent. Your computer must be connected to the Internet at the time specified for delivery.

CERTIFICATION READY?
How do you delay the delivery of a message?
1.6.2

5. In the message area, key Sample delayed delivery.
6. Click the Send button. The message is moved to the Outbox. The message is sent at the specified time if your computer is connected to the Internet.

   PAUSE. LEAVE Outlook open to use in the next exercise.

In the previous exercise, you composed a message and delayed the delivery of the message. Be sure that Outlook is running and your computer is connected to the Internet at the specified delivery time.

■ Working with Voting Options

THE BOTTOM LINE

Do you need to ask employees if they plan to attend the company picnic? Use the voting options to poll the employees. If the standard voting buttons do not meet your need, you can create customized voting buttons.

TROUBLESHOOTING

Microsoft Exchange Server is required to use voting buttons.

Using Standard Voting Buttons

The standard sets of voting buttons include Approve and Reject; Yes and No; and Yes, No, and Maybe. These three standard sets of buttons can enable you to create a wide variety of polls.

USE STANDARD VOTING BUTTONS

GET READY. Before you begin these steps, be sure to launch Microsoft Outlook.

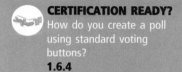 **ANOTHER WAY**
Click the *Use voting buttons* checkbox in the Message Options dialog box. To display the Message Options dialog box, click the *Message Option dialog box launcher* in the Options group on the Message tab.

1. Click the New button in the Standard toolbar. The Message window is displayed. By default, the Message tab is selected.
2. In the To field, key the addresses for three friends or coworkers.
3. In the Subject field, key Company picnic.
4. In the message area, key Do you plan to attend the company picnic next month? Press Enter.
5. Click the Options tab in the Ribbon. Click the Use Voting Buttons button on the Ribbon. The three sets of standard voting buttons are listed.
6. Click the Yes;No option.
7. Click the Send button. The message is moved to the Outbox and it is sent when your computer is connected to the Internet.

PAUSE. LEAVE Outlook open to use in the next exercise.

CERTIFICATION READY?
How do you create a poll using standard voting buttons?
1.6.4

When the message arrives in a recipient's mailbox, the InfoBar displays the text "Click here to vote." When the recipient clicks the InfoBar, the voting options are displayed as shown in Figure 3-19. The recipient simply clicks the choice she wants. A dialog box asks the recipient to confirm her choice. When the recipient confirms her choice, a message is automatically sent to the source of the poll. In this case, you are the source of the poll.

Figure 3-19

Recipient's voting options

On the sender's side of the voting process, the message used to send the poll is saved in the Sent Items folder like other sent messages. However, it is identified in the message list by the Tracking icon, which resembles the Tracking button. Double-click the message to open it. Click the Tracking button in the Ribbon as shown in Figure 3-20. As replies arrive, the votes are tracked in the original sent message containing the poll question.

Figure 3-20

Tracking poll results

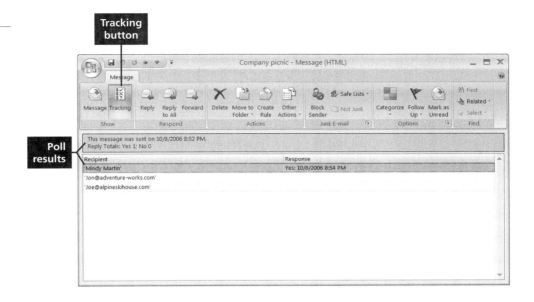

Figure 3-20

Tracking poll results

Using Custom Voting Buttons

When the standard voting buttons don't provide the options you need, you can create custom voting buttons. For example, if your company's holiday party is catered, you can ask employees who plan to attend if they want chicken or steak.

→ USE CUSTOM VOTING BUTTONS

GET READY. Before you begin these steps, be sure to launch Microsoft Outlook.

ANOTHER WAY

To display the Message Options dialog box, click the Message Option dialog box launcher in the Options group on the Message tab.

1. Click the New button in the Standard toolbar. The Message window is displayed. By default, the Message tab is selected.
2. In the To field, key the addresses for three friends or coworkers.
3. In the Subject field, key Company holiday dinner.
4. In the message area, key Select the meal you prefer for the company holiday party. Press Enter.
5. Click the Options tab in the Ribbon. Click the Use Voting Buttons button on the Ribbon. Click the Custom option. The Message Options dialog box is displayed. The *Use voting buttons* option is selected and Approve; Reject is displayed in the field as shown in Figure 3-21.

Figure 3-21

Message Options dialog box with *Use voting buttons* selected

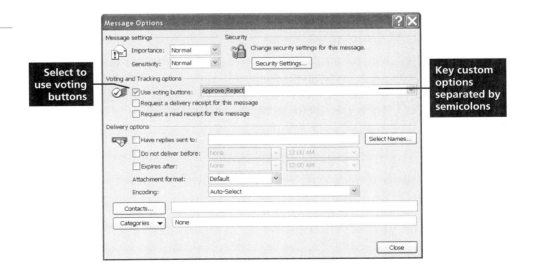

6. In the *Use voting buttons* field, key Chicken;Steak. Always insert a semicolon between the custom button labels. Click the Close button at the bottom of the dialog box to close the dialog box and return to the message.
7. Click the Send button. The message is moved to the Outbox and it is sent when your computer is connected to the Internet.
   PAUSE. LEAVE Outlook open to use in the next exercise.

CERTIFICATION READY?
How do you create a poll using custom voting buttons?
1.6.4

Customized buttons provide flexibility when conducting polls. Choosing dinner is only one of the many types of polls you can create. Any time you need to gather opinions from several people, consider using a poll.

■ Working with Security Settings

THE BOTTOM LINE

Microsoft Outlook provides several security features to protect your email correspondence. The features include encryption, a digital signature, and restricting permissions to a message.

TROUBLESHOOTING

To use a digital signature or encrypt a message, you must have a digital ID. If you do not have a digital ID, consult your system administrator or purchase a digital ID from a certificate authority.

Using a Digital Signature

A *digital ID* enables a recipient to verify that a message is really from you and decrypt any encrypted messages received from you. A digital ID contains a private key that remains on your computer and a public key you give to your correspondents to verify that you are the message sender.

➔ USE A DIGITAL SIGNATURE

GET READY. Before you begin these steps, you must acquire a digital ID and launch Microsoft Outlook.

ANOTHER WAY

Click the Digitally Sign Message button in the Options group on the Message tab.

1. Click the New button in the Standard toolbar. The Message window is displayed. By default, the Message tab is selected.
2. In the To field, key the address of a friend or coworker.
3. In the Subject field, key Digitally signed message.
4. On the Message tab, click the Options dialog box launcher. The Message Options dialog box shown in Figure 3-1 is displayed.
5. Click the Security Settings button. The Security Properties dialog box is displayed as shown in Figure 3-22.

Figure 3-22

Security Properties dialog box
with digital signature selected

**Select to add
your digital
signature to
this message**

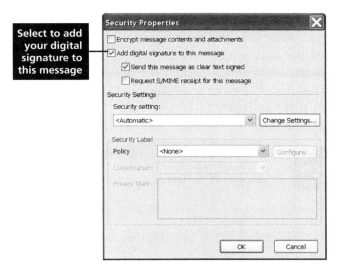

6. Click the Add digital signature to this message checkbox. Click OK to close the
   dialog box. Click the Close button to close the Message Options dialog box.

7. Click the Send button. The message is moved to the Outbox and it is sent when
   your computer is connected to the Internet.

   PAUSE. LEAVE Outlook open to use in the next exercise.

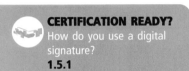

CERTIFICATION READY?
How do you use a digital
signature?
1.5.1

X REF

You can find more infor-
mation about contacts
in Lesson 6.

When a digitally signed message arrives in the Inbox, an icon in the message list indicates that
the message is digitally signed as shown in Figure 3-23. To save your certificate, the recipient
should use the digitally signed message to add you to the contact list or update the contact
information.

Figure 3-23

Digitally signed message

**The icon indicates
the message is
digitally signed**

Using Encryption

Protect the privacy of some messages by using encryption. *Encryption* scrambles the text
so that only the recipient with a key can decipher the message.

TROUBLESHOOTING

To send an encrypted message and decrypt an encrypted message, you must exchange
digital ID certificates with the recipient.

⊕ **USE ENCRYPTION**

GET READY. Before you begin these steps, be sure to launch Microsoft Outlook.

1. Click the New button in the Standard toolbar. The Message window is displayed. By
   default, the Message tab is selected.

2. In the To field, key the address of the friend or coworker who has exchanged
   digital ID certificates with you.

3. In the Subject field, key Sample encrypted message.

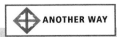
ANOTHER WAY

Click the Encrypt
button in the Options
group on the Message
tab.

CD

The **Content** document is available on the companion CD-ROM.

4. Open the *Content* file in the data files for this lesson. Select and copy all the text. Paste it in the message area.

5. On the Message tab, click the Options dialog box launcher. The Message Options dialog box shown in Figure 3-1 is displayed.

6. Click the Security Settings button. The Security Properties dialog box is displayed as shown in Figure 3-24.

Figure 3-24

Security Properties dialog box

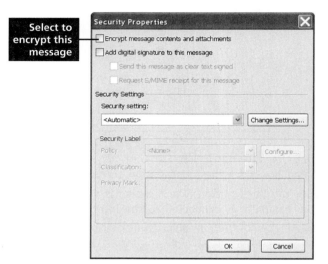

7. Click the Encrypt message contents and attachments checkbox. Click OK to close the dialog box. Click the Close button to close the Message Options dialog box.

8. Click the Send button. The message is moved to the Outbox and it is sent when your computer is connected to the Internet.

   PAUSE. LEAVE Outlook open to use in the next exercise.

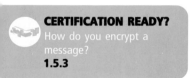

CERTIFICATION READY?
How do you encrypt a message?
1.5.3

When an encrypted message arrives in the Inbox, an icon in the message list indicates that the message is encrypted as shown in Figure 3-25. An encrypted message cannot be viewed in the Reading pane. It must be opened to be read.

Figure 3-25

Encrypted message

Restricting Permissions to a Message

Information Rights Management (IRM) has been improved in Outlook 2007. IRM allows you to control access to email messages.

TROUBLESHOOTING

Check with your instructor before beginning this activity; your computer system may not be set up to perform this activity.

Note: IRM for the 2007 Microsoft Office system requires Microsoft Windows Rights Management Services (RMS) for Windows Server 2003.

→ RESTRICT PERMISSIONS TO A MESSAGE

IMPORTANT. Check with your instructor before beginning this activity. You must have Microsoft Windows Rights Management Services (RMS) for Windows Server 2003 installed to perform this activity.

1. Click the New button in the Standard toolbar. The Message window is displayed. By default, the Message tab is selected.
2. In the To field, key the address of a friend or coworker.
3. In the Subject field, key Sample message with restricted permissions.

 **ANOTHER WAY**
To restrict permissions to a message, click the Permissions button in the Options group of the Message tab on the Ribbon.

4. Click the Microsoft Office Button in the message window. Click Permission and select the Do Not Forward option. An InfoBar is displayed in the message window as shown in Figure 3-26.

Figure 3-26

Creating a message with restricted permissions

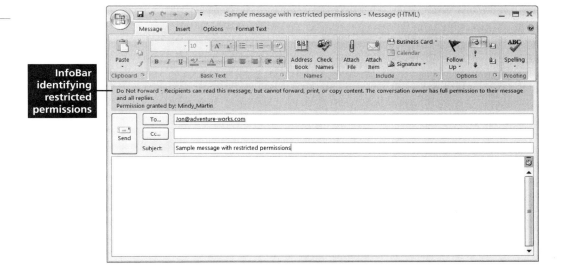

5. In the message area, key Sample message with restricted permissions.
6. Click the Send button. The message is moved to the Outbox and it is sent when your computer is connected to the Internet.

    PAUSE. LEAVE Outlook open to use in the next exercise.

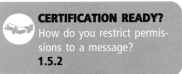
CERTIFICATION READY?
How do you restrict permissions to a message?
1.5.2

When a message with restricted permissions arrives in the Inbox, an icon in the message list indicates that the message has restricted permissions as shown in Figure 3-27. The same InfoBar that displayed in the message window as you created the message is displayed in the window pane when the message is received. Note that this does not provide security for the message content. Content can still be copied and distributed by a variety of methods such as keying the information into a new message.

Figure 3-27

Message with restricted permissions in the message list

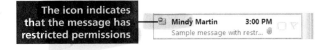

■ Locating Messages

THE BOTTOM LINE
What was the cost of that item? When is the project deadline? Important information is often exchanged through email messages. Finding important information quickly can be critical. Outlook provides tools to help you locate the right message when you need it.

Searching for Messages

Outlook 2007 utilizes the new Instant Search feature. As you search, each result is displayed immediately rather than waiting to complete the search to display the results.

TROUBLESHOOTING
Before you can enable Instant Search, the Windows Desktop Search components must be installed on your computer. If these components are not installed when you start Microsoft Office Outlook 2007, you will be prompted to download the software. After you download the software, you must restart Outlook to enable Instant Search.

Note: Windows Vista includes Windows Desktop Search. If you are using Office Outlook 2007 on a computer that runs Windows Vista, Instant Search is enabled automatically.

⊘ SEARCH FOR MESSAGES

GET READY. Before you begin these steps, be sure to launch Microsoft Outlook. Instant Search must be enabled.

1. If necessary, click the Mail button in the Navigation pane of the main Outlook window. The Instant Search box is displayed at the top of the Inbox, as shown in Figure 3-28.

Figure 3-28

Instant Search box

TAKE NOTE*
You can search any mail folder. To search all mail folders at the same time, click *All Mail Items* in the Navigation pane.

2. In the Navigation pane, click the Inbox folder to search.
3. In the Instant Search box, key Confidential. As you key the search text, Outlook displays the messages that match the text as shown in Figure 3-29.

Figure 3-29

Instant Search results

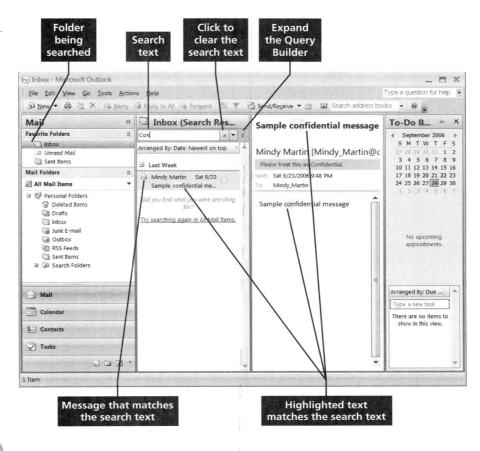

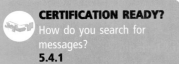

4. Click the `Clear Search` button.

   PAUSE. LEAVE Outlook open to use in the next exercise.

The Instant Search feature provides fast results. If you want to focus the search by adding additional criteria, click the Expand the Query Builder button shown in Figure 3-29. The Query Builder, shown in Figure 3-30, is displayed. Enter additional criteria to narrow search results. Matches are displayed below the Query Builder. Click the Query Builder button again to close the Query Builder.

Figure 3-30

Expanded Query Builder

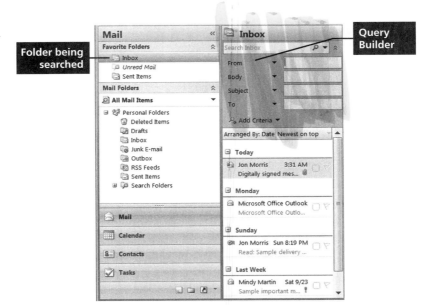

Sorting Messages by Attributes

In the message list, email messages are usually listed by date. The newest messages are displayed at the top of the message list. You can sort messages by other *attributes*, file characteristics such as size, subject, or sender.

⊙ SORT MESSAGES BY ATTRIBUTES

GET READY. Before you begin these steps, be sure to launch Microsoft Outlook.

1. If necessary, click the Mail button in the Navigation pane of the main Outlook window.
2. Click Arranged By above the message list. Select the From option. Messages are grouped by sender. Groups are listed in alphabetic order.
3. Click Arranged By above the message list. Select the Date option. Messages are grouped by date. Groups are listed in chronological order.

    PAUSE. LEAVE Outlook open to use in the next exercise.

ANOTHER WAY

To sort messages, click the View menu, point to Arrange By, and select an attribute.

By default, messages are sorted by the date they are received. Sometimes, you can get a better picture of a situation by viewing all the messages from a particular sender or subject. Sort by an attribute to organize the messages as needed.

■ Dealing with Spam

THE BOTTOM LINE

Unsolicited email sent to many email accounts is *spam* or junk email. It arrives at all times of the day containing offers of cheap medication, knock-off jewelry, and bad stock tips. If you don't manage the junk email, your Inbox could easily be buried in spam.

⊙ DEAL WITH SPAM

GET READY. Before you begin these steps, be sure to launch Microsoft Outlook.

1. If necessary, click the Mail button in the Navigation pane of the main Outlook window.
2. Click the Tools menu and click Options. The Options dialog box is displayed. The Preferences tab is active.
3. Click the Junk E-mail button. The Junk E-mail Options dialog box is displayed as shown in Figure 3-31. The current protection level is low. If you click the High option, less junk email will be delivered to your Inbox, but some messages that you want to see might be sent to the Junk E-mail folder.

Figure 3-31

Junk E-Mail Options dialog box

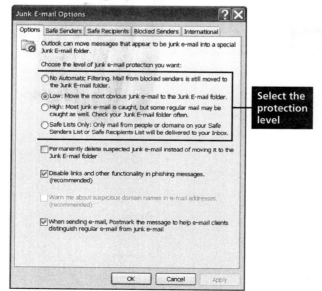

4. Click the Cancel button on both dialog boxes to return to the main Outlook window. For now, you will leave the setting at Low so you don't miss any important messages.

5. If a message from a friend or coworker is in your Inbox, right-click the message in the message list. Point to Junk E-mail on the shortcut menu and click the Add Sender to Safe Senders List option. A small dialog box tells you that the sender has been added to your Safe Senders List. Click OK to close the dialog box. CLOSE Outlook.

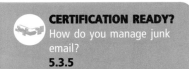

CERTIFICATION READY?
How do you manage junk email?
5.3.5

Increasing the level of protection decreases the amount of spam that will be directed to your Inbox. However, it increases the chance that a message from your boss or your brother will also be delivered to the Junk E-mail folder. If you choose to increase your protection level, check your Junk E-mail folder frequently. As you receive messages from people you want to correspond with, add their email addresses to the Safe Senders List. Messages from senders on the Safe Senders List are never directed to the Junk E-mail folder.

SUMMARY SKILL MATRIX

IN THIS LESSON YOU LEARNED	MATRIX SKILL	SKILL NUMBER
To select a format for messages you send	Select the default format for messages	5.6.3
To use advanced message options, including sensitivity, importance, and read receipts		
To set the sensitivity level	Set message sensitivity level	1.4.1
To set the importance level	Set mail importance level	1.4.2
To add a flag indicating the recipient should act	Add a or remove a flag for follow up	1.6.1
To request delivery and read receipts showing that messages were received and opened	Request read or delivery receipts	1.6.3
To receive replies at a specific address	Request that replies be sent to a specific e-mail address	1.6.5
To delay a message's delivery	Delay delivery of a message	1.6.2
To work with voting options to poll message recipients	Create e-mail polls using standard or custom voting buttons	1.6.4
To work with security settings, including digital signatures, encryption, and permissions		
To use a digital signature	Digitally sign a message	1.5.1
To encrypt messages you send	Encrypt a message	1.5.3
To restrict permissions to messages you send	Restrict permissions to a message	1.5.2
To locate messages by using Instant Search and sorting functions		
To search for messages by using Instant Search	Search all email folders in a single search	5.4.1
To use message attributes to sort messages		
To deal with spam by identifying junk mail and safe senders	Manage Junk e-mail messages	5.3.5

Matching

Match the term to the definition.

a. attribute	f. InfoBar
b. delivery receipt	g. plain text
c. digital ID	h. read receipt
d. encryption	i. sensitivity
e. Hypertext Markup Language (HTML)	j. spam

1. Suggests how the recipient should treat the message and the type of information in the message

2. Tells you that the message has arrived in the recipient's mailbox

3. Banner containing information added automatically at the top of a message

4. Junk email

5. File characteristic such as size, subject, or sender

6. Formatting language that enables you to format text and insert items such as horizontal lines, pictures, and animated graphics

7. Contains a private key that remains on your computer and a public key you give to your correspondents to verify that you are the message sender

8. Tells you that the message has been opened in the recipient's mailbox

9. Scrambles the text so that only the recipient with a key can decipher the message

10. Text without any formatting

(handwritten answers in left margin:) F B C J A E C H D G

True / False

Circle T if the statement is true or F if the statement is false.

T **(F)** **1.** Plain text is the default format for all messages.

(T) F **2.** An InfoBar is a banner containing information added automatically at the top of a message.

T **(F)** **3.** A red exclamation point is the icon used in the message list to indicate that a message is confidential.

T **(F)** **4.** A delivery receipt indicates that the message has been opened by the recipient.

(T) F **5.** When you delay the delivery of a message, it is held in the Outbox until it is time to be sent.

T **(F)** **6.** When you create custom voting buttons, insert a colon between the options.

T **(F)** **7.** An encrypted message can be previewed in the Reading pane when the message arrives.

(T) F **8.** Messages from senders on the Safe Senders List are never delivered to the Junk E-mail folder.

(T) F **9.** The Instant Search feature displays items matching the search criteria before the search is complete.

(T) F **10.** "Maybe" is one of the standard voting buttons.

■ Competency Assessment

Project 3-1: Create a Message in Plain Text Format

Mindy Martin, a co-owner of the Adventure Works resort, is supervising the arrangements for a wedding scheduled for next month at the resort. The bride's mother, Liz Keyser, sends messages to Mindy every day about a variety of details. Liz uses an older email program, so Mindy uses plain text format to correspond with her.

GET READY. Launch Outlook if it is not already running.

1. On the Standard toolbar, click the New button to create a new message.
2. In the Subject field, key Flowers for Keyser wedding.
3. In the message area, key the following message.

   Today's date Press [Enter] twice.

   Mrs. Keyser, Press [Enter] twice.

   Thank you for informing me that your family is providing the flowers for the reception. Flowers are currently listed on the wedding account. I will personally make sure that the wedding information is updated. Press [Enter] twice.

   Please let me know if you have any additional questions, Press [Enter] twice.

   Mindy Martin Press [Enter].

   Adventure Works Press [Enter].

4. Click the Options tab. Click the Plain Text button in the Format group. If the Microsoft Office Outlook Compatibility Checker dialog box is displayed, click the Continue button.
5. Click the Microsoft Office Button and select the Save As option. SAVE the message as *Flowers for Keyser wedding.txt*. Close the message without resaving, addressing, or sending it.

   LEAVE Outlook open for the next project.

Project 3-2: Create a Confidential Message

Doug Hite is the personal assistant for a well-known actor. The actor has reservations for next weekend. To avoid publicity, the actor will use the alias "Jeff Hay" when he registers. Create a confidential message confirming the reservation.

1. On the Standard toolbar, click the New button to create a new message.
2. In the Subject field, key Reservation confirmation.
3. In the message area, key the following message.

   Today's date Press [Enter] twice.

   Mr. Hite, Press [Enter] twice.

   This message confirms the reservation for Jeff Hay, arriving after 5 PM on Friday and leaving Sunday afternoon. As you requested, five pounds of dark chocolate nonpareils have been placed in the suite's refrigerator. Press [Enter] twice.

   Please contact me if you need any further assistance, Press [Enter] twice.

   Mindy Martin Press [Enter].

   Adventure Works Press [Enter].

4. Click the Options dialog box launcher in the Ribbon. The Message Options dialog box is displayed.
5. In the Message settings area, select Confidential from the Sensitivity list. Close the dialog box.

6. Click the Microsoft Office Button and select the Save As option. SAVE the message as *Reservation confirmation*. Close the message without resaving, addressing, or sending it.

LEAVE Outlook open for the next project.

■ Proficiency Assessment

Project 3-3: **Congratulations!**

Katie Jordan just won a weekend for two at Adventure Works! Prepare an email message informing Katie that she won the contest.

1. Before you compose your email message, apply stationery that fits the message content. Then open a new message window.

2. In the Subject field, key Congratulations.

3. In the message area, write a brief message telling Katie Jordan that she won a contest. Ask her to select any weekend in September for her visit.

4. On the Message tab, format the text.

5. On the Message tab, mark the message as High Importance.

6. SAVE the message as *Congratulations*. Close the message without resaving, addressing, or sending it.

LEAVE Outlook open for the next project.

Project 3-4: **Message Delivered**

The weather report calls for rain tomorrow. At Adventure Works, an outdoor luncheon meeting for 20 participants must be moved to an indoor conference room. Mindy needs to inform the staff member responsible for delivering and setting up the speaker's equipment and presentation materials.

1. OPEN a new message window.

2. In the Subject field, key Presentation Relocated.

3. In the message area, write a brief message telling the staff member that the presentation will be held in the Rose Room instead of the Bluebird Patio. Ask him to set up and test the equipment in the Rose Room by 10:00 AM.

4. On the Message tab, mark the message as High Importance.

5. On the Options tab, request a delivery receipt and a read receipt for the message.

6. SAVE the message as *Presentation Relocated*. Close the message without resaving, addressing, or sending it.

■ Mastery Assessment

LEAVE Outlook open for the next project.

Project 3-5: **Press Announcement**

The natural surroundings, luxurious facilities, and exceptional reputation have made Adventure Works a hometown favorite location for weddings. Later today, another well-known local couple will send wedding invitations to a few close friends and the press. Mindy wants to provide her contact information for the press, but it will be a busy afternoon. She

1. OPEN a new message window.
2. In the To field, key your email address.
3. In the Subject field, key Mello-Lloyd wedding.
4. In the message area, write a brief message stating that you are confirming that the Mello-Lloyd wedding will be held at Adventure Works. Provide a link to your Website at www.adventure-works.com and your contact information at 800-555-1234.
5. Set the delivery delay. (You must be able to leave the computer running and connected to the Internet until the specified time.)
6. Send the message without saving it.

LEAVE Outlook open for the next project.

Project 3-6: Send Your Digital Signature

A large corporation in a nearby city has decided to hold its Spring sales convention at Adventure Works. However, the Marketing Department in charge of the convention requires digital signatures on every message. You must exchange your digital signature with the marketing team member in charge of the convention.

1. OPEN a new message window.
2. In the To field, key the address for a friend or coworker.
3. In the Subject field, key Spring Conference.
4. In the message area, write a brief message stating that your digital signature has been added to the message.
5. Use the Message Options dialog box to access the security settings and add your digital signature to the message.
6. Send the message without saving it.

CLOSE Outlook.

INTERNET READY

A certificate authority sells digital IDs. Make a list of three to five certificate authorities. Compare the prices and functionality of the products they provide. (Hint: Click the Tools menu and click Trust Center. In the Trust Center dialog box, click E-mail Security and click the Get a Digital ID button.)

Sending a Message

Email is a common form of business correspondence. In many situations, it has replaced "snail mail," written correspondence delivered by the U.S. Post Office. Email software has made electronic messages a timely, creative, efficient method of communication.

Suppose you are the owner of a small candy company. You have a brick and mortar store in a small town in New Hampshire. It's a great place to raise a family, but your store does not get the amount of foot traffic in a month that a prime location in a big-city mall sees in a single day. To reach additional customers, you created an electronic storefront on the Internet.

As your business grows, the sales from your electronic storefront increase at a phenomenal rate. You communicate with customers daily as they place orders or request information.

To your surprise though, email messages are useful in running your brick and mortar store as well. You communicate with vendors, equipment providers, and other small business owners through email. In a single day, you might send dozens of messages.

- Respond to customer inquiries.
- Confirm orders from customers.
- Send invoices to customers.
- Send shipping notifications to customers.
- Send a list of monthly specials to customers subscribed to your mailing list.
- Set up a meeting with a vendor.
- Place orders for ingredients.
- Request information about new equipment.
- Place an ad for more employees in the local newspaper.

Yes, business is booming. Your small-town store has sold candy to customers in Los Angeles, Cincinnati, Phoenix, and Montreal.

↻ Circling Back

Fabrikam, Inc. is an older company. This family business was established by Rob Caron in 1973 to sell, install, and maintain swimming pools. As the second generation has taken over the company management, Fabrikam has expanded by increasing the Fabrikam line of products. Fabrikam now sells patio furniture, house awnings, and hot tubs. Over time, they plan to add almost every product that makes your back yard more fun or more comfortable.

⊙ Project 1: Signature

Nicole Caron, the Marketing manager, asked you to create a signature for email messages. She asked you to use a graphic she likes.

GET READY. Launch Outlook if it is not already running.

1. Click the New button. A new message window is opened.
2. Click in the message area. Click the Insert tab on the Ribbon.
3. Click the Table button in the Tables group. Click the second square in the fifth row of boxes in the drop-down list. An empty table with two columns and five rows is inserted in the message area.
4. Select all the cells in the first column of the table.
5. Click the Layout tab in the Ribbon. Because table cells are selected, the displayed layout options on the Ribbon apply to tables.
6. Click the Merge Cells button in the Merge group on the Ribbon. The cells in the first column are merged.
7. Click in the merged cell. Click the Insert tab on the Ribbon.
8. Click the Picture button in the Illustrations group. Select the *Sun.gif* file in the Data files. Click the Insert button on the dialog box. The image is inserted, but it is much too large to use in a signature. The image is automatically selected in the table.
9. With the picture still selected, click the Size button, and then click the Size Dialog Box Launcher. The Size dialog box is displayed.
10. In the Scale area, click the Lock aspect ratio checkbox to select the option if necessary. This option will keep the image in proportion as you resize it.
11. Click in the Height box. Key 5%, and press [Tab]. Click the Close button to return to the message window. The sun image has been resized.
12. Drag the vertical center border of the table to the left so the first column is barely wider than the sun image.
13. Click in the first row of the second column. Key Nicole Caron.
14. Click in the second row of the second column. Key Nicole Caron, Marketing Manager.
15. Click in the third row of the second column. Key Fabrikam, Inc.
16. Click in the fourth row of the second column. Key www.fabrikam.com.
17. Click in the fifth row of the second column. Key 800-555-8734 or Nicole@ fabrikam.com.
18. Select all the text in the table. Click the Message tab if necessary. In the Basic Text group, change the font to Verdana. (Use Arial font if you don't have Verdana.)
19. Select Nicole's name in the first row of the second column. Change the font to Freestyle Script. (If you don't have Freestyle Script font, use any font that looks like handwriting or leave the font unchanged.)

20. Increase the font size of Nicole's name to 20 and click the Bold button.

21. Select all the text in the table. Click the Font Color arrow. Click More Colors. In the displayed colors, click a dark red shade that coordinates with the color of the sun image. Click OK to close the dialog box.

22. Drag the right border of the table to the left so that the second column is barely wider than the widest text in the column.

23. Click the sun image. Click the Table Tools option displayed above the menu. Click the Layout tab. Click the Align Center button in the Alignment group.

24. Select the table. Click the Design tab. In the Table Styles group, click the Borders arrow. Click the No Border option.

25. With the table selected, press Ctrl + C to copy the table.

26. Click the Message tab. In the Include group, click the Signature button. Click the Signatures option to display the Signatures and Stationery dialog box.

27. Click the New button. The New Signature dialog box is displayed.

28. Key CB Project 1 and click OK to return to the Signatures and Stationery dialog box.

29. Click in the Edit signature area. Press Ctrl + V to paste the new signature into the box. Click the OK button to return to the message window.

LEAVE Outlook and the message window open for the next project.

Project 2: Theme

Add a theme to the "look" you are designing for Nicole Caron.

USE the message window that is open from the previous project.

1. Click the Message tab if necessary. In the Include group, click the Signature button. Click the Signatures option to display the Signatures and Stationery dialog box.

2. Click the Personal Stationery tab. Click the Theme button to display the Theme or Stationery dialog box.

3. In the list of themes and stationery, scroll down and click Journal. Click OK to close the dialog box.

4. Click OK to close the Signatures and Stationery dialog box. Note that changes to the theme or stationery are not displayed until you open a new message window.

5. Close the current message window without saving or sending the message.

LEAVE Outlook open for the next project.

Project 3: Send a Digital ID

Create and send a message using the new signature and theme. Include your digital ID. Mark the message as High Importance and flag the message for the recipient to follow up.

1. Click the New button. A new message window is opened. The Message tab is selected.

2. Click in the message area. Key Hi Jon, and press Enter twice. Notice that the theme you selected changed the fonts used in the message area.

3. Key I'm sending my digital ID. Press Enter twice.

4. Key I'm looking forward to our lunch appointment tomorrow. Press Enter twice.

5. In the Include group, click the Signature button. Click the CB Project 1 option to insert the signature.

6. In the To field, key the email address of a friend or coworker.

7. In the Subject field, key CB Project 3.

8. In the Options group, click the Follow Up button. Click the Flag for Recipients option. The Custom dialog box is displayed.

9. Click the Reminder checkbox so the option is not selected. Click OK to close the dialog box.

10. In the Options group, click the High Importance button.

11. In the Options group, click the Digitally Sign Message button.

12. Click the Microsoft Office Button. Click Save As to display the Save As dialog box.

13. Select HTML in the Save as type field if necessary. Click the Save button to save the file with the *CB Project 3* filename. If a warning box is displayed, click Yes.

14. Click the Send button. The message is moved to the Outbox and sent when the computer is connected to the Internet.

CLOSE Outlook.

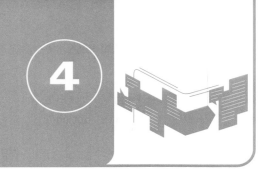

Managing Mail with Folders

LESSON SKILL MATRIX

SKILLS	MATRIX SKILL	SKILL NUMBER
Working with Folders		
Creating and Moving a Mail Folder	Create and move mail folders	5.3.1
Moving Messages to a Different Folder	Move mail between folders	5.3.2
Deleting and Archiving Outlook Items		
Emptying the Deleted Items Folder	Empty the Deleted Items and Sent Items folders	5.3.4

Mindy Martin, Adventure Works' co-owner, started using Outlook two months ago. She was amazed to see that her Inbox currently contains 180 messages. Clearly, she needs some way to organize them. After a bit of thought, she decides to mimic the organization she uses with her paper documents. She begins creating folders for the main categories of vendors, events, and guests.

KEY TERMS
archive
AutoArchive
Deleted Items folder
Drafts folder
Inbox folder
Junk E-mail folder
Outbox
restore
retention rules
Sent Items folder

■ SOFTWARE ORIENTATION

Microsoft Outlook's Folder List

The Folder List, shown in Figure 4-1, provides a complete list of your existing Outlook folders. It includes a folder for each Outlook component, such as the Calendar and Notes.

Figure 4-1

Folder List

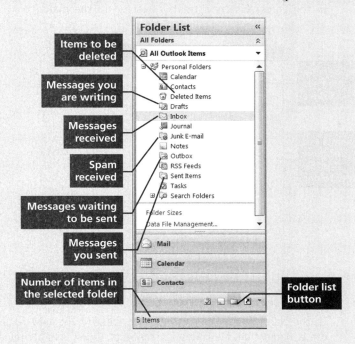

Although the Folder List includes every component, you will normally work only with the mail folders identified in Figure 4-1. The status bar at the bottom of the Outlook window displays the number of items in the selected folder. Create new folders to organize Outlook items by projects or individuals.

■ Working with Folders

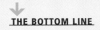
THE BOTTOM LINE

How often do you wander around your house looking for your car keys? If your answer is "rarely," you are already in the habit of putting things away so you know where to find them later. Organize your Outlook items in folders for the same reason. Items are easier to find when you put them away.

Creating and Moving a Mail Folder

In your office, new documents arrive in your Inbox regularly. You look at the document, perform the associated tasks, and file the paper in a folder you labeled for that type of item. You don't place it back in your Inbox. If you piled up all your documents in your Inbox, in a few weeks or months you would have a stack of paper that was several inches tall. In the same way, you don't want to keep all your messages in your Inbox in Microsoft Outlook.

CREATE AND MOVE A MAIL FOLDER

ANOTHER WAY

To create a new folder, right-click any folder in the folder list and select **New Folder**.

GET READY. Before you begin these steps, be sure to launch Microsoft Outlook.

1. Click the Folder List button in the bottom of the Navigation pane to display the Folder List shown in Figure 4-1.
2. Click the arrow next to New in the Standard toolbar. Click Folder. The Create New Folder dialog box is displayed, as shown in Figure 4-2. The folder that was selected in the Folder List is currently selected in the dialog box.

Figure 4-2

Create New Folder dialog box

3. In the Name field, key Lesson 4 to identify the new folder. When creating a folder, use a name that identifies its contents. Don't use abbreviations that you won't remember next week or six months from now.
4. Click Personal Folders. This determines the location where the new folder will be placed when it is created. If you do not have the correct location selected, you can move the new folder later.
5. Click the OK button to close the dialog box and create the folder. The new folder is added to the Folder List.
6. Click the Lesson 4 folder to select it and then drag the folder down and drop it in the Notes folder. A plus sign (+) is displayed next to the Notes folder, indicating that it contains a folder.
7. Click the plus sign (+) next to the Notes folder. The Folder List expands to display the Lesson 4 folder, as shown in Figure 4-3.

Figure 4-3

New folder created and moved into the Notes folder

CERTIFICATION READY?
How do you create and move a mail folder?

5.3.1

8. Drag the Lesson 4 folder and drop it on the Personal Folders icon in the Folder List. The Lesson 4 folder is placed alphabetically in the Personal Folders list, and the plus sign (+) is removed from the Notes folder.

PAUSE. LEAVE Outlook open to use in the next exercise.

Outlook provides several default mail folders that meet your most basic organizational needs. Table 4-1 identifies the default mail folders and describes their content.

Table 4-1

Default mail folders

FOLDER	DESCRIPTION
Deleted Items	Deleted items are held in this folder until the folder is emptied. Emptying the folder removes the items from your computer.
Drafts	Outlook messages you write but haven't sent are stored in this folder. You can return to a draft later to complete and send the message. If you close a message without sending it, a dialog box will ask if you want to save the draft. Click Yes to save the draft. Click No to discard the draft.
Inbox	By default, new messages to you are placed in this folder when they arrive.
Junk E-mail	Messages identified as spam are placed in this folder when they arrive.
Outbox	Outgoing messages are held in this folder until you are connected to the Internet. When an Internet connection is detected, the message is sent.
RSS Feeds	Really Simple Syndication (RSS) is a new Outlook 2007 feature that allows you to subscribe to content from a variety of Web sites offering the service. RSS is not covered in this book. Use Outlook's Help feature to find more information on RSS.
Sent Items	Items are automatically moved to this folder after they have been sent.

Deleting and Restoring a Folder

TROUBLESHOOTING

If you delete an item from the Deleted Items folder, the item is removed from your computer.

Because you can create new Outlook folders, you need the ability to delete folders. Delete a folder created accidentally or a folder you no longer need. Folders you delete are moved to the Deleted Items folder. Items in the Deleted Items folder are still on your computer. You can *restore* these items, that is, make them available for use again, by moving them out of the Deleted Items folder.

DELETE AND RESTORE A FOLDER

GET READY. Before you begin these steps, be sure to launch Microsoft Outlook.

TROUBLESHOOTING

Do not delete the default Outlook folders.

1. If necessary, click the Folder List button in the Navigation pane to display the complete list of Outlook folders.

2. Right-click the Lesson 4 folder created in the previous exercise. Click Delete "Lesson 4" from the shortcut menu. A warning dialog box is displayed, as shown in Figure 4-4.

Figure 4-4

Deleting a folder

3. Click Yes to close the warning dialog box. The Lesson 4 folder is moved to the Deleted Items folder. It will not be removed from your computer until the Deleted Items folder is emptied.

4. In the Folder List, click the plus sign (+) next to the Deleted Items folder. The Lesson 4 folder is displayed in the Folder List.

5. Drag the Lesson 4 folder and drop it on the Personal Folders icon in the Folder List. The Lesson 4 folder is placed in the Personal Folders, and the plus sign (+) is removed from the Deleted Items folder. The Lesson 4 folder has been restored, and it is now available for use.

   PAUSE. LEAVE Outlook open to use in the next exercise.

In the previous exercise, you deleted a folder you created earlier. Because deleted Outlook items are held in the Deleted Items folder until the folder is emptied, you were able to restore the Lesson 4 folder to the Personal Folders so it could be used again.

■ Moving Messages to a Different Folder

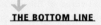

THE BOTTOM LINE

Messages arrive in the Inbox. Messages you send are stored in the Sent Items folder. To effectively organize your messages, create new folders for projects or individuals and move the related messages into the new folders.

MOVE MESSAGES TO A DIFFERENT FOLDER

GET READY. Before you begin these steps, be sure to launch Microsoft Outlook.

REF

In Lesson 5, you will create and use rules to move messages.

ANOTHER WAY

To move a message, you can drag the message from the message list and drop it on a folder in the Navigation pane.

1. If necessary, click the Mail button in the Navigation pane to display the Mail folder.

2. Click the New button in the Standard toolbar. The Message window is displayed. By default, the Message tab is selected.

3. In the To field, key your email address. In the Subject field, key Sample Message for Lesson 4.

4. In the message area, key Sample Message for Lesson 4.

5. Click the Send button. The message is moved to the Outbox, and it is sent when your computer is connected to the Internet.

6. Return to your Inbox, if necessary. Click the Send/Receive button if the message has not arrived yet. Because the message was sent to your email address, the message is moved to the Sent Items folder *and* it arrives in your Inbox. You will move both copies of the message into the Lesson 4 folder.

7. Right-click the Sample Message for Lesson 4 message that just arrived in your Inbox. Click Move to Folder on the shortcut menu. The Move Items dialog box is displayed, as shown in Figure 4-5.

Figure 4-5

Move Items dialog box

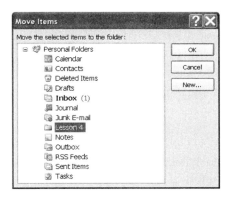

8. Click the Lesson 4 folder in the dialog box, if necessary. Click the OK button to close the dialog box and move the received message from the Inbox to the Lesson 4 folder.

9. Click the Sent Items folder in the Folder List. A list of the messages you sent is displayed in the message list.

10. Right-click the Sample Message for Lesson 4 message. Click Move to Folder on the shortcut menu. The Move Items dialog box is displayed.

11. Click the Lesson 4 folder in the dialog box, if necessary. Click the OK button to close the dialog box and move the sent message from the Sent Items folder to the Lesson 4 folder.

12. Click the Lesson 4 folder in the Folder List. The two messages you moved are displayed in the message list, as shown in Figure 4-6.

Figure 4-6

Messages moved to the Lesson 4 folder

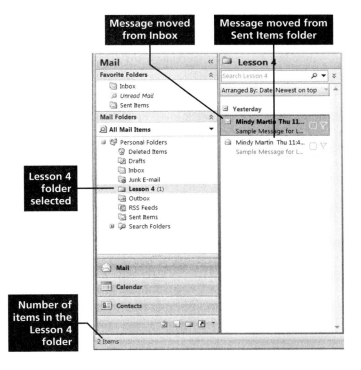

PAUSE. LEAVE Outlook open to use in the next exercise.

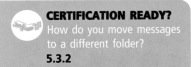

CERTIFICATION READY?
How do you move messages to a different folder?
5.3.2

In the previous exercise, you sent and received a message. When the message arrived in your Inbox, you moved the message to the Lesson 4 folder. It is a good idea to organize messages into folders based on projects or senders.

■ Deleting and Archiving Outlook Items

THE BOTTOM LINE

To maintain your folders, you should delete or archive old items. This prevents you from keeping old items past the date when they are useful.

Emptying the Deleted Items Folder

When you delete an Outlook item, it is moved to the Deleted Items folder. It is held in the Deleted Items folder until the folder is emptied. Emptying the Deleted Items folder removes its contents from your computer. The same procedure can be used to empty the Junk E-mail folder.

→ **EMPTY THE DELETED ITEMS FOLDER**

GET READY. Before you begin these steps, be sure to launch Microsoft Outlook.

1. If necessary, click the Mail button in the Navigation pane to display the Mail folder.
2. Right-click the Deleted Items folder in the Folder List. Click Empty "Deleted Items" Folder on the shortcut menu. A warning dialog box is displayed, as shown in Figure 4-7.

Figure 4-7

Emptying the Deleted Items folder

3. Click the OK button to remove the items from your computer.

PAUSE. LEAVE Outlook open to use in the next exercise.

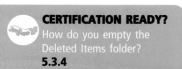
CERTIFICATION READY?
How do you empty the Deleted Items folder?
5.3.4

In the previous exercise, you emptied the Deleted Items folder. When you delete an Outlook item, it is not immediately removed from your computer. It is stored in the Deleted Items folder until the folder is emptied. Emptying the Deleted Items folder removes the items from your computer.

Archiving Outlook Items

It is easy to accumulate messages. Some messages are no longer related to your current projects, but you don't want to delete them. Also, some companies or departments have to follow *retention rules* that determine the length of time correspondence must be kept. To *archive* a message, you store it in a separate folder, reducing the number of messages in the folders you use most often. You can still access archived messages in Outlook. By default, items are archived automatically using the *AutoArchive* function, but you can change the AutoArchive settings and manually archive items.

→ **ARCHIVE OUTLOOK ITEMS**

GET READY. Before you begin these steps, be sure to launch Microsoft Outlook.

1. If necessary, click the Mail button in the Navigation pane to display the Mail folder. Click any mail folder.
2. Click the Tools menu and click Options. The Options dialog box is displayed.

3. Click the Other tab and click the AutoArchive button. The AutoArchive dialog box is displayed, as shown in Figure 4-8. This dialog box displays the AutoArchive options that are currently active.

Figure 4-8

AutoArchive dialog box

4. Click the Cancel button to close the AutoArchive dialog box without making any changes. Click the Cancel button to close the Options dialog without making any changes.

5. Right-click the Lesson 4 folder in the list of mail folders. Click Properties on the shortcut menu. The Properties dialog box is displayed. The information in this dialog box is specific to this folder.

6. Click the AutoArchive tab. The automatic archive settings for the Lesson 4 folder are displayed, as shown in Figure 4-9. Currently, this folder is not included in the AutoArchive process.

Figure 4-9

Default archive properties for the Lesson 4 folder

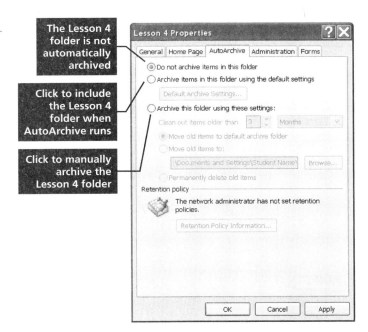

7. To change the AutoArchive settings for the Lesson 4 folder, click the Archive this folder using these settings option. This activates the dimmed options in this category.

8. In the *Clean out items older than* field, change the value to 1 and change the time period to *days*. Click the *Apply* button to apply the changes. Click the *OK* button to close the dialog box. Normally, you will set a longer time period.

9. To run the Archive process, click the *File* menu and click *Archive*. The Archive dialog box is displayed, as shown in Figure 4-10.

Figure 4-10

Archive dialog box

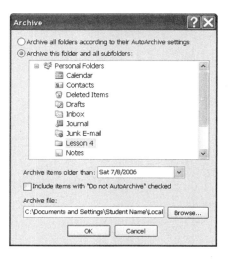

This process archives every folder that has the archive setting selected. If this is the first time you have archived your folders or you have many messages in folders that get archived, there might be a short delay until the process is complete.

10. In the *Archive items older than* field, click *tomorrow's date* so the messages you worked with today are included in the archive process.

11. Click the *OK* button. If you did not have archive folders because the archive process had not been run before, archive folders will be created. If the archive folders exist, the Lesson 4 folder will be added to the archive folders.

12. Click *Yes* to close the warning message. The warning message is displayed because you selected a future date. Normally, you will select a date in the past, so you won't see this warning message. In this exercise, you selected a future date to ensure that the messages created earlier in this lesson are moved to the archive folder.

13. Click the *Lesson 4* archive folder. The messages have been moved from the active Lesson 4 folder to the archived Lesson 4 folder, as shown in Figure 4-11.

Figure 4-11

Archive folders

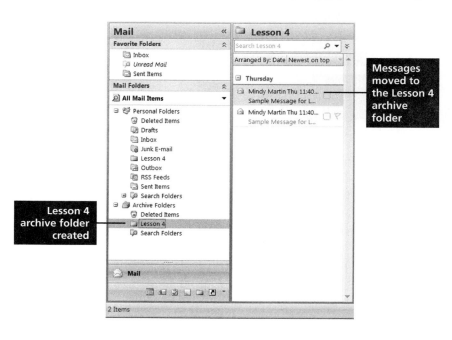

TROUBLESHOOTING

Check your state and company retention policies before deleting any business-related messages.

14. To clean up your folders from the changes in this lesson, delete the Lesson 4 folder in the Personal Folders and delete the Lesson 4 folder in the Archive Folders. Empty the Deleted Items folder.

    CLOSE Outlook.

In the previous exercise, you viewed your AutoArchive settings, added archive settings to a new folder, and manually archived a folder. At the end of the exercise, you deleted the Lesson 4 folder from the Personal Folders and the Archive Folders.

SUMMARY SKILL MATRIX

In this lesson you learned	Matrix Skill	Skill Number
To create, move, delete, and restore folders		
To create and move a mail folder	Create and move mail folders	5.3.1
To delete and restore a folder		
To move messages to a different folder	Move mail between folders	5.3.2
To delete and archive Outlook items		
To empty the Deleted Items folder	Empty the Deleted Items and Sent Items folders	5.3.4
To archive Outlook items		

■ Knowledge Assessment

Fill in the Blank

Complete the following sentences by writing the correct word or words in the blanks provided.

Junk-email

1. Spam is stored in the ______________ when it arrives.

Retention Rules

2. ______________ determine the length of time correspondence should be kept.

Inbox

3. By default, new messages are placed in the ______________ when they arrive.

Restored

4. A deleted item can be ______________ until it is completely removed from your computer.

Archive

5. ______________ your messages in a separate folder to reduce the number of messages stored in your active folders.

Outbox

6. Messages you send are stored in the ______________ until your computer is connected to the Internet.

Aoutarchive

7. The ______________ function automatically archives messages.

sent

8. Messages are automatically moved to the ______________ after they are sent.

deleted

9. Messages you delete are stored in the ______________ until it is emptied.

draft

10. The ______________ contains messages you have written but not sent.

Multiple Choice

Circle the correct choice.

B

1. What do you use to organize Outlook items?
   A. Archives
   B. Folders
   C. Search criteria
   D. Number of items

A

2. By default, where does email arrive?
   A. Inbox
   B. Outbox
   C. Junk E-Mail
   D. Sent Items

D

3. Which folders are displayed when you click the Folder List button in the Navigation pane?
   A. Mail folders
   B. Archive folders
   C. Personal folders
   D. All of the above

C

4. What should you consider when naming a folder?
   A. Use abbreviations to shorten the name
   B. The date the folder was created
   C. The content of the folder
   D. Use your initials so other users know you created the folder

B

5. Which folder is *not* one of the default Outlook folders?
   A. Outbox
   B. My Mail
   C. Drafts
   D. Sent Items

C

6. How do you restore a folder?
   A. Delete the folder
   B. Archive the folder
   C. Move the folder to the Personal Folders in the Folder List
   D. Delete items from the folder

A

7. How do you remove an Outlook item from your computer?
   A. Empty the Deleted Items folder
   B. Move the item to the Deleted Items folder
   C. Select the item and press the Delete key
   D. Delete the item and close Outlook

B

8. What company policies determine how long correspondence should be kept?
   A. Archival regulations
   B. Retention rules
   C. AutoArchive policy
   D. Correspondence policies

9. What attribute does AutoArchive use to determine which messages should be archived?
   A. Size
   B. Sender
   C. Attachments
   D. Date

10. How does AutoArchive identify which folders should be archived?
   A. Folder size
   B. Folder name
   C. Folder properties
   D. Folder location

■ Competency Assessment

Project 4-1: Create a Mail Folder

The Alpine Ski House is just a brisk walk away from Adventure Works. Joe Worden, Mindy Martin's cousin, is the owner of the Alpine Ski House. As the name implies, the Alpine Ski House sells ski equipment. However, the Alpine Ski House needs to attract and hold local customers when it isn't ski season. Joe started a ski club for local residents. During the off-season, club members meet to hike, bike, and exercise together to stay in shape for skiing. As the ski club becomes more active and gains more members, Joe decides he needs to organize his ski club messages.

GET READY. Launch Outlook if it is not already running.

1. Click the Folder List button in the Navigation pane to display the Folder List.
2. Click the arrow next to New in the standard toolbar. Click Folder. The Create New Folder dialog box is displayed.
3. In the Name field, key Ski Club to identify the new folder.
4. Click Personal Folders.
5. Click the OK button to close the dialog box and create the folder.
   LEAVE Outlook open for the next project.

Project 4-2: Move a Message into the Ski Club Folder

Joe Worden of the Alpine Ski House is planning a hike for the ski club members. Send a message about the hike and move the message to the Ski Club folder.

1. If necessary, click the Mail button in the Navigation pane to display the Mail folder.
2. Click the New button in the Standard toolbar. The Message window is displayed. By default, the Message tab is selected.
3. In the To field, key your email address. In the Subject field, key Ski Club Hike Saturday!
4. In the message area, key the following message:
   Hi Ski Club members! (Press Enter twice.)
   This is just a reminder. We'll be hiking the Mountain Dancer trail this Saturday. Meet in the Mountain Dancer camp site. Bring sandwiches for lunch and plenty of water for the hike. The weather forecast says it will be hot, hot, hot! Be sure you stay hydrated! (Press Enter twice.)

I'll see you Saturday at 9 AM! Call by Friday afternoon if you can't make it for the hike! (Press Enter twice.)

Joe Worden (Press Enter.)

Alpine Ski House (Press Enter.)

5. Click the Send button. The message is moved to the Outbox, and it is sent when your computer is connected to the Internet.

6. Return to your Inbox if necessary. Click the Send/Receive button if the message has not arrived yet.

7. Right-click the Ski Club Hike Saturday! message that just arrived in your Inbox. Click Move to Folder on the shortcut menu. The Move Items dialog box is displayed.

8. Click the Ski Club folder in the dialog box, if necessary. Click the OK button to close the dialog box and move the received message from the Inbox to the Ski Club folder.

   LEAVE Outlook open for the next project.

■ Proficiency Assessment

Project 4-3: **Change the AutoArchive Settings for the Ski Club Folder**

The ski club holds an event every month. Joe decided he wants to archive messages that are older than two months.

1. Right-click the Ski Club folder in the list of mail folders. Click Properties on the shortcut menu. The Properties dialog box is displayed.

2. Click the AutoArchive tab to view the automatic archive settings.

3. Click the Archive this folder using these settings option.

4. In the *Clean out items older than* field, change the value to 2 and change the time period to months, if necessary. Click the Apply button to apply the changes. Click the OK button to close the dialog box.

   LEAVE Outlook open for the next project.

Project 4-4: **Manually Archive the Ski Club Folder**

It isn't really time to archive the Ski Club folder, but Joe decides to run the archive process manually anyway.

1. Click the File menu and click Archive. The Archive dialog box is displayed.

2. In the *Archive items older than* field, click tomorrow's date so the message you worked with today is included in the archive process.

3. Click the OK button to run the archive process. Click Yes in the warning box. A warning message is displayed because you selected a future date.

4. Click the Ski Club archive folder. The messages have been moved from the active Ski Club folder to the archived Ski Club folder.

   LEAVE Outlook open for the next project.

■ Mastery Assessment

Project 4-5: **Delete and Restore the Ski Club Folder**

Joe Worden thought about the ski club while he sipped his coffee. With only one event per month, perhaps it wasn't necessary to create a folder just for the ski club.

1. If necessary, click the Folder List button in the Navigation pane to display the complete list of Outlook folders.
2. Right-click the Ski Club folder created in a previous project. Click Delete "Ski Club" from the shortcut menu. A warning dialog box is displayed.
3. Click Yes to close the warning dialog box. The Ski Club folder is moved to the Deleted Items folder. Now that the folder is deleted, Joe decides he should keep the folder.
4. In the Folder List, click the plus sign (+) next to the Deleted Items folder.
5. Drag the Ski Club folder and drop it on the Personal Folders icon in the Folder List. The Ski Club folder has been restored, and it is now available for use.

   LEAVE Outlook open for the next project.

Project 4-6: **Permanently Delete the Ski Club Folder**

This time, Joe is sure he wants to delete the Ski Club folder. If the correspondence about the club increases, he can always create the folder again.

1. Right-click the Ski Club folder created in a previous project. Click Delete "Ski Club" from the shortcut menu. A warning dialog box is displayed.
2. Click Yes to close the warning dialog box. The Ski Club folder is moved to the Deleted Items folder.
3. Right-click the Ski Club archive folder. Click Delete "Ski Club" from the shortcut menu. A warning dialog box is displayed.
4. Click Yes to close the warning dialog box. The Ski Club archive folder is moved to the Deleted Items folder.
5. Right-click the Deleted Items folder in the Folder List. Click Empty "Deleted Items" Folder on the shortcut menu. A warning dialog box is displayed.
6. Click the OK button to remove the items from your computer.

   CLOSE Outlook.

INTERNET READY

Find a business on the Internet that is similar to the Alpine Ski House. Make a list of the Outlook folders you would suggest for the owner.

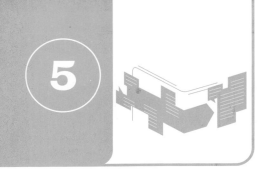

5

Processing Messages with Rules

SKILLS	MATRIX SKILL	SKILL NUMBER
Using Rule Templates		
Create a Rule to Move Messages from a Template	Create a rule to move email messages	5.5.1
Creating and Editing Rules		
Creating a Rule to Categorize Messages from a Selected Message	Categorize messages, appointments, meetings, contacts and tasks by color and Create a rule to categorize email messages	5.1.1 and 5.5.2
Creating a Rule to Forward Messages by Copying an Existing Rule	Create a rule to forward email	5.5.3
Creating a Rule to Delete Messages from Scratch	Create a rule to delete email	5.5.4

Mindy Martin is a co-owner of Adventure Works, a luxury resort near Cincinnati, Ohio. As with any business, a steady stream of information goes in and out of her office. Reservations, schedules, vendor orders, maintenance requests, and menus for the resort's restaurant are only a small sample of the information flying in and out of Mindy's email folders. To keep things straight, Mindy uses message rules to organize her messages as they arrive.

KEY TERMS
action
condition
exception
rule
template
Wizard

SOFTWARE ORIENTATION

Microsoft Outlook's Rules and Alerts Window

Message rules are displayed in the Rules and Alerts dialog box, as shown in Figure 5-1.

Figure 5-1

Outlook's Rules and Alerts window

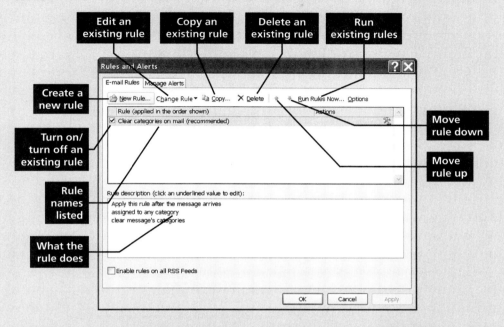

The rules that help you organize your messages are displayed in the Rules and Alerts window. In this window, you can edit existing rules, create new rules, enable rules, and disable rules.

■ Using Rule Templates

THE BOTTOM LINE

Using a template is the easiest method for creating a new rule. A ***template*** is an existing rule provided by Outlook that contains specific pieces of information that can be customized to create new rules. Usually, it is easier to use a template to create a rule than it is to create one from scratch.

Creating a Rule to Move Messages from a Template

A ***rule*** defines an action that happens automatically when messages are received or sent. Moving messages to specific folders to group related messages when they arrive is a basic method of organizing your messages. You can place messages about your active projects in project folders. You can place messages from vendors in separate folders. Create and use as many folders as you need to keep organized.

➔ CREATE A RULE TO MOVE MESSAGES FROM A TEMPLATE

GET READY. Before you begin these steps, be sure to launch Microsoft Outlook.

1. If necessary, click the Mail button in the Navigation pane to display the Mail folder. Then, right-click Personal Folders in the Folders List, and click New Folder in the shortcut menu. The Create New Folder dialog box is displayed.

2. In the Name field, key Lesson 5 Schedules. If necessary, click Personal Folders in the *Select where to place the folder* section. Click OK to create the folder and close the dialog box. You will create a rule to move messages into this folder.

3. Click the Tools menu, and click the Rules and Alerts option. The Rules and Alerts window shown in Figure 5-1 is displayed. Click the New Rule button. The Rules Wizard window is displayed, as shown in Figure 5-2. A ***Wizard*** consists of steps that walk you through completing a process in Microsoft Office applications.

Figure 5-2

Rules Wizard window with default selections

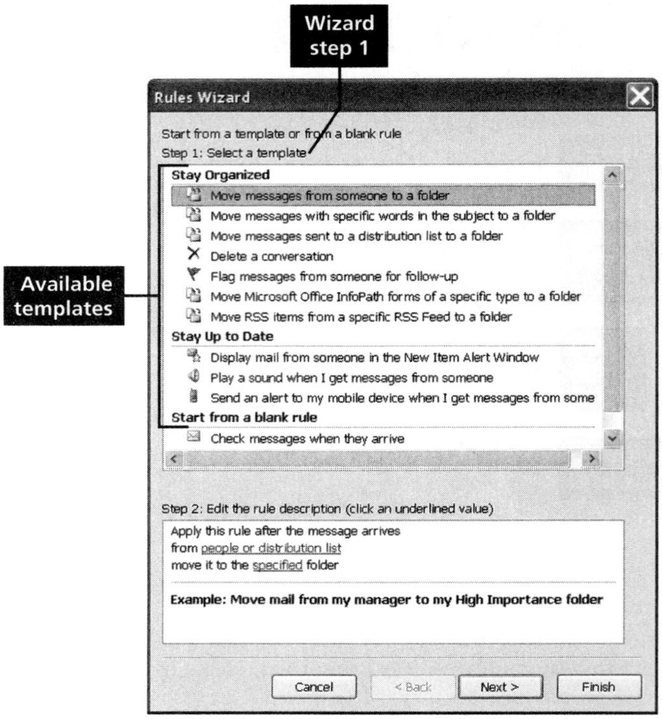

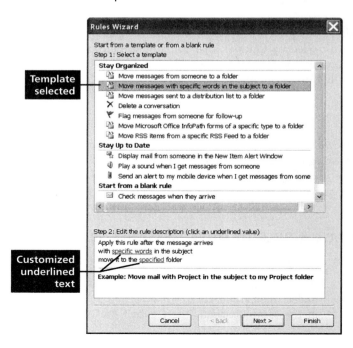

4. In the *Stay Organized* category, click Move messages with specific words in the subject to a folder. This rule will move messages about the selected topic. The rule description in the lower area of the window changes, as shown in Figure 5-3.

Figure 5-3

Rules Wizard window with template to move messages selected

TROUBLESHOOTING To ensure that a rule looking for a specific subject moves the messages, the subject line must contain the exact words.

5. In the *Step 2* area, click specific words. The Search Text window is displayed, as shown in Figure 5-4.

Figure 5-4

Search Text window

Key specific words that must appear in the subject

List of words that must be in the subject to move the message

Check to add keyed text to the search list

TAKE NOTE✻ In this exercise, you used a single phrase as the search text. To add more words or phrases to the search list, key the text into the Search Text window and click the Add button.

6. In the *Specify words or phrases to search for in the subject* field, key Lesson 5 Schedule. Click the Add button. The *Lesson 5 Schedule* phrase is enclosed by quotation marks and added to the search list for this rule. Click OK to close the Search Text window. The Rules Wizard window is displayed. The Lesson 5 Schedule search phrase is identified, as shown in Figure 5-5.

Figure 5-5

Rules Wizard window with the search phrase identified

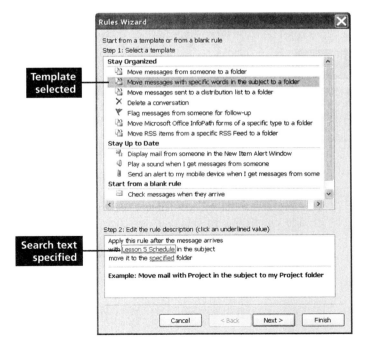

Template selected

Search text specified

7. In the *Step 2* area of the Rules Wizard window, click specified to identify the destination folder. The Folder List is displayed in the Rules and Alerts window, as shown in Figure 5-6.

Figure 5-6

Select the destination folder

Outlook folders

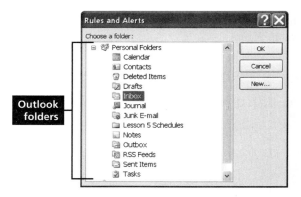

8. Click the Lesson 5 Schedules folder, and click OK. The specified destination folder is identified in the Rules Wizard window, as shown in Figure 5-7.

Figure 5-7

Rules Wizard window with the destination folder identified

Template selected

Template customized

Click the Next button to continue the Wizard

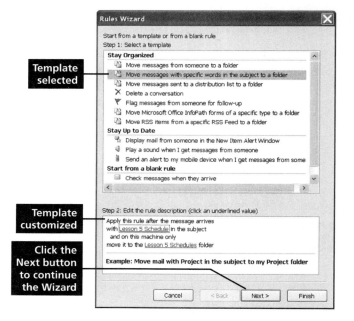

9. Click the Next button to continue the Wizard. Under *Step 1: Select condition(s)*, you will see a list of conditions that can be added to the rule. You don't want to add conditions to this rule, so click the Next button to continue the Wizard. Under *Step 1: Select action(s)*, you will see a list of actions that can be taken. You don't want to add actions to this rule, so click the Next button to continue the Wizard. A list of exceptions to the rule is displayed, as shown in Figure 5-8.

Figure 5-8

Rules Wizard window with
exceptions that can be added
to the rule

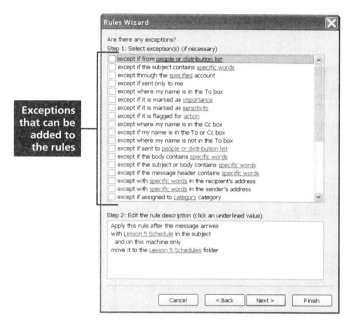

**Exceptions
that can be
added to
the rules**

10. Click the except if the subject contains specific words checkbox. This option
   is second on the list. Text is added to the rule description at the bottom of the
   Rules Wizard window.

11. In the rule description area at the bottom of the window, click specific words.
   The Search text window shown in Figure 5-4 is displayed.

12. In the *Specify words or phrases to search for in the subject* field, key RE:. Click the
   Add button. The *RE:* text is enclosed by quotation marks and added to the search
   list for this rule. Click OK to close the Search Text window. The Rules Wizard
   window is displayed. The exception is added to the rule, as shown in Figure 5-9.
   Making RE: an exception prevents replies to the Lesson 5 Schedule messages from
   being moved to the destination folder.

Figure 5-9

Rules Wizard window with
exception added to the rule

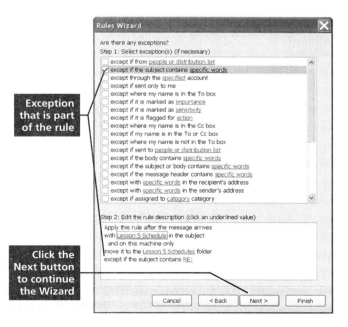

**Exception
that is part
of the rule**

**Click the
Next button
to continue
the Wizard**

13. Click the Next button to continue the Wizard. The rule is displayed for your
   approval, as shown in Figure 5-10.

Figure 5-10

Rules Wizard window with
rule displayed for approval

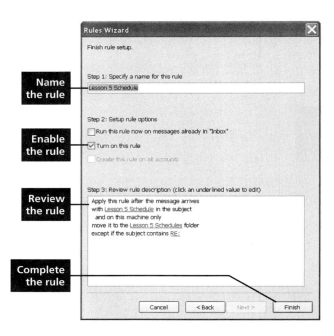

Figure 5-10

Rules Wizard window with
rule displayed for approval

14. Examine the rule carefully to verify that it is correct. Click the Finish button. The
    new rule is displayed in the Rules and Alerts window, as shown in Figure 5-11.

Figure 5-11

Rules and Alerts window
with the new rule displayed

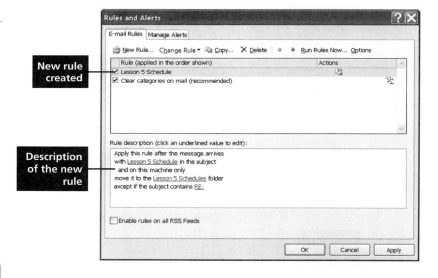

CERTIFICATION READY?
How do you create a rule to
move messages?
5.5.1

15. Click the OK button to close the Rules and Alerts window.
    PAUSE. LEAVE Outlook open to use in the next exercise.

In the previous exercise, you used a Wizard to create a new rule to move arriving messages
about a specific subject to a selected destination folder. Using the wizard to create a new rule
simplifies the process. If you try to advance to the next step without completing the current
step, an error message is displayed. It instructs you to finish the current step.

A rule consists of three parts: a condition, an action, and an exception. In simple terms, a rule
says **if A** happens (the condition) **then B** (the action) **unless C** (the exception.) Table 5-1
describes the parts of a rule.

Table 5-1

Parts of a rule

PART	DESCRIPTION
Condition	The *condition* identifies the characteristics used to determine the messages affected by the rule. Use caution when you define the conditions. If your conditions are too broad, the rule will affect more messages than intended. If your conditions are too narrow, the rule will not identify messages that should be affected.
Action	The *action* determines what happens when a message meets the conditions defined in the rule. For example, the message can be moved, forwarded, or deleted.
Exception	The *exception* identifies the characteristics used to exclude messages from being affected by the rule.

Running a Rule

Rules run automatically when new messages arrive. You can also run rules manually to test them. Send yourself a message that meets the rule's conditions. Verify that the action is carried out as intended.

⊕ RUN A RULE

GET READY. Before you begin these steps, be sure to complete the previous exercise creating a rule.

1. Click the Tools menu, and click the Rules and Alerts option. The Rules and Alerts window shown in Figure 5-1 is displayed.

2. Click the Run Rules Now button. The Run Rules Now dialog box is displayed, as shown in Figure 5-12.

Figure 5-12

Run Rules Now dialog box

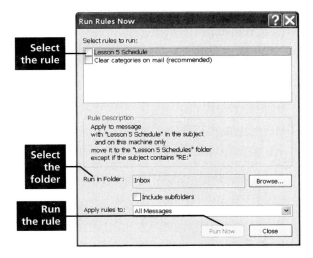

3. In the *Select rules to run* section, click the Lesson 5 Schedule checkbox. Click the Run Now button. Because you don't have any messages that meet the condition, no action is taken. To test this rule, you need to receive a message that meets the condition.

4. Click the Close button, and click the OK button to return to the main Outlook window.

5. Click the New button in the Standard toolbar. The Message window is displayed.

6. Click the To field. Key your email address.

7. Click the Subject field. Key Lesson 5 Schedule. When this message arrives, it will meet the condition defined in the Lesson 5 Schedule rule.

8. In the message area, key Lesson 5 Schedule rule test.

9. Click the Send button. The message is moved to the Outbox and sent when the computer is connected to the Internet.

10. If necessary, click the Send/Receive button to receive the message. When the message arrives, the rule runs automatically and places the message in the Lesson 5 Schedules folder, as shown in Figure 5-13.

Figure 5-13

Rule moved the received message

PAUSE. LEAVE Outlook open to use in the next exercise.

After creating a rule, test the rule to verify that it works. For example, to test the rule created in the previous exercise you sent a message with *Lesson 5 Schedule* as the subject to yourself. Over time, you might need to add conditions to the rule because everyone who sends schedules to you does not use the correct subject. You can add a condition such as the *Lesson 5 Schedule* phrase in the body of the message or add a condition identifying any message with the word *schedule* in the subject.

■ Creating and Editing Rules

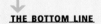

THE BOTTOM LINE

In many situations, creating a rule from a template is one of the easiest methods for creating a rule. However, rules can be created in a number of different ways. You can create a rule from an existing message or copy an existing rule and edit one or more of the rule's components. If a rule is simple, it can be created quickly from scratch.

Creating a Rule to Categorize Messages from a Selected Message

Repeating the same action over and over is one of the most common reasons for creating a rule. The next time you select a message on which you plan to perform an often-repeated action, use the message to create a rule. For example, categorizing messages is a common organizational task. A rule can automate this repetitive task.

⊕ **CREATE A RULE TO CATEGORIZE MESSAGES FROM A SELECTED MESSAGE**

USE the message you sent in the previous exercise.

1. In the Navigation pane, click the Lesson 5 Schedules folder. One message is in the folder. It is highlighted in the Message List.

2. Right-click the message. Click Create Rule on the shortcut menu. The Create Rule dialog box is displayed, as shown in Figure 5-14. The characteristics of the selected message are displayed in the dialog box.

Figure 5-14
_____

Create Rule dialog box

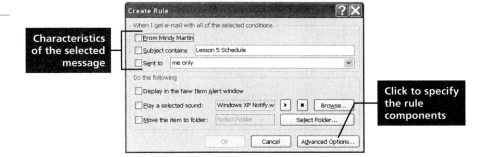

3. Click the Subject contains checkbox. The field contains *Lesson 5 Schedule*, the subject of the selected message. Click the Advanced Options button to specify additional rule components. The Rules Wizard window is displayed.

4. The condition about the message's subject is already selected. Click the Next button. The Rules Wizard window lists the available actions for the rule. Actions based on the selected message are displayed at the top of the list. Click the assign it to the category category checkbox. The selected action is moved to the lower area of the window, as shown in Figure 5-15.

Figure 5-15
_____

Rules Wizard window with available actions based on the selected message

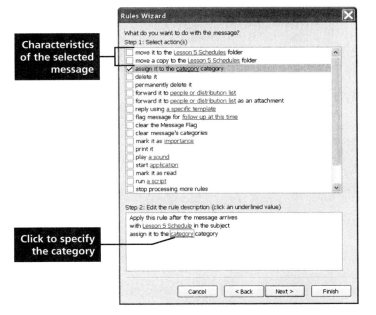

X REF Color Category is a new feature in Outlook 2007. You can find more information on Color Categories in Lesson 12.

5. In the *Step 2: Edit the rule description* area, click the underlined category. The Color Categories dialog box is displayed, as shown in Figure 5-16.

Figure 5-16

Color Categories dialog box

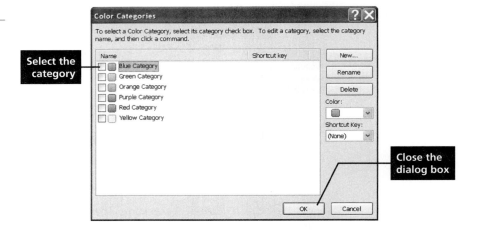

TAKE NOTE*

You can rename categories, but it isn't necessary in this lesson.

CERTIFICATION READY?
How do you categorize messages by color?
5.1.1

6. Click the Blue Category checkbox. Click OK. If a Rename Category window is displayed, click the No button. The Color Categories dialog box is closed, and you are returned to the Rules Wizard window.

7. The condition and action for the rule are complete. You don't want to identify any exceptions. Click the Finish button. The rule is saved. The Rules Wizard window is closed, and you are returned to the main Outlook window. In the following steps, you will rename and test the new rule.

8. Click the Tools menu and click the Rules and Alerts option. The Rules and Alerts dialog box is displayed, as shown in Figure 5-17. The new rule you just created is identified as *Lesson 5 Schedule (1)*. The name was inherited from the rule already applied to the message when you selected the message.

Figure 5-17

Rule created from a selected message

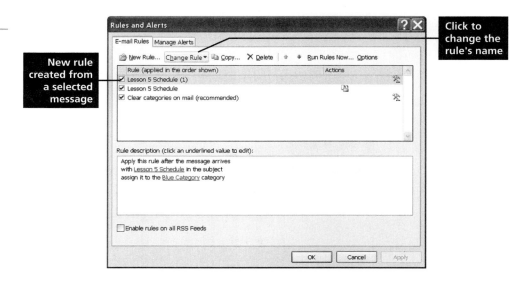

9. If necessary, select the Lesson 5 Schedule (1) rule. Click the Change Rule button, and click the Rename Rule option. The Rename dialog box is displayed, as shown in Figure 5-18.

Figure 5-18

Rename a rule

10. In the *New name of rule* field, key Blue Lesson 5 Schedule. Click OK. The Rename dialog box is closed. The name of the rule has been changed.
11. Click the Run Rules Now button. The Run Rules Now dialog box is displayed.
12. Click the Blue Lesson 5 Schedule checkbox. Click the Run Now button.
13. Click the Close button. Click OK to return to the main Outlook window. In the Messages List, the Blue Category has been assigned to the message. See Figure 5-19.

Figure 5-19

Blue Category assigned to a message

PAUSE. LEAVE Outlook open to use in the next exercise.

CERTIFICATION READY?
How do you create a rule to categorize messages?
5.5.2

Creating a rule from a selected message has advantages. As you create the rule, the characteristics of the selected message are offered as rule components. This saves time and increases the rule's accuracy.

Creating a Rule to Forward a Message by Copying an Existing Rule

Forwarding messages is another common task that can be performed by a rule. When many of the rule components are similar to an existing rule, you can copy the existing rule to create the new rule.

CREATE A RULE TO FORWARD A MESSAGE BY COPYING AN EXISTING RULE

USE the message and the rule created in a previous exercise.

1. Click the Tools menu. Click the Rules and Alerts option. The Rules and Alerts window shown in Figure 5-1 is displayed.
2. Click the Blue Lesson 5 Schedule rule. Click the Copy button. The Copy rule to dialog box is displayed, as shown in Figure 5-20.

Figure 5-20

Copying a rule

TAKE NOTE * If your Outlook profile accesses more than one email account, you can choose the Inbox affected by the rule. Refer to Outlook's Help for more information about Outlook profiles.

3. Click OK. This identifies the Inbox affected by the rule. A copy of the selected rule is created and added to the list of rules, as shown in Figure 5-21.

Figure 5-21

Copied rule created

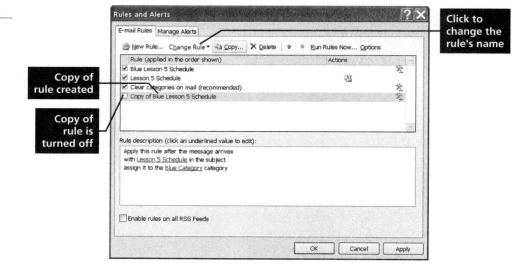

4. Select the Copy of Blue Lesson 5 Schedule rule, if necessary. Click the Change Rule button, and click Rename Rule. The Rename dialog box is displayed.

5. In the *New name of rule* field, key Forward Lesson 5 Schedule. Click OK. The dialog box is closed, and the rule's name is changed.

6. With the Forward Lesson 5 Schedule rule selected, click the Change Rule button, and click the Edit Rule Settings option. The Rules Wizard window is displayed.

7. The condition about the message's subject is already selected. Click the Next button. The Rules Wizard window lists the available actions for the rule.

8. Click the assign it to the category category checkbox to deselect the action. Click the forward it to people or distribution list checkbox. The *forward it to people or distribution list* action is moved to the rule description in the lower area of the Rules Wizard window.

9. In the *Step 2: Edit the rule description* area, click the underlined people or distribution list text. The Rule Address dialog box is displayed.

X REF Rather than keying an email address into the To field, you can select a person from your Outlook Contacts. You will learn more about contacts in Lesson 6.

10. In the To field, key the email address of a friend or coworker. Click the OK button to close the dialog box. The Rules Wizard window is updated, as shown in Figure 5-22.

Figure 5-22

Rule to forward messages

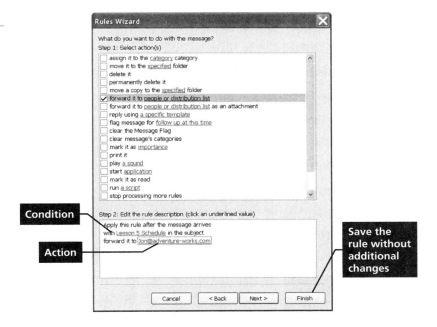

Figure 5-22

Rule to forward messages

Condition

Action

Save the rule without additional changes

11. This rule does not have exceptions. Click the Finish button to save the rule and return to the Rules and Alerts window.

12. Click the Forward Lesson 5 Schedule checkbox to turn on the rule.

13. Click the Run Rules Now button. The Run Rules Now dialog box is displayed.

14. Click the Forward Lesson 5 Schedule checkbox. Click the Run Now button.

15. Click the Close button. Click OK to return to the main Outlook window. The forwarded message is listed in the Sent Items folder.

PAUSE. LEAVE Outlook open to use in the next exercise.

CERTIFICATION READY?
How do you create a rule to forward messages?
5.5.3

So far, you have created a rule to move a message, a rule to assign a category, and a rule to forward messages. Rather than creating three separate rules, you could create a single rule that performs all three actions.

How do you decide which actions can be combined into a single rule? You can turn individual rules on and off. If you turn off a rule with several actions, none of the actions are performed. When you combine actions into a single rule, don't include components that you might need to turn off separately.

Suppose that Jon, the addressee for the forwarded messages, goes on a two-week business trip followed by a two-week vacation in Hawaii. He asked you to stop forwarding schedules to him for four weeks. If the three actions were combined into one rule, you would need to create new rules or edit the combined rule so that the messages are still moved and categorized, but *not* forwarded to Jon. If you keep the forwarded action in a separate rule, you can turn off the forwarding rule until Jon returns with a tan and too many vacation photos.

Creating a Rule to Delete Messages from Scratch

Some rules are simple to write. You want to find messages that meet one condition and perform one action without exceptions. For example, a simple rule might be "Delete all the messages in the Blue Category." You can quickly create simple rules like this from scratch.

➔ CREATE A RULE TO DELETE MESSAGES FROM SCRATCH

USE the message you sent in the previous exercise.

1. Click the Tools menu, and click the Rules and Alerts option. The Rules and Alerts window shown in Figure 5-1 is displayed.

2. Click the New Rule button. The Rules Wizard window is displayed, as shown in Figure 5-23.

Figure 5-23

Creating a rule from scratch

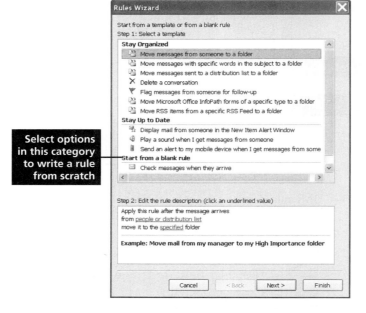

3. In the *Start from a blank rule* section, click Check messages when they arrive. This identifies when the rule will run automatically. Click the Next button to continue creating the rule.

> **TAKE NOTE** *
>
> To delete all messages from a specific sender, select the *from people or distribution list* condition in the Step 1 area. In the Step 2 area, click *people or distribution list*. Then, you can key the sender's email address into the From field and click OK to continue creating the rule.

4. In this Rules Wizard window, you identify the conditions of the rule. Click with specific words in the subject. This rule will identify messages about the selected topic.

5. In the *Step 2* area, click specific words. The Search Text window is displayed.

6. In the *Specify words or phrases to search for in the subject* field, key Lesson 5 Schedule. Click the Add button. The *Lesson 5 Schedule* phrase is enclosed by quotation marks and added to the search list for this rule. Click OK to close the Search Text window. The Rules Wizard window is displayed. The *Lesson 5 Schedule* search phrase is identified. Click the Next button to continue creating the rule.

7. Available actions are listed in the Rules Wizard window. Click the delete it check-box. You don't want to add any additional conditions, actions, or exceptions. Click the Finish button. The rule is complete: When a message arrives with *Lesson 5 Schedule* in the subject, delete it.

8. Select the Lesson 5 Schedule (1) rule, if necessary. Click the Change Rule button, and click Rename Rule. The Rename dialog box is displayed.

9. In the *New name of rule* field, key Delete Lesson 5 Schedule. Click OK. The dialog box is closed, and the rule's name is changed.

10. Click the Delete Lesson 5 Schedule checkbox to clear the checkbox. Click the OK button to close the Rules and Alerts window.

PAUSE. LEAVE Outlook open to use in the next exercise.

In the previous exercise, you created a rule from scratch. This is the best method to create simple rules with one condition, one action, and no exceptions.

■ Managing Rules

THE BOTTOM LINE Rules manage your messages. To manage your rules, change their sequence or turn them on or off.

Sequencing Rules

The sequence in which rules are processed can be important. For example, you can change the importance of a message before forwarding it to a coworker. Also, you want to forward a message before you delete it.

→ SEQUENCE RULES

USE the rules you created in the previous exercises.

1. Click the Tools menu, and click the Rules and Alerts option. The Rules and Alerts window shown in Figure 5-1 is displayed.

2. Click the Delete Lesson 5 rule. Click the Move Down button (blue arrow pointing down) four times. The *Delete Lesson 5 Schedule* rule is last on the list of rules.

3. Click the Clear categories on mail (recommended) rule. Click the Move Up button (blue arrow pointing up) two times. The sequence of your rules should match the rule sequence in Figure 5-24.

Figure 5-24

Sequenced rules

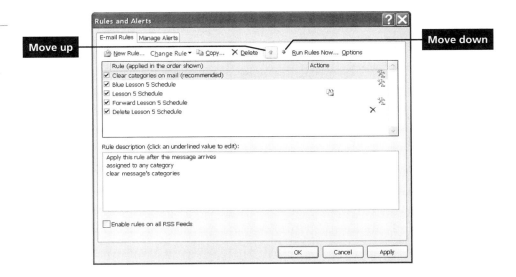

4. Click OK to save the changes and close the Rules and Alerts window.

PAUSE. LEAVE Outlook open to use in the next exercise.

In the previous exercise, you moved two rules. The *Clear categories on mail (recommended)* rule is first on the list of rules. This clears the categories of the arriving message so you can apply your own category in the *Blue Lesson 5 Schedule* rule.

Turning Off a Rule

In the Rules and Alerts window, the checkbox in front of the rule's name controls its status. A rule is either off or on. If a rule is on, the checkbox in front of the rule is filled. If a rule is off, the checkbox in front of the rule is empty.

→ TURN OFF A RULE

USE the rules you created in the previous exercises.

1. Click the Tools menu, and click the Rules and Alerts option. The Rules and Alerts window shown in Figure 5-1 is displayed.
2. Click the Delete Lesson 5 Schedule checkbox so the checkbox is empty.
3. Click OK to save the changes and close the Rules and Alerts window.
   PAUSE. LEAVE Outlook open to use in the next exercise.

Turning off a rule rather than deleting it enables you to turn on the rule if it is needed later. It also enables you to keep a rule turned off and run it at a time of your choice.

Deleting a Rule

Turning off a rule rather than deleting it has advantages. However, if you created a rule that you will not use again, delete it. This keeps your list of rules organized and reduces confusion caused by a long list of old rules that are not used.

→ DELETE A RULE

USE the rules you created in the previous exercises.

1. Click the Tools menu, and click the Rules and Alerts option. The Rules and Alerts window shown in Figure 5-1 is displayed.
2. Click the Delete Lesson 5 Schedule rule. Click the Delete button. Click Yes in the dialog box.
3. Click OK to save the changes and close the Rules and Alerts window.
4. To clean up your folders from the changes in this lesson, delete the Lesson 5 Schedules folder in the Personal Folders, and delete the rules created in this lesson. The rules to delete include *Blue Lesson 5 Schedule, Lesson 5 Schedule,* and *Forward Lesson 5 Schedule.* Do not delete the *Clear categories on mail (recommended)* rule. Empty the Deleted Items folder.
   CLOSE Outlook.

CERTIFICATION READY?
How do you delete a rule?
5.5.1

Use caution when deleting a rule rather than disabling it. You don't want to spend time recreating a rule that you carelessly deleted. Managing your rules also manages your messages.

SUMMARY SKILL MATRIX

IN THIS LESSON YOU LEARNED	MATRIX SKILL	SKILL NUMBER
To use a rule template		
To create a rule from a template	Create a rule to move email messages	5.5.1
To run a rule		
To create and edit rules		
To create a rule to categorize messages from a selected message	Categorize messages, appointments, meetings, contacts and tasks by color and Create a rule to categorize email messages	5.1.1 and 5.5.2
To create a rule to forward messages by copying an existing rule	Create a rule to forward email	5.5.3
To create a rule to delete messages from scratch	Create a rule to delete email	5.5.4
To manage rules		
To sequence rules		
To turn off a rule		

■ Knowledge Assessment

Fill in the Blank

Complete the following sentences by writing the correct word or words in the blanks provided.

1. _____ manage your messages.
2. A(n) _____ is taken only if the conditions are met.
3. Many rules do not have _____.
4. A(n) _____ walks you through a process.
5. The first part of a rule is the _____.
6. A(n) _____ provides structure for a rule.
7. A(n) _____ is easy to see because it is colored.
8. The _____ of the rules changes when you move a rule up or down.
9. An existing rule can be _____ to create a new rule.
10. A rule has _____ parts.

Handwritten answers in left margin:
Rules
Action
exceptions
wizard
conditions
template
color category
sequence
copied
3

Multiple Choice

Circle the correct choice.

1. What window enables you to add steps in a rule?
   A. Rules and Alerts
   B. Rules Wizard
   C. Steps
   D. New Rule

Handwritten in left margin: B

2. How does a rule identify the messages it affects?
   A. Actions
   B. Cues
   C. Conditions
   D. Phrases

3. What part of a rule is not required?
   A. Actions
   B. Conditions
   C. Exceptions
   D. All of the above

4. What happens if a rule's conditions are too broad?
   A. The rule will affect more messages than intended.
   B. The rule will affect fewer messages than intended.
   C. The rule will not run.
   D. The affected messages are deleted.

5. How do you test a rule?
   A. Read the rule.
   B. Create a message that meets the rule's exceptions.
   C. Create a separate folder for testing.
   D. Run the rule manually.

6. Why would you use an existing message to create a rule?
   A. The message is part of the rule.
   B. The message is not affected by the rule.
   C. Only the selected message is affected by the rule.
   D. The message's characteristics are used to create the rule.

7. Why would you copy an existing rule to create a new rule?
   A. Many of the new rule's characteristics are similar to the existing rule.
   B. The new rule replaces the existing rule.
   C. The existing rule does not work correctly.
   D. This process tests the existing rule.

8. How do you decide which actions can be combined in a single rule?
   A. The conditions are the same for all of the actions.
   B. The exceptions are the same for all the actions.
   C. A rule with combined actions is easier to write.
   D. The actions won't need to be turned off separately.

9. Why would you change the sequence of your rules?
   A. Rules should be in alphabetic order.
   B. Short rules should be processed first.
   C. Some actions should be performed before others.
   D. Rules should be processed in the order they were created.

10. Why would you turn off a rule?
    A. The rule is no longer needed.
    B. The rule should only be run periodically.
    C. You don't want the rule to run automatically.
    D. All of the above

■ Competency Assessment

Project 5-1: Create Folders and Messages to Test Rules

Jack Creasey owns a small Internet-based gift shop with a big name. World-Wide Importers sells a variety of crafted objects created by small crafters across the country and one vendor in Canada, justifying the "World-Wide" portion of his company's name. Jack regularly receives pictures of crafted items from his suppliers and sends invoices to customers who buy his products. Jack decided to create rules to manage his messages automatically. First, he needs to create two folders and a message.

GET READY. Launch Outlook if it is not already running.

1. If necessary, click the Mail button in the Navigation pane to display the Mail folder.

2. Right-click Personal Folders in the Folders List. Click New Folder in the shortcut menu. The Create New Folder dialog box is displayed.

3. In the Name field, key P5 Products. If necessary, click Personal Folders in the *Select where to place the folder* section. Click OK to create the folder and close the dialog box. You will create a rule to move messages into this folder.

4. Right-click Personal Folders in the Folders List. Click New Folder in the shortcut menu. The Create New Folder dialog box is displayed.

5. In the Name field, key P5 Invoices. If necessary, click Personal Folders in the *Select where to place the folder* section. Click OK to create the folder and close the dialog box.

6. Click the New button in the Standard toolbar. The Message window is displayed.

7. Click the To field. Key your email address.

8. Click the Subject field. Key New ceramic statue!

9. In the message area, key Take a look at this new flying pig birdfeeder! It's sure to be a big hit!

10. Click the Attach File button. Navigate to the data folders for this lesson. Click the *Flying Pig Birdfeeder* file, and click the Insert button.

11. Click the Send button. The message is moved to the Outbox and sent when the computer is connected to the Internet.

LEAVE Outlook open for the next project.

The *Flying Pig Birdfeeder* image is available on the companion CD-ROM.

Project 5-2: Create a Rule from Scratch to Categorize Messages

Jack wants to create a rule that categorizes the messages he sends with "Invoice" in the Subject field. Assign the messages to the Yellow Category. Complete Project 5-1 before starting this project.

1. Click the Tools menu, and click the Rules and Alerts option. The Rules and Alerts window is displayed.

2. Click the New Rule button. The Rules Wizard window is displayed.

3. In the *Start from a blank rule* section, click Check messages after sending. Click the Next button.

4. In the *Step 1: Select condition(s)* area, click the with specific words in the subject checkbox.

5. In the *Step 2* area, click specific words. The Search Text window is displayed.

6. In the *Specify words or phrases to search for in the subject* field, key Invoice. Click the Add button. *Invoice* is enclosed by quotation marks and added to the search list for this rule. Click OK to close the Search Text window.

7. In the Rules Wizard window, click the Next button.

8. In the *Step 1: Select action(s)* area, click the assign it to the category category checkbox.

9. In the *Step 2* area, click the underlined category.

10. Click the Yellow Category checkbox. Click OK. If a Rename Category window is displayed, click the No button. The Color Categories dialog box is closed, and you are returned to the Rules Wizard window.

11. In the Rules Wizard window, click the Finish button. The new Invoice rule is listed in the Rules and Alerts window. Click OK to close the Rules and Alerts window.

    LEAVE Outlook open for the next project.

■ Proficiency Assessment

Project 5-3: Test a Rule

To test the Invoice rule, Jack sends a message to himself with the word "Invoice" in the Subject field. Complete Project 5-1 before starting this project.

1. Create a new message addressed to yourself.

2. In the Subject field, key Invoice.

3. In the message area, key Testing.

4. Send the message.

5. Click the Sent Items folder. Verify that the Invoice message in the Sent Items folder was assigned to the Yellow Category.

6. Click the Inbox. When the *Invoice* message arrives, it is not assigned to the Yellow Category because categories are cleared for arriving messages by the *Clear categories on mail (recommended)* rule.

7. Click the Tools menu, and click the Rules and Alerts option. The Rules and Alerts window is displayed.

8. Click the Invoice checkbox to clear the checkbox. This turns off the Invoice rule. Click OK to close the Rules and Alerts window.

    LEAVE Outlook open for the next project.

Project 5-4: Use a Template to Create a Rule that Moves Messages

Jack wants to move messages about invoices into the P5 Invoices folder. Complete Projects 5-1 and 5-3 before starting this project.

1. Open the Rules and Alerts window.

2. Click the New Rule button. The Rules Wizard window is displayed.

3. In the *Stay Organized* category, click Move messages with specific words in the subject to a folder.

4. In the *Step 2* area, click specific words. The Search Text window is displayed.

5. In the *Specify words or phrases to search for in the subject* field, key Invoice. Click the Add button. Click OK to close the Search Text window.

6. In the *Step 2* area of the Rules Wizard window, click specified to identify the destination folder.

7. Click the P5 Invoices folder, and click OK.

8. Click the Finish button.

9. In the Rules and Alerts window, click Change Rule, and click the Rename Rule option. Key Move Invoices in the *New name of rule* field.

10. Close the dialog boxes and return to the main Outlook window.

11. If necessary, click the Send/Receive button to receive the Invoice message sent in Project 5-3. The rule is run automatically when messages are received, so skip to step 13.

12. If the Invoice message was already received before you created the Move Invoices rule, click the Tools menu, and click the Rules and Alerts option. The Rules and Alerts window is displayed. Click the Run Rules Now button. In the Run Rules Now dialog box, click the Move Invoices checkbox so the checkbox is filled, and click the Run Now button. Close the dialog boxes and return to the main Outlook window.

13. Click the P5 Invoices folder to verify that the received Invoice message was moved to the P5 Invoices folder.

14. Click the Move Invoice checkbox to clear the checkbox in the Rules and Alerts window. This turns off the Invoice rule. Click OK to close the Rules and Alerts window.

    LEAVE Outlook open for the next project.

■ Mastery Assessment

Project 5-5: Use a Message to Create a Rule that Moves Messages

Suppliers frequently send pictures of new products to Jack. He wants to move these messages to the P5 Products folder. Complete Project 5-1 before starting this project.

1. In the Inbox, right-click the New ceramic statue! message, and click Create Rule on the shortcut menu.

2. In the Create Rule dialog box, click the Subject contains checkbox. Click in the *Subject contains* field and modify the value to the single word *New*.

3. Click the Move to folder checkbox and select P5 Products as the destination folder.

5. Click the OK button. In the Success dialog box, click the checkbox to run the rule. Click the OK button to close the Success dialog box.

6. Click the P5 Products folder to verify that the *New ceramic statue!* message was moved to the P5 Products folder.

7. Change the name of the rule you just created to Move Products.

8. Turn off the Move Products rule. Close the Rules and Alerts window and return to the main Outlook window.

    LEAVE Outlook open for the next project.

Project 5-6: Copy a Rule to Create a New Rule Assigning a Category

Jack wants to apply a Color Category to the arriving messages that have attachments. He can copy the Move Products rule and edit the action to move the messages. Complete Projects 5-1 and 5-5 before starting this project.

1. In the Rules and Alerts window, click the Move Products rule. Click the Copy button. In the *Copy rule to* dialog box, verify that your Inbox is selected and click OK.

2. Scroll down to select the new rule, if necessary. Change the name of the rule to *Categorize Products*.

3. Click Change Rule, and then click Edit Rule Settings. The Rules Wizard window is displayed.

4. You don't want to change the conditions, so continue the Wizard to the list of actions.

5. Turn off the *move it to the specified folder* action. Click the assign it to the category category checkbox.

6. In the *Step 2* area, select the Purple Category.

7. Click the Finish button.

8. In the Rules and Alerts window, move the rules to place them in the following sequence:

   Clear categories on mail (recommended)

   Categorize Products

   Move Products

   Invoice

   Move Invoices

9. Activate and run all the rules for Projects 5-1 to 5-6. After running the rules, your folders should contain the following items:

   P5 Invoices folder: *Invoice* message without an assigned category

   P5 Products folder: *New ceramic statue!* message assigned to the Purple Category

   Sent Items: Sent *Invoice* message assigned to the Yellow Category

10. To clean up after completing these projects, delete the P5 Invoices and P5 Products folders. Delete the Categorize Products, Move Products, Invoice, and Move Invoices rules.

    CLOSE Outlook.

INTERNET READY

Another common way to organize messages is based on the sender. Create an email account with a free Website such as Yahoo.com. Create a rule to manage messages from the Web-based account. Test the rule by sending a message from the Web-based account to your Outlook account.

Contact Basics

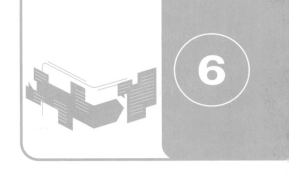

LESSON SKILL MATRIX

SKILLS	MATRIX SKILL	SKILL NUMBER
Creating and Modifying Contacts		
Creating a Contact from a Blank Contact	Create a contact from a blank contact	4.1.1
Modifying Contact Information	Modify contact information	4.1.5
Sending and Receiving Contacts		
Saving a Contact Received as a Contact Record	Save a contact received as a contact record	4.1.4
Creating a Contact from a Message Header	Create a contact from a message header	4.1.2
Viewing and Deleting Contacts		
Creating and Modifying a Distribution List	Create and modify distribution lists	4.3

Like many business executives, Mindy Martin will tell you that *who* you know is just as important as *what* you know. Mindy refers to Outlook's contact information dozens of times every day. She calls, writes, and sends messages to suppliers, guests, and other business organizations. Direct contact with the right people can avoid problems or solve small problems before they become catastrophes.

KEY TERMS
contact
Contacts folder
distribution list
duplicate contact
message header
ScreenTip
spoofing

■ SOFTWARE ORIENTATION

Microsoft Outlook's Contacts Window

The main Contact window displays basic information about the contacts in your Contacts folder, as shown in Figure 6-1.

Figure 6-1

Outlook's Contacts folder

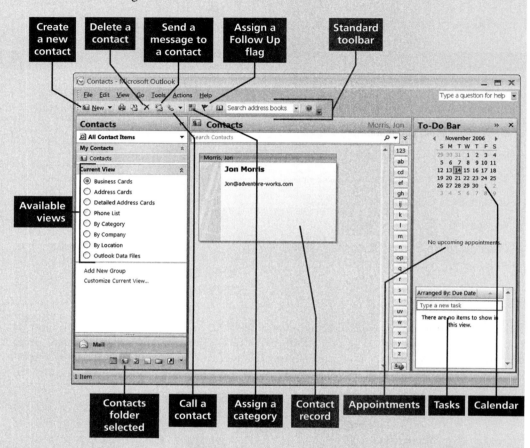

The Contacts folder enables you to organize and maintain information about the individuals and businesses you communicate with regularly. In this window, you can select a contact record, create a new contact record, view appointments, view tasks, send a message to a contact, call a contact, assign a contact to a category, and assign a follow-up flag to a contact.

■ Creating and Modifying Contacts

THE BOTTOM LINE

A *contact* is a collection of information about a person or company. The *Contacts folder* is an electronic organizer that enables you to create, view, and edit contact information.

Contacts can be added in many different ways. For example, Mindy Martin's Contacts folder contains a contact for Jon Morris. The contact for Jon was created automatically when Jon and Mindy exchanged digital signatures. If you exchanged digital signatures with a coworker or friend in Lesson 3, your Contacts folder contains a contact for that individual.

Creating a Contact from a Blank Contact

You can use a variety of methods to create contacts. The most basic method of creating a contact is opening a new contact and keying the information into the Contact window.

⊕ CREATE A CONTACT FROM A BLANK CONTACT

GET READY. Before you begin these steps, be sure to launch Microsoft Outlook.

1. If necessary, click the Contacts button in the Navigation pane to display the Contacts folder shown in Figure 6-1.

TAKE NOTE* The Standard toolbar in the Contacts folder differs from the Standard toolbar in the Mail folder. The options on the toolbars reflect the actions you can take in the folder.

2. Click New on the Standard toolbar. The Untitled – Contact window is displayed, as shown in Figure 6-2. The blank Contact window is ready to store data for a new contact.

Figure 6-2

Untitled – Contact window

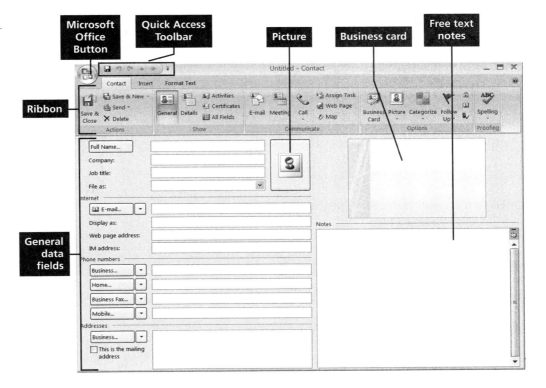

3. Move your mouse over each button in the Ribbon on the new Contact window. The Ribbon is a new feature in outlook 2007. *ScreenTip* providing a brief description of an item's purpose is displayed as the mouse hovers over each button.

4. Click the Full Name field, if necessary. Key Gabe Mares and press Tab. The insertion point moves to the Company field. The *File as* field is automatically filled with *Mares, Gabe,* and *Gabe Mares* is displayed in the business card. The name of the window is changed to Gabe Mares – Contact.

5. In the Company field, key Wingtip Toys and press Tab. The insertion point moves to the *Job title* field. The company's name is added to the business card.

6. In the *Job title* field, key Software Support Manager and press Tab. Gabe's job title is added to the business card. The insertion point moves to the *File as* field, highlighting the current value.

7. Click the dropdown arrow in the *File as* field. A short list of alternative ways of filing the contact is displayed. Some methods use the company name to file the contact. Other alternatives file the contact by the contact's first name. Release the mouse button without selecting a different option.

TROUBLESHOOTING

The email addresses provided in these exercises belong to unused domains owned by Microsoft. When you send a message to these addresses, you will receive an error message stating that the message could not be delivered. Delete the error messages when they arrive.

8. Click the E-mail field. Key Gabe@wingtiptoys.com and press [Tab]. The *Display as* field is automatically filled, and Gabe's email address is added to the business card.

9. You don't want to change the way Gabe's email address is displayed, so press [Tab]. The insertion point moves to the *Web page address* field.

TAKE NOTE *

It isn't necessary to key spaces or parentheses in phone numbers. Outlook automatically formats phone numbers when the insertion point leaves the field.

10. In the *Web page address* field, key www.wingtiptoys.com.

11. Below the *Phone numbers* heading, click the Business field. When you move the insertion point out of the *Web page address* field, the Web page address is automatically added to the business card. Key 6155551205.

12. Below the Addresses heading, click the Business field. Key 7895 First Street. Press [Enter]. Key Nashville, TN 76534. Press [Tab]. The business card is automatically updated. The Gabe Mares–Contact window is displayed in Figure 6-3.

Figure 6-3

Gabe Mares – Contact window

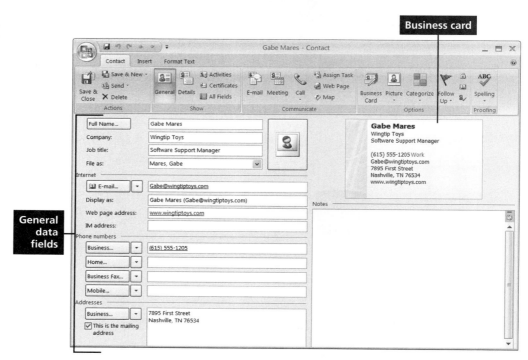

If you press Tab in the Address field before keying at least two lines of text, the Check Address dialog box is displayed. Because Outlook expects at least two lines of text in an address, the text you have already keyed might be displayed in the wrong fields in the Check Address dialog box. Click the Cancel button to close the dialog box and continue keying the address.

TROUBLESHOOTING

13. In the Actions group on the Ribbon, click the Save & Close button. Gabe Mares' contact information is saved, and you are returned to the main Contacts window.

PAUSE. LEAVE Outlook open to use in the next exercise.

In a contact record, using the postal abbreviation for a state makes it easier to use the information in a mailing list or other data exports.

In the previous exercise, you keyed the basic information for a contact. You do not have to key information into every field. To save contact information, you should have a value in the *File as* field. If the *File as* field is empty, a warning message is displayed when you try to save the contact. The warning tells you that the *File as* field is empty and asks if you want to save the contact with an empty *File as* field. If you save the contact, it will be placed before any other contacts saved with a value in the *File as* field, because a blank is sorted as a value that occurs before any other value.

Creating a Contact from an Existing Contact

Often, you will have several contacts who work for the same company. Rather than keying the same data for a new contact, you can create the new contact from the existing contact.

→ CREATE A CONTACT FROM AN EXISTING CONTACT

GET READY. Before you begin these steps, be sure to complete the previous exercise creating a contact.

1. If necessary, click the Contacts button in the Navigation pane to display the Contacts folder shown in Figure 6-1.

2. Double-click the Gabe Mares contact. The Gabe Mares – Contact window shown in Figure 6-3 is displayed.

3. In the Actions group on the Ribbon, click the Save & New arrow. In the dropdown list of options, click New Contact from Same Company. A new window titled Wingtip Toys – Contact is displayed.

4. Click the Full Name field if necessary. Key Diane Tibbott and press Tab. The insertion point moves to the Company field. The *File as* field is automatically filled with *Tibbott, Diane*, and *Diane Tibbott* is displayed in the business card. The name of the window is changed to Diane Tibbott – Contact.

5. Click the Job title field. Key Marketing Representative and press Tab. Diane's job title is added to the business card. The insertion point moves to the *File as* field, highlighting the current value.

6. Click the E-mail field. Key Diane@wingtiptoys.com and press Tab. The *Display as* field is automatically filled, and Diane's email address is added to the business card.

7. In the Actions group on the Ribbon, click the Save & Close button. Diane Tibbott's contact information is saved. Close Gabe's contact record to return to the main Contacts window.

PAUSE. LEAVE Outlook open to use in the next exercise.

When you create a new contact for a person from the same company, the company name, File as, Website, phone number, and address are carried over to the new contact. The name, job title, and email address are not carried over to the new contact, because these fields will usually differ between contacts, even though they work for the same company.

Modifying Contact Information

People move. They change jobs. They retire. To keep the information in your Contacts folder current, you will need to modify the information for existing contacts. You can modify an existing contact and save it as a new contact rather than overwriting the existing contact.

→ MODIFY CONTACT INFORMATION

GET READY. Before you begin these steps, be sure to complete the first exercise creating a contact for Gabe Mares.

ANOTHER WAY

To open a contact, right-click the *contact* in the Contacts folder and click *Open* on the shortcut menu.

1. If necessary, click the Contacts button in the Navigation pane to display the Contacts folder shown in Figure 6-1.

2. Double-click the Gabe Mares contact. The Gabe Mares – Contact window shown in Figure 6-3 is displayed.

3. Click the following fields and replace the existing values with the new values.

Company	Tailspin Toys
Job title	Software Development Manager
E-mail	Gabe@tailspintoys.com
Web page address	www.tailspintoys.com
Business phone number	6155550195
Business address	5678 Park Place
	Nashville, TN 76502

4. In the Actions group on the Ribbon, click the Save & Close button. The modified contact information is saved, and you are returned to the main Contacts window.

5. Double-click the Diane Tibbott contact. The Diane Tibbott – Contact window is displayed.

6. Click the Job title field. Select the existing value, key Software Support Manager, and press Tab. Diane's job title is modified on the business card.

7. In the Actions group on the Ribbon, click the Save & Close button. The modified contact information is saved, and you are returned to the main Contacts window.

8. Compare your Contacts folder to Figure 6-4. In your Contacts folder, Jon Morris' contact record is replaced by the individual with whom you exchanged digital signatures in Lesson 3.

Figure 6-4

Modified contacts

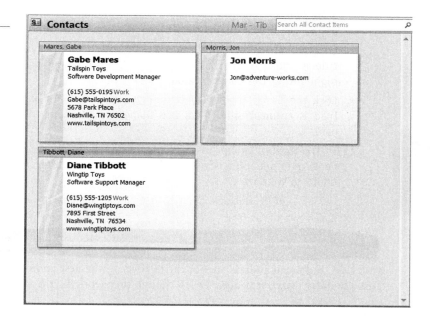

PAUSE. LEAVE Outlook open to use in the next exercise.

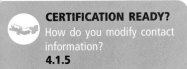

CERTIFICATION READY?
How do you modify contact information?
4.1.5

In the previous exercise, you updated the information for two contacts. The following changes occurred.

- Gabe Mares left Wingtip Toys. He was hired by Tailspin Toys as the Software Development Manager. Most of his contact information has changed.
- Diane Tibbott was promoted to Gabe's previous position as Software Support Manager. Her email address and phone number remain the same. Only her title has changed. The corner office with a view that came with the promotion is not part of her contact information.

■ Sending and Receiving Contacts

THE BOTTOM LINE

It is easy to exchange contact information via email. You can send and receive contacts as attachments. Every time you send a message, you are sending your contact information. In Outlook, you can create a contact for the sender of any message you receive.

Sending a Contact as an Attachment

You already know that you can send documents and files as attachments. You can also send a contact as an attachment.

➔ SEND A CONTACT AS AN ATTACHMENT

GET READY. Before you begin these steps, be sure to complete the first exercise creating a contact for Gabe Mares.

1. If necessary, click the Contacts button in the Navigation pane to display the Contacts folder shown in Figure 6-1.
2. Double-click the Gabe Mares contact. The Gabe Mares – Contact window shown in Figure 6-3 is displayed.
3. In the Actions group on the Ribbon, click the Send button. Click the In Outlook Format option. A new message window is displayed. In the Subject field, the topic is automatically identified as FW: Gabe Mares, and Gabe's contact record is attached to the message, as shown in Figure 6-5.

Figure 6-5

Sending a contact as an attachment

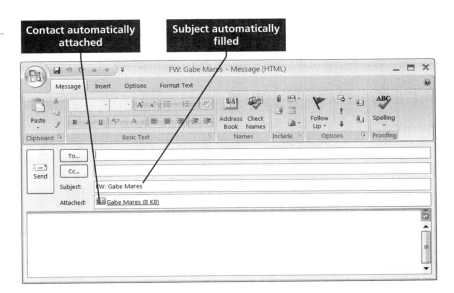

TROUBLESHOOTING If a message is displayed stating that you must save the original item, click *OK* to continue.

4. In the message area, key Gabe Mares' contact information is attached.
5. In the To field, key your email address.

TAKE NOTE* When you send contact information, any text in the Notes area of the contact record and items attached to the contact record are also sent. Before you send the contact record, delete any information in the Notes area and attachments that you don't want the recipient to see.

6. Click the Send button. The message is moved to the Outbox, and it is sent when your computer is connected to the Internet.
7. CLOSE the Gabe Mares - Contact window.

PAUSE. LEAVE Outlook open to use in the next exercise.

In the previous exercise, you sent contact information directly from the Contacts folder as an attachment to a message. This enables you to send contact information without keying it as text in a message.

TROUBLESHOOTING If the recipient does not use Outlook 2007, the contact information might not be displayed correctly and the recipient might not be able to create a contact from the attachment.

X REF

You will learn more about electronic business cards in Lesson 7.

Saving a Contact Received as a Contact Record

When you request contact information from a coworker's Contacts folder, the coworker can send the information as a business card or a contact record in Outlook format. If the contact record is sent in Outlook format, you can open the attachment, view the information, and save it as a contact record.

⊙ SAVE A CONTACT RECEIVED IN OUTLOOK FORMAT

USE the FW: Gabe Mares message sent in the previous exercise.

1. If necessary, click the Mail button in the Navigation pane to display the Mail folder. If the FW: Gabe Mares message has not arrived yet, click the Send/Receive button on the Standard toolbar.
2. Click the FW: Gabe Mares message. The message is displayed in the Reading pane.
3. In the Reading pane, right-click the Gabe Mares attachment. Click Open on the shortcut menu. The attachment opens in the Gabe Mares – Contact window.
4. In the Actions group on the Ribbon, click the Save & Close button. Because you received this contact information at the same email address used to send the contact information, the contact record is already in your Contacts folder. Therefore, Outlook detects that this is a *duplicate contact*. The Duplicate Contact Detected window shown in Figure 6-6 is displayed. If the contact record was not a duplicate, the contact would be saved without any further action needed.

Figure 6-6

Duplicate Contact Detected window

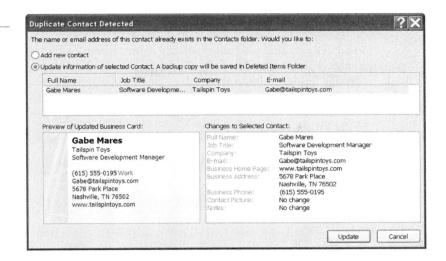

5. You want to create a new contact, so select the Add new contact option at the top of the window, and click the Add button at the bottom of the window. The Duplicate Contact Detected window is closed, the contact record is created, and you are returned to the Mail folder.

6. Click the Contacts button in the Navigation pane to display the Contacts folder. Now, you have the original Gabe Mares contact record you created by keying the data and the Gabe Mares contact record you created from the attachment. Your Contacts folder should be similar to Figure 6-7. In your Contacts folder, Jon Morris' contact record is replaced by the individual with whom you exchanged digital signatures in Lesson 3.

Figure 6-7

Duplicate contact record created

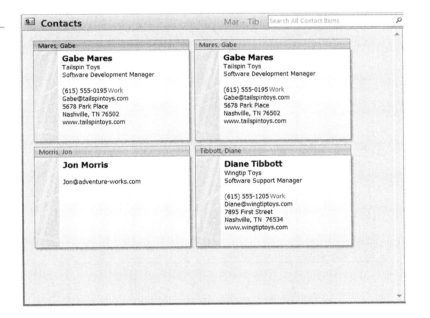

PAUSE. LEAVE Outlook open to use in the next exercise.

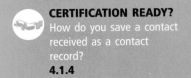

CERTIFICATION READY?
How do you save a contact received as a contact record?
4.1.4

In the previous exercise, you saved a contact in Outlook format that was sent to you as an attachment. You used the same account in an earlier exercise to send the contact record. Therefore, when you received the contact record Outlook recognized it as a duplicate of an existing contact. If this had been a new contact record that you did not have in your Contacts folder, you would have been finished after you clicked the Save & Close button.

Creating a Contact from a Message Header

Every message you send automatically contains your contact information in the message header. The ***message header*** is the text automatically added at the top of a message. The message header contains the sender's email address, the names of the servers used to send and transfer the message, the subject, the date, and other basic information about the message. You can use the message header to create a contact record in your Contacts folder for the message's sender.

⊕ CREATE A CONTACT FROM A MESSAGE HEADER

USE the FW: Gabe Mares message sent in a previous exercise.

1. If necessary, click the Mail button in the Navigation pane to display the Mail folder.

2. Click the FW: Gabe Mares message. The message is displayed in the Reading pane.

3. In the Reading pane, right-click the sender's name or email address. Click the Add to Outlook contacts option on the shortcut menu. A contact window containing the sender's name and email address is displayed, as shown in Figure 6-8. Because you sent the FW: Gabe Mares message, it is your contact information in the Contact window.

Figure 6-8

Creating a contact from a message header

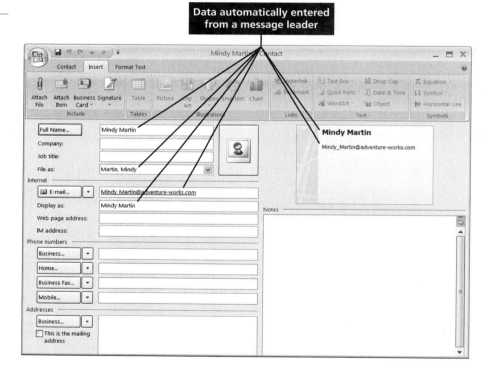

4. In the Actions group on the Ribbon, click the Save & Close button. The contact record is created, and you are returned to the Mail folder.

5. Click the Contacts button in the Navigation pane to display the Contacts folder. Now, you have the original Gabe Mares contact record you created by keying the data, the Gabe Mares contact record you created from the attachment, the contact record created when you received a digital signature in Lesson 3, Diane Tibbott's contact record created from Gabe's record, and your contact record created from a message header.

PAUSE. LEAVE Outlook open to use in the next exercise.

CERTIFICATION READY?
How do you create a contact from a message header?
4.1.2

In the previous exercise, you created a contact from a message header. Although a message header contains important information, it is important to note that false information can be provided in the message header. This is known as *spoofing*. Many junk messages contain false information in the message header.

■ Viewing and Deleting Contacts

THE BOTTOM LINE

By default, contacts are displayed as business cards. However, other views are available. Select a different view to focus on specific information. Prevent clutter in your Contacts folder. When a contact is no longer useful or you found a duplicate contact, delete the contact record.

→ **VIEW AND DELETE CONTACTS**

USE the contacts you created in the previous exercises.

1. If necessary, click the Contacts button in the Navigation pane to display the Contacts folder shown in Figure 6-1. This is the Business Cards view. It is the only view that displays any graphics on the business card.

2. Click the Address Cards button in the Navigation pane. The view is modified, as shown in Figure 6-9. Job title and company information is hidden. Any graphics on the Business Card view are also hidden. The address cards contain only text.

Figure 6-9

Contact in Address Cards view

3. Click the Detailed Address Cards button in the Navigation pane. The view is modified to display additional information.

4. Click the Phone List button in the Navigation pane. The view is modified, as shown in Figure 6-10. Use this view if you need to call several contacts in your Contacts folder.

Figure 6-10

Contacts in Phone List view

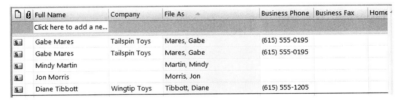

REF

You will learn more about categories in Lesson 12.

5. Click the By Category button in the Navigation pane. The view is modified to group the contacts by category. Use this view if you need to see all the contacts assigned to a specific category.

6. Click the By Company button in the Navigation pane. The view is modified to group the contacts by company name, as shown in Figure 6-11. Use this view to see all the contacts working for a specific company.

Figure 6-11

Contacts grouped by company name

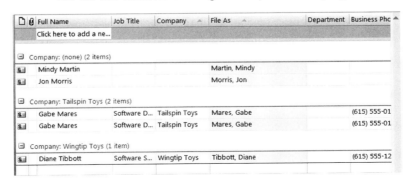

You will learn more about Outlook data files in Lesson 12.

To delete a contact record, right-click the contact and click Delete on the shortcut menu.

7. Click the By Location button in the Navigation pane. The view is modified to group the contacts by country/region. Use this view to see contacts with an address in a particular area. This is more useful if your contacts are not located in the same geographic area.

8. Click the Outlook Data Files button in the Navigation pane. The view is modified to display the contacts as they would appear in a data file.

9. Click the Business Cards button in the Navigation pane to return to the default view of the contacts.

10. Click the first Gabe Mares contact record. On the Standard toolbar, click the Delete button. The contact record is moved to the Deleted Items folder. It will not be removed from your computer until the Deleted Items folder is emptied.

PAUSE. LEAVE Outlook open to use in the next exercise.

Because several views are available, select the view that targets the information you need to see. When you are viewing contact records, you can minimize the clutter by deleting contacts that are no longer useful or duplicates that have been accidentally created.

8 ways to view contacts

■ Creating and Modifying a Distribution List

THE BOTTOM LINE

A *distribution list* is a group of individual contacts saved together as a single contact. A distribution list simplifies the task of regularly sending the same message to a group of people. For example, suppose that you manage a group of seven sales representatives. Every week, you send every sales representative a message that summarizes the sales revenue for the previous week and sets the sales goals for the current week. To address the message, you must select seven email addresses. If you create a distribution list, you can add the seven individual contacts to the distribution list. Next week, you can use the distribution list as the address for the sales message. You make one selection in the To field to send the message to the seven members of the distribution list.

Creating a Distribution List

To create a distribution list, you create a contact that is identified as a distribution list. Then you select the members of the distribution list and save the distribution list. To send a message to all the members of the distribution list, simply select the distribution list as the recipient.

⊕ CREATE A DISTRIBUTION LIST

USE the contacts you created in the previous exercises.

1. If necessary, click the Contacts button in the Navigation pane to display the Contacts folder shown in Figure 6-1.

2. On the Standard toolbar, click the New arrow to display the dropdown menu. Click the Distribution List option. The Untitled – Distribution List window is displayed, as shown in Figure 6-12. The Members button in the Show group on the Ribbon is selected.

Figure 6-12

Untitled – Distribution List window

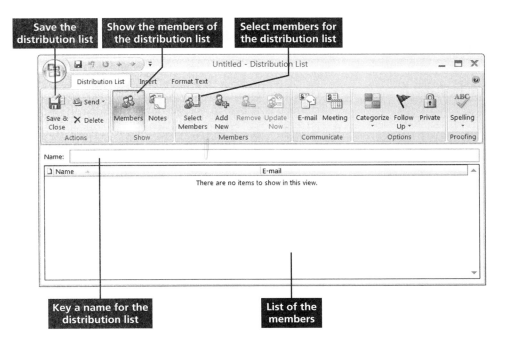

3. In the Members group on the Ribbon, click the Select Members button. The Select Members: Contacts window is displayed, as shown in Figure 6-13. The contacts in your Contacts folder are listed. The first contact is already selected.

Figure 6-13

Select Members: Contacts window

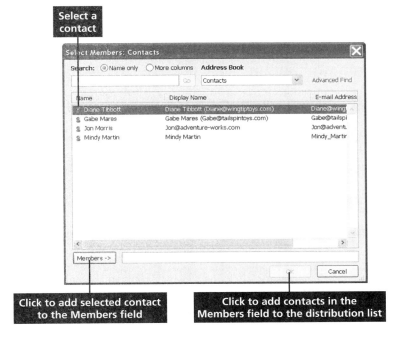

4. Because the first contact you want to include in the distribution list is already selected, click the Members button. The contact's name is added to the Members field at the bottom of the window.

5. Click the second contact in the list. Click the Members button. The second contact is added to the Members field.

6. Click the third contact on the list. Click the Members button. The third contact is added to the Members field.

TROUBLESHOOTING You have three contacts if you did not exchange digital signatures in Lesson 3. Skip step 7 and continue.

7. Click the fourth contact on the list. Click the Members button. The fourth contact is added to the Members field.
8. Click OK. The Select Members: Contacts window is closed, and you are returned to the Untitled – Distribution List window. The four contacts are listed in the lower area of the window.
9. Click the Name field. Key Wingtip Toys List. This name is used to identify the distribution list in the Contacts folder.
10. Click the Save & Close button. The distribution list is saved. The window is closed, and you are returned to the Contacts folder. The Wingtip Toys List contact is displayed, as shown in Figure 6-14.

Figure 6-14

Distribution list created

TAKE NOTE * When you view the distribution list in the Contacts folder, the list of members is not visible. To see the list of members, open the contact record.

PAUSE. LEAVE Outlook open to use in the next exercise.

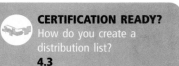

CERTIFICATION READY?
How do you create a distribution list?
4.3

In the previous exercise, you created a distribution list that contains all of your contacts. Normally, a distribution list contains multiple members, but it won't contain all of your contacts.

Modifying a Distribution List

Any distribution list used over time will eventually require changes. In fact, the distribution list you just created already requires a change.

➔ MODIFY A DISTRIBUTION LIST

USE the contacts you created in the previous exercises.

1. If necessary, click the Contacts button in the Navigation pane to display the Contacts folder shown in Figure 6-1.
2. Double-click the Wingtip Toys List contact. The Wingtip Toys List – Distribution List window is displayed.
3. Click Gabe's name in the lower area of the window. In the Members group on the Ribbon, click the Remove button. Gabe is removed from the distribution list.
4. In the list of members, double-click your name. Your contact record is displayed.
5. Click the Company field. Key the name of your company.
6. Click the Save & Close button in your contact window. Your modified contact record is saved and closed.
7. Click the Save & Close button in the distribution list window. The distribution list is saved. The window is closed, and you are returned to the Contacts folder.

8. Double-click the Wingtip Toys List contact to reopen it. The Wingtip Toys List – Distribution List window is displayed.

9. In the Communicate group on the Ribbon, click the E-mail button. A blank Message window is displayed. In the To field, the Wingtip Toys List contact is automatically entered, as shown in Figure 6-15. The rest of the fields are empty.

Figure 6-15

Message addressed to the distribution list created

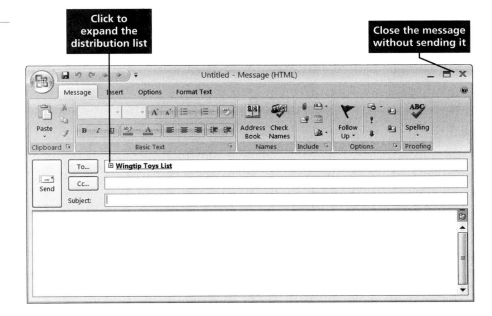

10. Click the plus sign in the To field. A warning box is displayed stating that the list will be replaced with its members. Click OK. The individual addressees are displayed in the To field.

TROUBLESHOOTING It is not necessary to expand the distribution list in a message. You expanded the distribution list in this exercise for demonstration purposes.

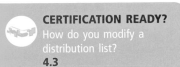

CERTIFICATION READY?
How do you modify a distribution list?
4.3

11. Click the Close button to close the message without sending it. Do not save changes to the message.
CLOSE Outlook.

When you created the Wingtip Toys distribution list, you included Gabe Mares. However, he works for Tailspin Toys now. In the previous exercise, you removed Gabe from the distribution list. You also accessed and modified your contact record through the distribution list. Finally, you created a message that could be sent to the members of the distribution list. After all, sending a message to multiple recipients quickly and easily is the purpose of creating and maintaining a distribution list.

SUMMARY SKILL MATRIX

In This Lesson You Learned	Matrix Skill	Skill Number
To create new contact records and modify existing contact records		
To create a new contact from scratch	Create a contact from a blank contact	4.1.1
To create a new contact for a different individual from the same company as an existing contact	Create a contact from a blank contact	4.1.1
To modify information in an existing contact record	Modify contact information	4.1.5
To send and receive contact records via email		
To send a contact record as a message attachment		
To create a contact record from a contact record received as a message attachment	Save a contact received as a contact record	4.1.4
To create a contact record from the message header of any message you receive	Create a contact from a message header	4.1.2
To select a different view to see specific information in your contact records and delete unneeded contact records		
To create a distribution list and modify an existing distribution list	Create and modify distribution lists	4.3

■ Knowledge Assessment

Fill in the Blank

Complete the following sentences by writing the correct word or words in the blanks provided.

1. The ______________ is an electronic organizer that enables you to create, view, and edit contact information.
2. Like documents and files, contact information can be sent as a(n) ______________.
3. The text automatically added at the top of a message is the ______________.
4. A(n) ______________ is a collection of information about a person or company.
5. The default view in the Contacts folder is the ______________ view.
6. A(n) ______________ provides a brief description of an item's purpose.
7. If you try to add a contact that already exists in your Contacts folder, Outlook detects a(n) ______________.
8. Providing false information in a message header is called ______________.
9. A(n) ______________ is a group of individual contacts saved together as a single contact.
10. Contact records in a distribution list are known as ______________ of the distribution list.

contacts folder
attachment
message header
contact
business card
screen tip
duplicate contact
spoofing
distribution list
members

Multiple Choice

Circle the correct choice.

C

1. What window is displayed when the mouse hovers over a button?
   A. the contact's name
   B. Online Help
   C. ScreenTip
   D. enlarged view of the button

A

2. Which field should contain a value when you save a contact?
   A. File as
   B. Display as
   C. Full Name
   D. E-mail

D

3. What value is not carried over to the new contact when you create a new contact record from the same company?
   A. Address
   B. Website
   C. Phone number
   D. Email address

C

4. A duplicate contact should be
   A. created for every contact.
   B. displayed before the original contact.
   C. deleted.
   D. modified.

D

5. When you key a phone number in a contact record,
   A. key the parentheses around the area code.
   B. don't key the area code.
   C. key a hyphen between each group of numbers.
   D. don't key spaces in the number.

D

6. Which of the following is a way to create a contact record?
   A. Key information into a blank contact record.
   B. Modify an existing contact record and save it as a new contact.
   C. Create a contact from a message header.
   D. All of the above

A

7. What does a recipient need to save a contact received in Outlook format?
   A. Outlook 2007
   B. Existing contact records
   C. Any email program
   D. All of the above

C

8. What provides the information to create a contact from any message you receive?
   A. The attachment
   B. The subject
   C. The message header
   D. The Subject field

A

9. How many views are available in the Contacts folder?
   A. Eight
   B. One
   C. It depends on the number of contact records you have saved
   D. Five

D

10. How can you simplify the task of regularly sending messages to the same group of contacts?
    A. Resend the message to each contact.
    B. Use nicknames for the contacts.
    C. Set a predetermined time for sending the messages.
    D. Create a distribution list.

■ Competency Assessment

Project 6-1: Create Contacts from Blank Contacts

Gabe Mares recently started a new job at Tailspin Toys. As part of the training program, he will be travelling to different divisions to examine their procedures. At his first stop in Pittsburgh, PA, Gabe collected contact information for the team leader.

GET READY. Launch Outlook if it is not already running.

1. If necessary, click the Contacts button in the Navigation pane to display the Contacts folder.
2. Click New on the Standard toolbar. The Untitled – Contact window is displayed.
3. Click the Full Name field if necessary. Key Mandar Samant and press Tab.
4. In the Company field, key Tailspin Toys and press Tab.
5. In the Job title field, key Software Development Team Lead and press Tab.
6. Click the E-mail field. Key Mandar@tailspintoys.com and press Tab.
7. In the Web page address field, key www.tailspintoys.com.
8. Below the Phone numbers heading, click the Business field. Key 4125551117. Press Tab.
9. Below the Addresses heading, click the Business field. Key 4567 Broadway. Press Enter. Key Pittsburgh, PA 14202. Press Tab.
10. In the Actions group on the Ribbon, click the Save & Close button.
    LEAVE Outlook open for the next project.

Project 6-2: Create a Contact from a Contact at the Same Company

While Gabe was in Pittsburgh, he interviewed a software developer in Mandar Samant's team. Although Gabe doesn't usually contact developers directly, he wants to save her contact information in case an opening occurs as a team leader.

1. If necessary, click the Contacts button in the Navigation pane to display the Contacts folder.
2. Double-click the Mandar Samant contact. The contact window is displayed.
3. In the Actions group on the Ribbon, click the Save & New arrow. In the dropdown list of options, click New Contact from Same Company.
4. Click in the Full Name field if necessary. Key Jamie Reding and press Tab.
5. In the Job title field, key Software Developer and press Tab.

6. In the *E-mail* field, key Jamie@tailspintoys.com and press Tab.

7. In the *Notes* field, key Potential team lead.

8. In the Actions group on the Ribbon, click the Save & Close button.

9. CLOSE the Mandar Samant contact record without saving changes.

   LEAVE Outlook open for the next project.

■ Proficiency Assessment

Project 6-3: Modify Contact Information

Two months later, Jamie Reding was promoted to a team leader in the Pittsburgh office. Gabe modified her contact information.

1. If necessary, click the Contacts button in the Navigation pane to display the Contacts folder.

2. Double-click the Jamie Reding contact. The contact window is displayed.

3. Click the Job title field. Change her title to Software Development Team Lead and press Tab.

4. Click the Notes field. Change the text to Monitor her progress.

5. In the Actions group on the Ribbon, click the Save & Close button.

   LEAVE Outlook open for the next project.

Project 6-4: Send a Contact as an Attachment

Gabe's manager asked for information about a team leader for a new project. Gabe sends Jamie's contact record.

1. If necessary, click the Contacts button in the Navigation pane to display the Contacts folder.

2. Double-click the Jamie Reding contact. The Contact window is displayed.

3. In Actions group on the Ribbon, click the Send button. If a message is displayed stating that you must save the original item, click OK to continue. Click the In Outlook Format option.

4. Click the To button. In the Select Names: Contacts window, click your contact record. Click the To button. Click OK.

5. Click in the message area. Key The contact information you requested is attached.

6. Click the Send button.

7. CLOSE Jamie Reding's contact record without saving changes.

   LEAVE Outlook open for the next project.

■ Mastery Assessment

Project 6-5: Create a Distribution List

Gabe sends several messages to the team leaders each day. To simplify the task, Gabe creates a distribution list.

1. If necessary, click the Contacts button in the Navigation pane to display the Contacts folder.

2. On the Standard toolbar, click the New arrow and then click the Distribution List option on the shortcut menu.

3. In the Members group on the Ribbon, click the Select Members button.
4. Add all the Tailspin Toys employees to the Members field, including Gabe, and click OK.
5. Name the distribution list Tailspin Team Leaders.
6. Click the Save & Close button.
   LEAVE Outlook open for the next project.

Project 6-6: Modify a Distribution List

Gabe was not surprised to determine that the Tailspin Team Leaders distribution list needs to be changed. Gabe needs to remove himself from the distribution list and add Diane Tibbott. Diane just accepted the position of Software Development Team Lead for Tailspin Toys. She will work in the Nashville office with Gabe.

1. If necessary, click the Contacts button in the Navigation pane to display the Contacts folder.
2. Use Gabe's contact record to create a new contact record from the same company for Diane Tibbott. Use the following information.

Full Name	Diane Tibbott
Job title	Software Development Team Lead
E-mail	Diane@tailspintoys.com

3. Delete Diane Tibbott's outdated contact record from Wingtip Toys.
4. Open the Tailspin Team Leaders contact record.
5. Click Gabe Mares in the list of members and click the Remove button.
6. Click the Select Members button. In the Select Members: Contacts window, add Diane Tibbott to the Members field and click OK.
7. SAVE the changes to the distribution list.
   CLOSE Outlook.

INTERNET READY

Looking for a new job with better pay, the right amount of travel, better hours, and a larger office? Use the Internet. Research some companies that interest you. Create contact records for the Human Resources offices in those companies.

Advanced Contact Management

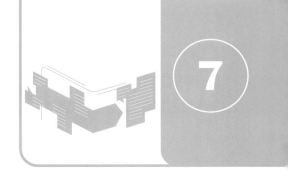

7

The Marketing department at Tailspin Toys is holding a contest that is open to all employees. To compete, employees must design an electronic business card. Gabe Mares, the Software Development Manager, wasn't planning to enter the contest. However, he had an idea for an electronic business card that he couldn't resist. He thumbed through the Tailspin Toys catalog until he found the perfect picture for his design. After all, who can resist a teddy bear?

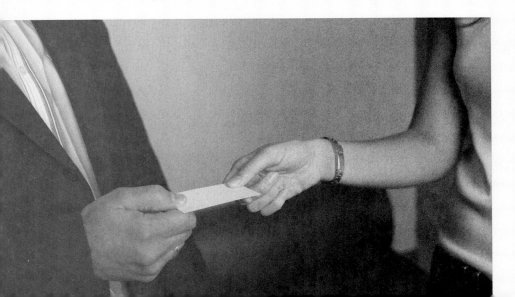

KEY TERMS
address book
Categorized Mail
electronic business cards
import
Large Mail
Search Folder
secondary address book
Unread Mail
virtual folder

133

SOFTWARE ORIENTATION

Microsoft Outlook's Edit Business Card Window

The default view in the Contacts folder is the Business Cards view. It displays all of the contacts in your Contacts folder as business cards. By default, the text appears on the right and the left side of the card contains a gray bar, as shown in Figure 7-1.

Figure 7-1

Outlook's Edit Business Card window

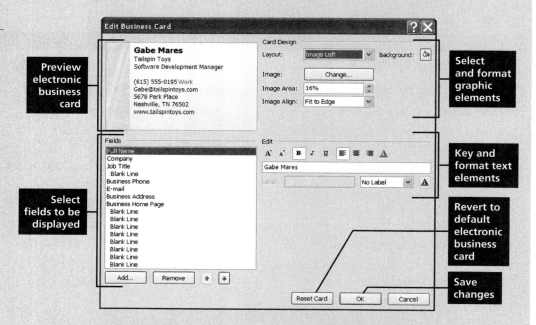

Use the Edit Business Card window to create a business card that fits your company image. Refer to Figure 7-1 as you complete the following exercises.

■ Using Electronic Business Cards

THE BOTTOM LINE

The electronic business card is a new feature in Outlook 2007. *Electronic business cards* are the digital version of paper business cards. They can be sent as attachments, used as signatures, and used to create a contact record. Because the default view in the Contacts folder displays the electronic business cards, it is important to design an electronic business card that is memorable and easy to find when several electronic business cards are displayed on the screen.

Editing an Electronic Business Card

"Here's my card. Give me a call sometime." How many times have you shaken hands and exchanged business cards with new contacts? Electronic business cards are the paper-less version of the business cards you currently have stashed in your wallet, falling out of your address book, choking your Rolodex, and marking the page in the latest novel you're reading.

EDIT AN ELECTRONIC BUSINESS CARD

GET READY. Before you begin these steps, be sure to launch Microsoft Outlook. The Greg Mares contact record was created in Lesson 6.

 An electronic business card is created automatically when you create a contact. It is basically another view of the contact record. If you delete the electronic business card, you delete the contact. Changes made to the information on the electronic business card are changed for the contact as well.

1. If necessary, click the Contacts button in the Navigation pane to display the Contacts folder. Minimize the To-Do Bar to provide additional room to display your contact records.

2. Double-click the Gabe Mares contact. The Gabe Mares – Contact window is displayed.

TROUBLESHOOTING The email addresses provided in these exercises belong to unused domains owned by Microsoft. When you send a message to these addresses, you will receive an error message stating that the message could not be delivered. Delete the error messages when they arrive.

3. In the Options group on the Ribbon, click the Business Card button. The Edit Business Card window is displayed, as shown in Figure 7-1.

4. In the Card Design area in the upper-right of the window, verify that Image Left is selected in the Layout field and Fit to Edge is selected in the Image Align field. This defines the position of the graphic. Currently, the graphic is the default gray bar.

The *bear side* image is available on the companion CD-ROM.

5. Click the Change button. The Add Card Picture dialog box is displayed. Navigate to the data files for this lesson. Click the *bear side* file and click OK. The bear image is added to the card preview.

6. In the Card Design area, click the Image Area field. Change the value to 25%, if necessary. In the card preview, the image area widens to 25% of the card's width.

7. In the Card Design area, click the Image Align field. In the dropdown list, click Bottom Center. In the card preview, the image is resized and repositioned.

8. In the Card Design area, click the Image Align field. In the dropdown list, click Fit to Edge. In the card preview, the image is resized and placed in its original position.

9. In the Fields area, click Business Home Page in the list of fields. Click the Add button. In the dropdown menu, point to Internet Address and then click IM Address. IM Address is added to the list of fields. The IM Address field is used for an instant messaging address.

10. With IM Address selected in the list of fields, click the empty field in the Edit area. Key GabeTailspinToys, as shown in Figure 7-2.

Figure 7-2

Modified Edit Business Card window

11. Click OK. The Edit Business Card window is closed. Click the Save & Close button to return to the Contacts folder. Gabe's business card is displayed, as shown in Figure 7-3.

Figure 7-3

Modified business card

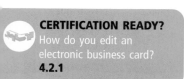

CERTIFICATION READY?
How do you edit an electronic business card?
4.2.1

PAUSE. LEAVE Outlook open to use in the next exercise.

In the previous exercise, you modified the default electronic business card to create a memorable business card that can easily be picked out of the crowd of electronic business cards many users store in their Contacts folders. Gabe wants to present an image of fun and safety for Tailspin Toys. A teddy bear presents that image.

The Edit Business Card window has four separate areas, as identified in Table 7-1. The four areas work together to provide a flexible tool that can create an amazing variety of customized electronic business cards.

Table 7-1

Edit Business Card window

AREA	DESCRIPTION
Preview	View the effect of the changes you make.
Fields	Identify the fields you want to display on the electronic business card. Use the Add button to insert a new field. Select a field in the list and click the Remove button to delete a field. To move a field up or down on the card, select the field and click the Move Field Up (Up arrow) button or the Move Field Down (Down arrow) button .
Card Design	Insert and position a graphic or select a background color for the card. Position the image and define the amount of the card that can be used for the graphic. Graphics cannot be edited in Outlook 2007. The image must be ready to be placed before it is used in the electronic business card.
Edit	Key the value to be displayed in the field. Limited text formatting options are available.

 Sending an Electronic Business Card

Electronic business cards can be shared with others. Insert one or more business cards in a message and click the Send button.

 SEND AN ELECTRONIC BUSINESS CARD

USE the Gabe Mares contact record.

1. If necessary, click the Mail button in the Navigation pane to display the Mail folder.
2. Click the New button in the Standard toolbar. The Message window is displayed. By default, the Message tab is selected.
3. Click the To field. Key your email address.
4. Click the Subject field. Key Business cards attached.
5. Click in the message area. Key I attached the electronic business cards you requested. Press Enter.

6. In the Include group on the Ribbon, click the Insert Business Card button. A dropdown list is displayed.
7. Click Other Business Cards in the dropdown list. The Insert Business Card window is displayed, as shown in Figure 7-4.

 If the contact name is displayed in the dropdown list, you can click the name to insert the electronic business card.

Figure 7-4

Insert Business Card window

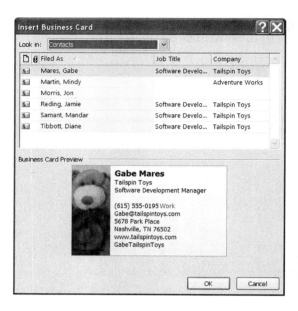

8. Click the Gabe Mares contact. Press [Ctrl] and click the Diane Tibbott contact. Click OK. The electronic business cards are inserted into the message. In the Attached field, the contact records are attached as .vcf files, as shown in Figure 7-5.

Figure 7-5

Electronic business cards inserted into a message

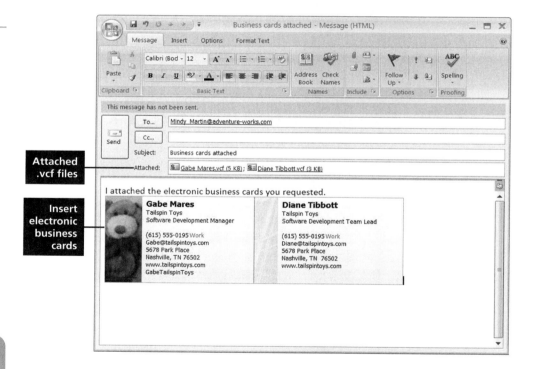

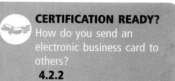

CERTIFICATION READY?
How do you send an electronic business card to others?
4.2.2

9. Click the Send button.

PAUSE. LEAVE Outlook open to use in the next exercise.

In the previous exercise, you sent an electronic business card in a message. Outlook 2007 users will be able to create contact records from the electronic business records. Users of other email applications will be able to get the contact information from the .vcf files that were automatically created by Outlook and attached to the message when you inserted the electronic business cards.

You can find more information on other methods of creating contacts in Lesson 6.

Creating a Contact from an Electronic Business Card

When you receive an electronic business card, you can use the card to create a contact record. All of the information on the electronic business card and the card's appearance are saved in your Contacts folder.

CREATE A CONTACT FROM AN ELECTRONIC BUSINESS CARD

USE the message you sent in the previous exercise.

1. If necessary, click the Mail button in the Navigation pane to display the Mail folder.
2. Click the Send/Receive button if the *Business cards attached* message has not arrived yet.
3. Click the Business cards attached message in the message list to display it in the Reading pane. The electronic business cards are displayed in the message body.
4. Right-click the Gabe Mares electronic business card in the message body. Click the Add to Outlook Contacts option in the shortcut menu. A Gabe Mares – Contact window is displayed that contains the information displayed on the electronic business card, including the preview image of the card.
5. Click the Save & Close button in the Actions group on the Ribbon. Because you received this contact information at the same email address used to send the contact information, the contact record is already in your Contacts folder. Therefore, Outlook detects that this is a duplicate contact, and the Duplicate Contact Detected window shown in Figure 7-6 is displayed. If the contact record was not a duplicate, the contact would be saved without any further action needed.

Figure 7-6

Duplicate Contact Detected window

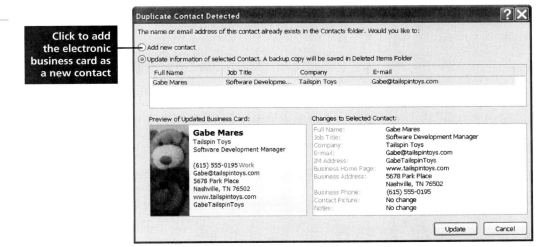

6. You want to create a new contact, so select the Add new contact option at the top of the window and click the Add button at the bottom of the window. The Duplicate Contact Detected window is closed, the contact record is created, and you are returned to the Mail folder.
7. Click the Contacts button in the Navigation pane to display the Contacts folder. Now, you have the original Gabe Mares contact record and the Gabe Mares contact record you created from the electronic business card in the message.

8. In the Contacts folder, click the first Gabe Mares contact record and click the Delete button in the Standard toolbar. The contact record is moved to the Deleted Items folder. It will not be removed from your computer until the Deleted Items folder is emptied.

   PAUSE. LEAVE Outlook open to use in the next exercise.

In the previous exercise, you created a contact from an electronic business card you received in a message. However, you used the same email account in an earlier exercise to send the electronic business card. Therefore, when you tried to create a contact Outlook recognized it as a duplicate of an existing contact. If this had been a new contact record that you did not have in your Contacts folder, you would have been finished after you clicked the Save & Close button.

Normally, when you receive a duplicate record you will use the received information to update the contact in your Contacts folder. You can compare the information in your contact record with the information sent to you in the message. Before you update contact information, be sure that the new data is accurate.

Using an Electronic Business Card in a Signature

A signature can be added automatically in every message you send. Include your electronic business card in your signature to provide an easy way for the recipient to add the contact to the Contacts folder.

USE AN ELECTRONIC BUSINESS CARD IN A SIGNATURE

USE the Gabe Mares electronic business card you modified in a previous exercise.

1. If necessary, click the Mail button in the Navigation pane to display the Mail folder.
2. Click the New button in the Standard toolbar. The Message window is displayed. By default, the Message tab is selected.
3. Click the Signature button in the Include group on the Ribbon. In the dropdown list, click Signatures. The Signatures and Stationery window is displayed.
4. Click the New button to create a new signature. The New Signature dialog box is displayed.
5. To name the new signature, key Gabe into the *Type a name for this signature* field. Click OK. The New Signature dialog box is closed, and Gabe is highlighted in the *Select signature to edit* list box.
6. Click in the empty Edit signature box. Key Gabe Mares and press Enter. Key Software Development Manager and press Enter. Key Tailspin Toys and press Enter. Key Gabe@tailspintoys.com and press Enter.
7. Click the Insert Business Card button above the Edit Signature box. The Insert Business Card window in Figure 7-4 is displayed.
8. Click the Gabe Mares contact record and click OK. The electronic business card is inserted into the signature, as shown in Figure 7-7.

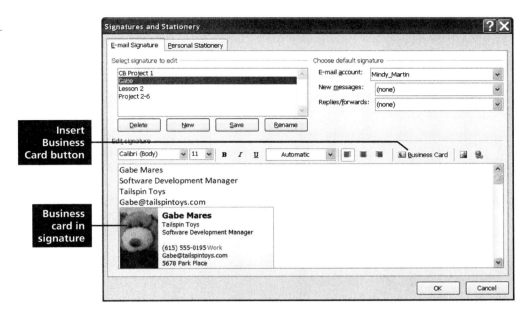

Figure 7-7

Signature containing an
electronic business card

Insert Business Card button

Business card in signature

9. Click OK to close the Signatures and Stationery window.

10. In the Message window, click the To field, if necessary, and then key your email address.

11. In the Subject field, key New Signature Test.

12. In the message body, key Testing new signature and press Enter.

13. In the Include group on the Ribbon, click the Signature button and then click Gabe. The signature is inserted into the message, as shown in Figure 7-8.

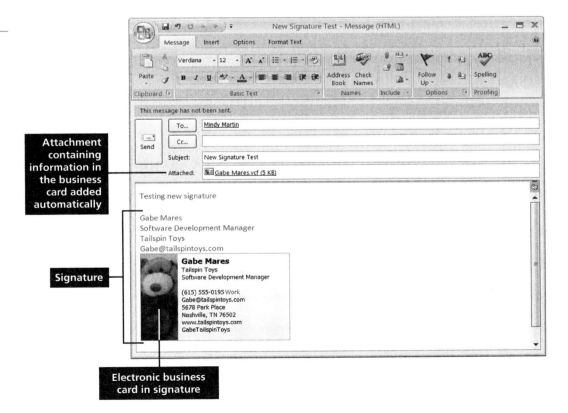

Figure 7-8

Message containing
Gabe signature

Attachment containing information in the business card added automatically

Signature

Electronic business card in signature

14. Click the Send button.

PAUSE. LEAVE Outlook open to use in the next exercise.

CERTIFICATION READY?
How do you use an
electronic business card as
an automatic signature in
messages?
4.2.3

In the previous exercise, you created a signature containing an electronic business card. Any recipient using Outlook 2007 can create a contact directly from the electronic business card.

Recipients using other email programs might not be able to view the electronic business card or save it as a contact record. Outlook automatically attaches the .vcf file containing the contact information. However, you can key the contact information into the signature so that it is displayed in the message. You can also delete the attachment before sending the message. Some people avoid opening messages with attachments. Deleting the attachment prevents the recipient from ignoring your message simply because it has an attachment.

■ Finding Contact Information

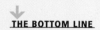 Memory can be unreliable. How often have you recognized a face but couldn't match it to a name? Or you remembered that nice woman who just moved into the office down the hall, but you can't remember the name of her company? Outlook's search features can help you. Use the information you know to find the information you can't remember.

Searching for Contacts

When you search the Contacts folder, you can use any information in a contact record to identify a particular contact or several contacts. You can search for contacts containing text such as Diane, Pittsburgh, or Lead. Using the new Instant Search feature, matching contacts are displayed as they are found.

→ SEARCH FOR CONTACTS

GET READY. Before you begin these steps, be sure to launch Microsoft Outlook. Instant Search must be enabled. The contacts used in this exercise were entered in Lesson 6.

1. If necessary, click the Contacts button in the Navigation pane to display the Contacts folder.

2. In the Instant Search box, key Pittsburgh. As you key the search text, Outlook displays the matching contacts, as shown in Figure 7-9. The two contacts located in Pittsburgh are displayed.

Figure 7-9

Search for contacts

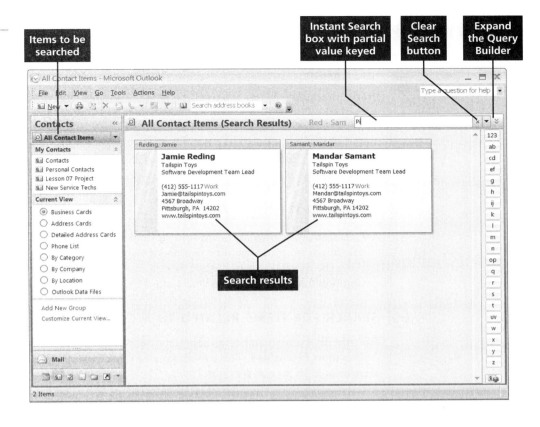

3. Click the Expand the Query Builder button. The Query Builder is expanded, as shown in Figure 7-10.

Figure 7-10

Expanded Query Builder

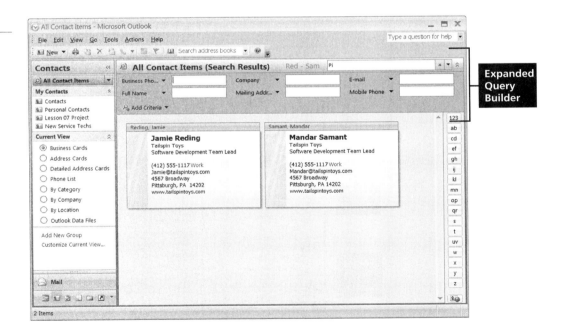

TROUBLESHOOTING   The size and layout of the Query Builder depend on the size and resolution of your monitor and the amount of the screen occupied by the Outlook application.

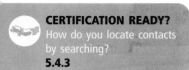

CERTIFICATION READY?
How do you locate contacts by searching?
5.4.3

4. Click the Clear Search button and collapse the Query Builder. The search criteria are cleared and all contacts are displayed.

   PAUSE. LEAVE Outlook open to use in the next exercise.

In the previous exercise, you used the new Instant Search feature. Results are immediately displayed when items matching the search criteria are located. Your Contacts folder currently contains very few contacts. As you add contacts, you might need to narrow the search results by using the expanded Query Builder. In the Query Builder, you can key *Pittsburgh* into the Mailing Address field so that results containing the letters in other fields are not displayed in the search results.

Searching for Items Related to a Contact

Occasionally, you will want to find all Outlook items related to a contact. For example, you might want to view messages about a specific meeting and the Calendar item scheduling the meeting. Using Instant Search in the Folder List enables you to search all Outlook folders at the same time to find items related to your search criteria.

⊕ SEARCH FOR ITEMS RELATED TO A CONTACT

GET READY. Before you begin these steps, be sure to launch Microsoft Outlook. Instant Search must be enabled. The contacts used in this exercise were entered in Lesson 6. Messages were created in previous lessons.

1. If necessary, click the Folder List button in the Navigation pane to display the Folder List and select All Outlook Items in the Instant Search dropdown list.

2. In the Instant Search box, key **Gabe**. As you key the search text, Outlook displays the matching Outlook items. The Gabe Mares contact record and the related messages are displayed, as shown in Figure 7-11.

Figure 7-11

Outlook items related to Gabe

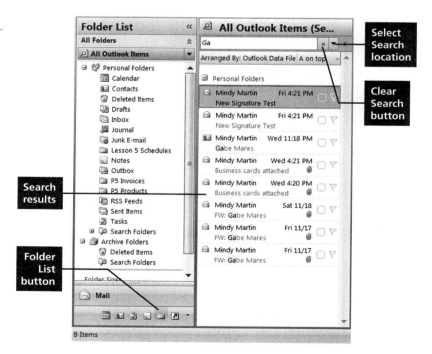

TROUBLESHOOTING Your search results might vary if you deleted any messages sent or received in previous lessons.

3. Click the Clear Search button to clear the search criteria.

   PAUSE. LEAVE Outlook open to use in the next exercise.

In the previous exercise, you searched all Outlook items for the items related to Gabe Mares. As you keyed Gabe's name in the Instant Search box, items related to Gabe were found and displayed. In each item, the search text is highlighted in the result.

Creating a Custom Search Folder

Instant Search quickly finds Outlook items. However, you have to key the search text every time you perform a search. A **Search Folder** is a virtual folder that searches your email folders to locate items that meet the saved search criteria. A **virtual folder** is a folder that does not contain the actual items it displays. The items are actually located in other folders.

CREATE A CUSTOM SEARCH FOLDER

GET READY. Before you begin these steps, be sure to launch Microsoft Outlook. The contacts used in this exercise were entered in Lesson 6. Messages were created in previous lessons.

1. If necessary, click the Mail button in the Navigation pane to display the Mail folder.

2. On the Standard toolbar, click the New arrow to display the dropdown list. Click the Search Folder option. The New Search Folder window is displayed. Scroll to the bottom of the list of options and click Create a custom Search Folder, as shown in Figure 7-12.

Figure 7-12

New Search Folder window

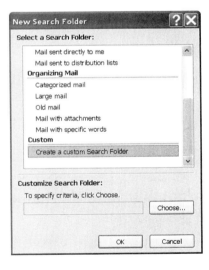

3. Click the Choose button to display the Custom Search Folder window shown in Figure 7-13.

Figure 7-13

Custom Search Folder window

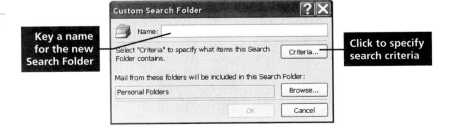

4. In the Name field, key Messages about Jamie. When naming a Search Folder, create a name that reflects the search criteria.

5. Click the Criteria button to display the Search Folder Criteria window shown in Figure 7-14.

Figure 7-14

Search Folder Criteria window

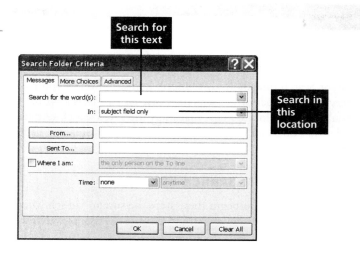

6. In the *Search for the word(s)* field, key Jamie. In the *In* field, select subject field and message body from the dropdown list. Click OK in each window to return to the Mail folder. The new Search Folder and the search results are automatically displayed, as shown in Figure 7-15.

Figure 7-15

Search Folder created

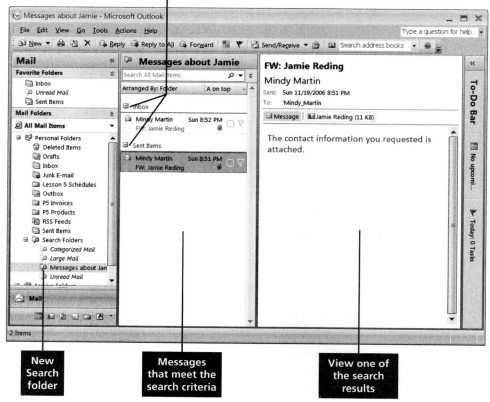

PAUSE. LEAVE Outlook open to use in the next exercise.

In the previous exercise, you created a custom Search Folder to identify any messages about Jamie Reding, one of your contacts. You can easily create Search Folders that identify messages exchanged with a specific contact or messages about a project or meeting.

TAKE NOTE* Search Folders are virtual folders. You can delete a Search Folder without deleting the displayed messages because the messages are actually located in other folders. However, if you click a message in the Search Folder and then delete the message, the message is deleted.

Outlook has several standard Search Folders as well. They are Categorized Mail, Large Mail, and Unread Mail. The folders are described in Table 7-2.

Table 7-2

Standard Search Folders

SEARCH FOLDER	CONTENT
Categorized Mail	Messages that have an assigned color category are displayed in this folder.
Large Mail	Messages larger than 100 kilobytes are displayed in this folder.
Unread Mail	Messages that are marked as Unread are displayed in this folder.

■ Creating a Secondary Address Book

THE BOTTOM LINE

Previous versions of Outlook allowed you to create a private address book by creating an Outlook file with the .pab extension. Because the Contacts folder has more functionality and features than the private address book, Outlook 2007 does not allow you to create or use a personal address book. Instead, you can create a secondary address book.

Every Contacts folder has its own Outlook address book. Therefore, to keep your personal contacts separate from your business contacts, create an additional Contacts folder that has its own address book. The address book for an additional Contacts folder is a ***secondary address book***. This provides all the functionality of the familiar Contacts folder and separates your personal information from your business information.

Creating a Secondary Address Book for Personal Contacts

Each Outlook Contacts folder has an associated Outlook address book. To create a secondary address book for personal contacts, create a secondary Contacts folder that contains the personal contact records.

➔ CREATE A SECONDARY ADDRESS BOOK FOR PERSONAL CONTACTS

GET READY. Before you begin these steps, be sure to launch Microsoft Outlook.

1. If necessary, click the Folder List button in the Navigation pane to display the Folder List.
2. Click the Contacts folder in the Folder List.
3. Click the New arrow to display the dropdown menu and click Folder. The Create New Folder window is displayed.

4. In the Name field, key My Contacts. Because you selected the Contacts folder before creating a new folder, Contact Items is already displayed in the *Folder contains* field and the Contacts folder is selected in the *Select where to place the folder* list. Click OK. The My Contacts folder is created in the Contacts folder. It is slightly indented in the Folder List to indicate that it is in the Contacts folder, as shown in Figure 7-16.

Figure 7-16

My Contacts folder created

New My Contacts folder

CERTIFICATION READY?

How do you create a secondary address book for personal contacts?

4.4.1

5. Click the My Contacts folder in the Folder List. Contacts are not displayed in the main pane because this folder does not contain any contacts yet.

PAUSE. LEAVE Outlook open to use in the next exercise.

An ***address book*** stores names and email addresses. When you key an address in the To, Cc, or Bcc field in a new message, the address book displays potential matches. If the name is a match, you can click the displayed name to fill the address field.

Importing a Secondary Address Book from a File

Manually keying a large number of contacts can be tedious. It's much easier to import the contact information. When you ***import*** a file, you bring information into a file from an external source. In this case, you import contact information from a Microsoft Excel file.

→ **IMPORT A SECONDARY ADDRESS BOOK FROM A FILE**

USE the My Contacts folder you created in the previous exercise.

1. Click the My Contacts folder in the Folder List, if necessary.
2. Click the File menu and then click the Import and Export option. The Import and Export Wizard is displayed.
3. Click Import from another program or file, if necessary, in the list of available actions. Click the Next button.
4. Click Microsoft Excel 97-2003 in the list of available import file types. Click the Next button.
5. Click the Browse button. Navigate to the data files for this lesson and click the *Source Personal Contacts* file. Click OK to close the Browse window and return to the Import a File window. Click the Next button.
6. Verify that My Contacts is selected as the destination folder. Click the Next button.

CD

The *Source Personal Contacts* file is available on the companion CD-ROM.

7. Click the Finish button. The contacts are imported and displayed in the My Contacts folder, as shown in Figure 7-17.

Figure 7-17

My Contacts folder

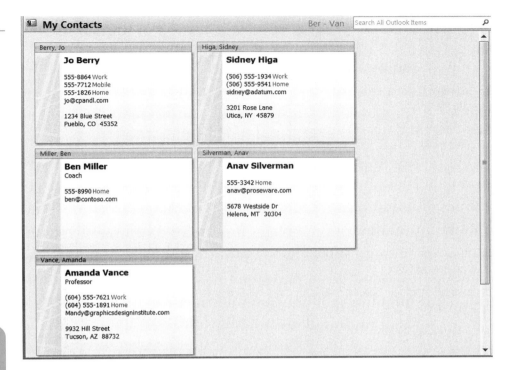

CERTIFICATION READY?
How do you import a secondary address book from a file?
4.4.2

CLOSE Outlook.

 If you are switching to Outlook 2007 from another program, Outlook's Import feature could save you time and effort.

Importing contact information is obviously much easier than keying the data into the fields. It also prevents errors from keying incorrect letters or numbers. One typographical error could result in calling a complete stranger instead of Great-Grandma Mabel on her birthday.

SUMMARY SKILL MATRIX

IN THIS LESSON YOU LEARNED	MATRIX SKILL	SKILL NUMBER
To use electronic business cards		
To modify electronic business cards by adding an image and changing fields	Edit an electronic business card	4.2.1
To send electronic business cards as message attachments	Send an electronic business card to others	4.2.2
To create a contact from electronic business cards received in a message	Create a contact from an electronic business card	4.1.3
To create a signature containing an electronic business card	Use an electronic business card as an automatic signature in messages	4.2.3
To find contact information		
To find a contact using Instant Search	Locate tasks or contacts by searching	5.4.3
To find Outlook items related to a specific contact using Instant Search	Locate all items related to a specific person by searching	5.4.2
To find messages that meet specific criteria by creating a Search Folder	Create a custom Search Folder	5.4.5
To create a secondary address book		
To create a secondary address book to hold your personal contacts	Create a secondary address book for personal contacts	4.4.1
To import the data for a secondary address book from an external source	Import a secondary address book from a file	4.4.2

■ Knowledge Assessment

Fill in the Blank

Complete the following sentences by writing the correct word or words in the blanks provided.

import
virtual folder
electronic business cards
Address Book
Secondary Address book
Search folder
Signature
Instant search
folder list
Contacts

1. You can _____ contact information from an external source.

2. Outlook items are not stored in a(n) _____.

3. _____ can contain an image to set them apart from other contact records.

4. The _____ stores names and addresses.

5. The _____ can be used to contain information about personal contacts.

6. A(n) _____ identifies items in other folders that meet specific criteria.

7. A(n) _____ containing an electronic business card can be added automatically in every message you send.

8. _____ displays search results as they are identified.

9. The _____ displays all the Outlook folders.

10. The _____ folder contains contact records.

Multiple Choice

Circle the correct choice.

C

1. What is the default view in the Contacts folder?
   A. Address Cards
   B. Detailed Address Cards
   C. Business Cards
   D. Phone List

D

2. What can you do with an electronic business card?
   A. Send it as an attachment
   B. Include it in your signature
   C. Create a contact record from it
   D. All of the above

A

3. When is an electronic business card created?
   A. When the contact record is created
   B. When the electronic business card is viewed
   C. When the electronic business card is modified
   D. When the electronic business card is sent with a message

C

4. How many areas are in the Edit Business Card window?
   A. One
   B. Three
   C. Four
   D. Eight

B

5. Why is a .vcf file automatically attached to a message containing an electronic business card?
   A. Outlook 2007 requires the .vcf file to create a new contact.
   B. Users of other email applications can use the .vcf file.
   C. The .vcf file contains the graphic used in the electronic business card.
   D. The .vcf file contains your signature.

D

6. Which Outlook search feature displays results immediately?
   A. Immediate Search
   B. Fast Find
   C. Search Folder
   D. Instant Search

A

7. Which folder is a virtual folder?
   A. Search Folder
   B. Contacts folder
   C. Secondary Contacts folder
   D. Sent Items folder

C

8. Which folder is *not* a standard Search Folder?
   A. Categorized Mail
   B. Unread Mail
   C. Mail with Attachments
   D. Large Mail

9. Where can you store personal contacts in Outlook 2007?

   A. Private address book

   B. Personal address book

   C. Search Folder

   D. Secondary address book

10. Which of the following is an easy way to enter contact information stored in another application?

   A. Import

   B. Key the data

   C. Send the data in an email message

   D. All of the above

■ Competency Assessment

Project 7-1: **Edit an Electronic Business Card**

Diane Tibbott was recently hired by Tailspin Toys. She decided to use the teddy bear image to brighten up her electronic business card.

GET READY. Launch Outlook if it is not already running.

1. If necessary, click the Contacts button in the Navigation pane to display the Contacts folder. Click the Contacts folder if necessary.

2. Double-click the Diane Tibbott contact. The Diane Tibbott – Contact window is displayed.

3. In the Options group on the Ribbon, click the Business Card button to display the Edit Business Card window.

4. In the Card Design area in the upper-right of the window, select Background Image in the Layout field.

5. Click the Change button. The Add Card Picture dialog box is displayed. Navigate to the data files for this lesson. Click the bear background file and click OK. The bear image is added to the card preview.

6. In the Card Design area, click the Image Align field. Change the value to Fit to Edge. In the card preview, the image fills the card.

7. Click OK to close the Edit Business Card window. Click the Save & Close button to return to the Contacts folder.

   LEAVE Outlook open for the next project.

CD

The *bear background* image is available on the companion CD-ROM.

Project 7-2: **Send an Electronic Business Card**

Diane Tibbott wants to stay in touch with her friends at Wingtip Toys. She decided to send her new electronic business card to her former supervisor.

1. If necessary, click the Mail button in the Navigation pane to display the Mail folder.

2. Click the New button in the Standard toolbar. The Message window is displayed. By default, the Message tab is selected.

3. Click the To field. Key Molly@wingtiptoys.com.

4. Click the Subject field. Key Let's keep in touch!

5. Click in the message area. Key I attached my new electronic business card. Write when you have time. Press Enter.

6. In the Include group on the Ribbon, click the Insert Business Card button. A dropdown list is displayed.

7. Click Diane Tibbott. The electronic business card is inserted and the .vcf file is attached.

8. Click the Send button.

LEAVE Outlook open for the next project.

■ Proficiency Assessment

Project 7-3: Use an Electronic Business Card in a Signature

Management has decided that every message sent to clients must include an electronic business card. Rather than manually inserting the electronic business card into every message, Diane decided to create a signature containing her electronic business card.

1. If necessary, click the Mail button in the Navigation pane to display the Mail folder.

2. Click the New button in the Standard toolbar to open a new Message window.

3. Click the Signature button in the Include group on the Ribbon. In the dropdown list, click Signatures to display the Signatures and Stationery window.

4. Click the New button to display the New Signature dialog box.

5. To name the new signature, key Diane into the *Type a name for this signature* field. Click OK.

6. Click the empty Edit signature box. Key Diane Tibbott and press Enter. Key Software Development Team Lead and press Enter. Key Tailspin Toys and press Enter. Key Diane@tailspintoys.com and press Enter.

7. Click the Insert Business Card button above the Edit Signature box to display the Insert Business Card window.

8. Click the Diane Tibbott contact record and click OK to insert the electronic business card into the signature.

9. Click OK to close the Signatures and Stationery window and return to the Message window.

10. In the Include group on the Ribbon, click the Signature button and then click Diane. The signature is inserted in the message.

11. CLOSE the message without saving or sending it.

LEAVE Outlook open for the next project.

Project 7-4: Create a Custom Search Folder

Diane wants to monitor messages about the team's new software development project. The project has been nicknamed 007 for the fictional character James Bond. All messages about the project must contain "007" in the Subject field. Diane decided to create a Search Folder to collect messages about the project.

1. If necessary, click the Mail button in the Navigation pane to display the Mail folder.

2. On the Standard toolbar, click the New arrow to display the dropdown list. Click the Search Folder option to display the New Search Folder window. Scroll to the bottom of the list of options and click Create a custom Search Folder.

3. Click the Choose button to display the Custom Search Folder window.

4. In the Name field, key Project 007.

5. Click the Criteria button to display the Search Folder Criteria window.

6. In the *Search for the word(s)* field, key 007. In the *In* field, select in subject field only from the dropdown list if necessary. Click OK in each window to return to the Mail folder.

7. Create a new message. In the To field, key your email address. In the Subject field, key 007. In the message body, key Testing Search Folder. Click the Send button.

8. Click the Send/Receive button if the 007 message has not arrived. After the message arrives, click the Project 007 folder to view its content. It should contain the 007 message in the Sent Items folder and the 007 message in the Inbox.

   LEAVE Outlook open for the next project.

■ Mastery Assessment

Project 7-5: Create a Secondary Address Book

Diane works for a new company, but she wants to stay in touch with friends she made at Wingtip Toys. Diane decided to create a secondary address book before she imports personal contacts for her friends.

1. If necessary, click the Folder List button in the Navigation pane to display the Folder List.

2. Click the Contacts folder in the Folder List.

3. Click the New arrow to display the dropdown menu and click Folder. The Create New Folder window is displayed.

4. In the Name field, key Diane's Contacts. Because you selected the Contacts folder before creating a new folder, Contact Items is already displayed in the *Folder contains* field and the Contacts folder is selected in the *Select where to place the folder* list. Click OK. The Diane's Contacts folder is created in the Contacts folder.

   LEAVE Outlook open for the next project.

Project 7-6: Import a Secondary Address Book from a File

After creating the Diane's Contacts folder, Diane can import contact records for her friends at Wingtip Toys.

1. Click the Diane's Contacts folder in the Folder List, if necessary.

2. Click the File menu and then click the Import and Export option to display the Import and Export Wizard.

3. Click Import from another program or file in the list of available actions. Click the Next button.

4. Click Microsoft Excel 97-2003 in the list of available import file types. Click the Next button.

The **Source Diane's Contacts** file is available on the companion CD-ROM.

5. Click the Browse button. Navigate to the data files for this lesson and click the *Source Diane's Contacts* file. Click OK to close the Browse window and return to the Import a File window. Click the Next button.

6. Verify that Diane's Contacts is selected as the destination folder. Click the Next button.

7. Click the Finish button. The contacts are imported and displayed in the Diane's Contacts folder.

   CLOSE Outlook.

INTERNET READY

Microsoft provides templates for a wide variety of electronic business cards. Sophisticated, casual, fun, and serious designs are available. Go to www.Microsoft.com. Search for electronic business cards. Download a style that appeals to you. Modify the card and use it as your electronic business card.

Workplace Ready

Organizing Outlook Items

Nicole Holliday is an instructor at the School of Fine Arts. Every session, a batch of fresh students registers for Nicole's classes. Nicole teaches several classes that require students to submit electronic files. The school doesn't set up mailboxes for each class, so Nicole uses Outlook to organize her messages.

Every session, Nicole sets up a new email folder for each class. She creates rules that sort messages from each student into the correct folder. A few weeks after classes end, Nicole archives the class folders that are no longer needed.

Because Nicole also teaches at a second school, she created a secondary address book to separate the contact information between the two schools. Incorrectly addressing a message to a staff member at the wrong school would be embarrassing.

↻ Circling Back

Kim Ralls was promoted to Shift Supervisor and transferred to the downtown office at City Power & Light. Although Kim was transferred, her computer and other equipment did not move with her. She needs to set up Outlook 2007 with new rules and contacts to help her manage her new responsibilities. She also needs to update her electronic business card to display her new title and contact information.

⊕ Project 1: Create Mail and Contacts Folders

Kim starts the process of customizing Outlook 2007 to meet her needs by creating new folders. One mail folder will contain messages about requests for new service. Another folder will contain contact information for the CP&L service technicians responsible for establishing service at new homes and businesses.

GET READY. Launch Outlook if it is not already running.

1. Click the Folder List button in the bottom of the Navigation pane to display the Folder List.
2. Click the arrow next to New in the standard toolbar. Click Folder. The Create New Folder dialog box is displayed.
3. In the Name field, key New Service to identify the new folder. Verify that Mail and Post Items is selected in the *Folder contains* field. If necessary, click Personal Folders in the *Select where to place the folder* list. Click OK to create the folder.
4. Click the arrow next to New in the standard toolbar. Click Folder. The Create New Folder dialog box is displayed.
5. In the Name field, key New Service Techs to identify the new folder. Select Contact Items in the *Folder contains* field. If necessary, click Contacts in the *Select where to place the folder* list. Click OK to create the folder.

   LEAVE Outlook open for the next project.

⊕ Project 2: Create a Rule

Kim receives messages requesting new service from the Customer Service department. Messages could come from a dozen different Customer Service representatives. However, the Subject field for every message contains the words "New Service Request." Kim decided to create a rule moving all of the requests to the New Service folder.

USE the New Service folder created in the previous project. Your computer must be connected to the Internet to test the rule at the end of this project.

1. If necessary, click the Mail button in the Navigation pane to display the Mail folder.
2. Click the Tools menu, and click the Rules and Alerts option. The Rules and Alerts window is displayed. Turn off all rules except the *Clear categories on mail* rule.
3. Click the New Rule button. The Rules Wizard window is displayed.
4. In the *Stay Organized* category, click Move messages with specific words in the subject to a folder.
5. In the *Step 2* area, click specific words. The Search Text window is displayed.
6. In the *Specify words or phrases to search for in the subject* field, key New Service Request. Click the Add button. Click OK to close the Search Text window. The Rules Wizard window is displayed.
7. In the *Step 2* area of the Rules Wizard window, click specified to identify the destination folder. The Folder List is displayed in the Rules and Alerts window.

8. Click the New Service folder, and click OK. The specified destination folder is identified in the Rules Wizard window. Click the Next button to continue the Wizard.

9. Click the Next button twice to continue the Wizard without modifying conditions or actions.

10. Under *Select exceptions*, click the except if the subject contains specific words checkbox. Text is added to the rule description at the bottom of the Rules Wizard window.

11. In the rule description area, click specific words. The Search text window is displayed.

12. In the *Specify words or phrases to search for in the subject* field, key RE:. (Be sure to include the colon in the specified words or any message subject containing the letters *re* will be an exception.) Click the Add button. The *RE:* text is enclosed by quotation marks and added to the search list for this rule. Click OK to close the Search Text window. The Rules Wizard window is displayed.

13. Click the Next button to continue the Wizard. The rule is displayed for your approval. Examine the rule carefully to verify that it is correct. Click the Finish button. The new rule is displayed in the Rules and Alerts window. Verify that the only active rules are the *New Service Request* and *Clear categories on mail* rules. Click the OK button to close the Rules and Alerts window.

14. Click the New button to display a new Message window. Address the message to your email address. In the Subject field, key New Service Request. Send the message. Create and send a second message to your email address using RE: New Service Request in the Subject field.

15. Click the Send/Receive button, if necessary, to receive the messages. Verify that the New Service Request message was moved to the New Service folder and the RE: New Service Request message remained in the Inbox.

16. Click the Tools menu, and click the Rules and Alerts option. The Rules and Alerts window is displayed. Turn off all rules except the *Clear categories on mail* rule. Click OK to close the Rules and Alerts window.

LEAVE Outlook open for the next project.

Project 3: Create Contact Records

Kim needs to create contact records for herself and the two new Service Technicians in her department.

USE the New Service Techs folder created in the first project.

1. If necessary, click the Contacts button in the Navigation pane to display the Contacts folder. Under My Contacts in the Navigation pane, click New Service Techs to open the new folder created in Project 1.

2. Click New on the Standard toolbar to display a blank Contact window.

3. Click the Full Name field, if necessary. Key Kim Ralls and press Tab.

4. In the *Company* field, key City Power & Light and press Tab.

5. In the *Job title* field, key Shift Supervisor and press Tab.

TROUBLESHOOTING The email addresses provided in these projects belong to unused domains owned by Microsoft. When you send a message to these addresses, you will receive an error message stating that the message could not be delivered. Delete the error messages when they arrive.

6. Click the E-mail field. Key Kim@cpandl.com and press [Tab].

7. In the *Web page address* field, key www.cpandl.com.

8. Below the *Phone numbers* heading, click the Business field. Key 2175559821.

9. Below the Addresses heading, click the Business field. Key 324 Main Street. Press [Enter]. Key Springfield, IL 68390. Press [Tab].

10. In the Actions group on the Ribbon, click the Save & New arrow. In the dropdown list of options, click New Contact from Same Company.

11. Click the Full Name field, if necessary. Key Jay Henningsen and press [Tab]. Click the Job title field. Key New Service Technician and press [Tab]. Click the E-mail field. Key Jay@cpandl.com and press [Tab].

12. In the Actions group on the Ribbon, click the Save & New arrow. In the dropdown list of options, click New Contact from Same Company.

13. Click the Full Name field, if necessary. Key Julia Moseley and press [Tab]. Click the Job title field. Key New Service Technician and press [Tab]. Click the E-mail field. Key Julia@cpandl.com and press [Tab].

14. In the Actions group on the Ribbon, click the Save & Close button.

15. CLOSE any open contact records.

    LEAVE Outlook open for the next project.

⊙ Project 4: Edit an Electronic Business Card

Now that Kim has created new contact records, she decides to dress up her electronic business card.

1. If necessary, click the Contacts button in the Navigation pane to display the Contacts folder.

2. Double-click the Kim Ralls contact. The Kim Ralls – Contact window is displayed.

3. In the Options group on the Ribbon, click the Business Card button. The Edit Business Card window is displayed.

4. In the Card Design area in the upper-right of the window, verify that Image Left is selected in the Layout field.

CD

The *lights on* image is available on the companion CD-ROM.

5. Click the Change button. The Add Card Picture dialog box is displayed. Navigate to the data files for this project. Click the *lights on* file and click OK.

6. In the Card Design area, click the Image Area field. Change the value to 25%, if necessary.

7. In the Card Design area, click the Image Align field. In the dropdown list, click Fit to Edge.

8. In the Card Design area, click the Background button. The Color dialog box is displayed. Click the yellow color swatch in the second row. Click OK.

9. In the Fields area, click Business Phone in the list of fields. Click the Bold button.

10. In the Fields area, click E-mail in the list of fields. Click the Bold button.

11. Click OK. The Edit Business Card window is closed. Click the Save & Close button to return to the Contacts folder.

    CLOSE Outlook.

Calendar Basics

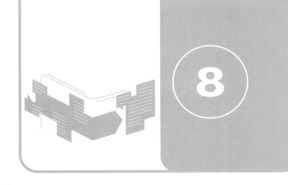

LESSON SKILL MATRIX

SKILLS	MATRIX SKILL	SKILL NUMBER
Managing Appointments		
Creating a One-Time Appointment	Create a one-time appointment, meeting, or event	2.1.1
Scheduling a Recurring Appointment	Create a recurring appointment, meeting, or event	2.1.2
Creating an Appointment from a Message	Create an appointment, meeting, or event from an email message	2.1.3
Creating an Appointment from a Task	Create an appointment, meeting, or event from a task	2.1.4
Marking an Appointment as Private	Mark an appointment, meeting, or event as private	2.1.5
Managing Events	Create a recurring appointment, meeting, or event and Mark an appointment, meeting, or event as private	2.1.2, 2.1.5

As a marketing assistant, Terry Eminhizer knows the value of time. Terry manages her schedule and the schedules of two marketing representatives who are constantly on the road. Setting up travel arrangements, confirming appointments with clients, and generally smoothing out the bumps for the marketing representatives gives them more time to make bigger sales. Time is money.

KEY TERMS
appointment
banner
busy
event
free
out of office
private
recurring appointment
tentative

■ SOFTWARE ORIENTATION

Microsoft Outlook's Appointment Window

The Appointment window displayed in Figure 8-1 enables you to schedule an appointment or event. Scheduled appointments and events are displayed on your calendar.

Figure 8-1

Outlook's Appointment window

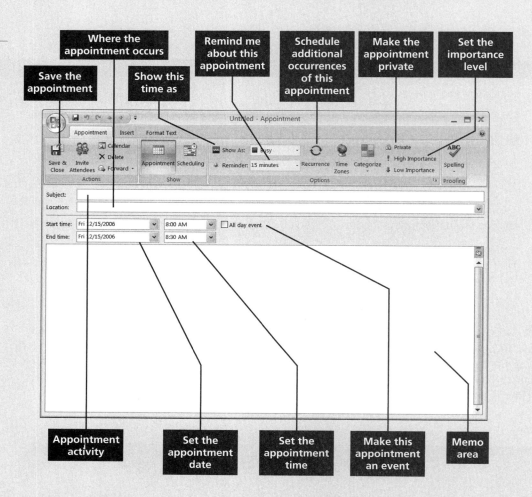

Use the Appointment window to create an appointment or event. Refer to Figure 8-1 as you complete the following exercises.

■ Managing Appointments

THE BOTTOM LINE

An *appointment* is a scheduled activity that does not require sending invitations to other people or resources. An appointment can occur once or occur at regular intervals.

Creating a One-Time Appointment

Appointments can involve other people, but they do not require invitations sent through Outlook. Appointments can include activities such as doctor appointments and picking up your daughter after soccer practice.

X REF

You can find more information on the Calendar folder in Lesson 10.

CREATE A ONE-TIME APPOINTMENT

GET READY. Before you begin these steps, be sure to launch Microsoft Outlook.

1. Click the Calendar button in the Navigation pane to display the Calendar folder. Click the Month button to display the Month view, if necessary.
2. Click next Friday's date on the monthly calendar.

 **ANOTHER WAY** You can also select the date in the Appointment window. If the date is displayed in the monthly calendar, it is easier to select the date there. For appointments that occur several months in the future, it is easier to select the date in the Appointment window.

3. On the Standard toolbar, click the New button. The Appointment window in Figure 8-1 is displayed. The date selected in the monthly calendar is already displayed in the *Start time* and *End time* fields.
4. In the Subject field, key Blood Drive.
5. In the Location field, key Van in the South parking lot.
6. In the *Start time* fields, select or key 2:00 PM. By default, each appointment is 30 minutes long. Because you need to fill out forms before donating and eat a few cookies after donating, select an End time of 3:00 PM.
7. Click the Save & Close button in the Actions group on the Ribbon. The appointment is displayed on the calendar.

PAUSE. LEAVE Outlook open to use in the next exercise.

CERTIFICATION READY?
How do you create a one-time appointment, meeting or event?
2.1.1

In the previous exercise, you created a one-time appointment to donate blood at the company blood drive. By default, when you select a future date in the calendar, the displayed time of the appointment in the Appointment window will be the start of the work day.

The *Show as* field in the Appointment window determines how the time is displayed on your calendar. When others look at your calendar, this tells them if you are available and how definite your schedule is for a specific activity. You can choose from four options displayed in Table 8-1.

Table 8-1

Show time as options

SHOW AS	DESCRIPTION
Free	No activities are scheduled for this time period. You are available.
Busy	An activity is scheduled for this time period. You are not available for other activities.
Tentative	An activity is scheduled for this time period, but the activity might not occur. You might be available for other activities.
Out of Office	You are out of the office.

Scheduling a Recurring Appointment

A *recurring appointment* is an appointment that occurs at regular intervals. Recurrences can be scheduled based on daily, weekly, monthly, and yearly intervals.

SCHEDULE A RECURRING APPOINTMENT

GET READY. Before you begin these steps, be sure to launch Microsoft Outlook.

1. Click the Calendar button in the Navigation pane to display the Calendar folder. Click the Month button to display the Month view, if necessary.

2. Click the third Monday of the month on the monthly calendar. If the third Monday of this month has passed, click the third Monday of next month.

TAKE NOTE *In the Month view, click the lower part of the square to select the day. Clicking the top part of the square displays the Day view for that date.*

3. On the Standard toolbar, click the New button. The Appointment window in Figure 8-1 is displayed. The date selected in the monthly calendar is already displayed in the *Start time* and *End time* fields.

4. In the Subject field, key Engineering Lunch.

5. In the Location field, key Conference Room B.

6. In the *Start time* fields, key 12:15 PM. Key or select an End time of 1:15 PM.

7. Click the Memo area. Key New techniques and troubleshooting.

8. Click the Recurrence button in the Options group on the Ribbon. The Appointment Recurrence window is displayed, as shown in Figure 8-2.

Figure 8-2

Appointment Recurrence window

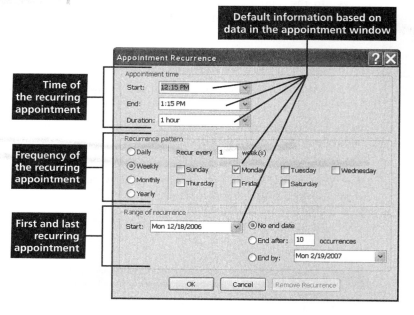

9. In the Appointment Recurrence window, click Monthly in the Recurrence pattern area. Selecting a different frequency changes the patterns available for selection on the right side in the Recurrence pattern area.

10. On the right side in the Recurrence pattern area, click the radio button to select The third Monday of every 1 month(s). Because the date of the first recurring appointment was the third Monday of the month, the third Monday of every month is offered as a likely pattern.

11. Click OK to set the recurrence pattern and return to the Appointment window. The recurrence pattern is displayed in the Appointment window, as shown in Figure 8-3.

Figure 8-3

Recurring appointment

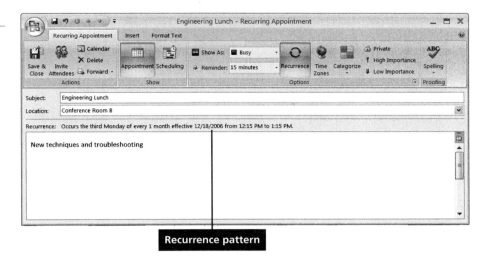

Recurrence pattern

12. Click the Save & Close button in the Actions group on the Ribbon. The appointment is displayed on the monthly calendar. Click the Forward button at the top of the monthly calendar to verify that the recurring appointment is displayed in next month's calendar. Click the Back button at the top of the monthly calendar to return to the current month.

PAUSE. LEAVE Outlook open to use in the next exercise.

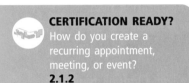

CERTIFICATION READY?
How do you create a recurring appointment, meeting, or event?
2.1.2

In the previous exercise, you created a recurring appointment. Recurring appointments are common in many calendars. Weekly soccer games, monthly lunch dates with an old friend, and semi-annual company dinners are examples of recurring appointments.

Creating an Appointment from a Message

Sometimes, a message can lead to an appointment. For example, your son's cross-country running coach sends you a message about the awards banquet or you receive a message that a farewell lunch will be held Thursday for a coworker in your department. Simply use the email message to create an appointment.

⊕ CREATE AN APPOINTMENT FROM A MESSAGE

GET READY. Before you begin these steps, be sure to launch Microsoft Outlook.

1. If necessary, click the Mail button in the Navigation pane to display the Mail folder.

2. Click the New button in the Standard toolbar to display the Message window.

3. In the To field, key your email address. In the Subject field, key Vice President Duerr visiting Thursday afternoon. In the message area, key Vice President Bernard Duerr is visiting this division on Thursday. An employee meeting will be held in the company cafeteria from 2:00 PM to 4:00 PM. Attendance is mandatory. Click the Send button.

4. Return to your Inbox, if necessary. Click the Send/Receive button if the message has not arrived yet.

5. Double-click the Vice President Duerr visiting Thursday afternoon message to open it.

6. Click the Move to Folder button in the Actions group on the Ribbon. In the drop-down list, click Other Folder. The Move Item to window is displayed, as shown in Figure 8-4.

Figure 8-4

Move Item to window

Click the Calendar folder

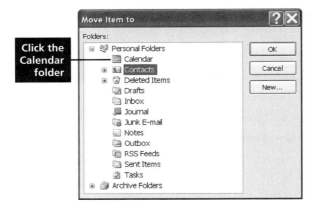

7. In the *Move Item to* window, click Calendar and then click OK. An Appointment window is opened. The message text is displayed in the Memo area of the Appointment window. The message subject is displayed in the Subject field in the Appointment window.

8. In the Appointment window, key Company cafeteria into the Location field.

9. Key Thursday into the *Start time* field instead of a date. Key or select a Start time of 2:00 PM.

TAKE NOTE*

You can key text in the *Start time* and *End time* fields rather than a date. Outlook translates the text into a date.

10. In the *End time* field, key an End time of 4:00 PM. The Appointment window should be similar to Figure 8-5.

Figure 8-5

Creating an appointment from a message

Subject created automatically from message subject

Message used to create appointment

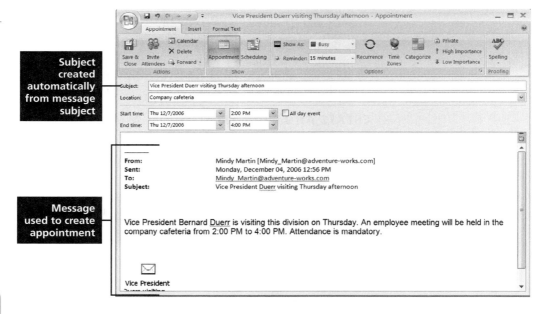

11. Click the Save & Close button in the Actions group on the Ribbon.

12. Click the Calendar button in the Navigation pane to display the Calendar folder. The appointment created from the message is displayed.

PAUSE. LEAVE Outlook open to use in the next exercise.

In the previous exercise, you created an appointment from a message you received. The message text is saved automatically in the Appointment window's memo area. This stores the related message with the appointment.

Creating an Appointment from a Task

Tasks describe activities you have to do. Appointments tell you when activities are performed. Tasks frequently become appointments when the time to perform a task is scheduled.

You can find more information on tasks in Lesson 11.

⊕ CREATE AN APPOINTMENT FROM A TASK

GET READY. Before you begin these steps, be sure to launch Microsoft Outlook.

1. Click the Calendar button in the Navigation pane to display the Calendar folder. Click the Month button to display the Month view, if necessary.

2. Click the View menu. Point to To-Do Bar and then click Normal. The To-Do Bar is displayed to the right of the monthly calendar. Your scheduled appointments are listed in the To-Do Bar. No tasks are displayed as shown in Figure 8-6.

Figure 8-6

To-Do Bar displayed

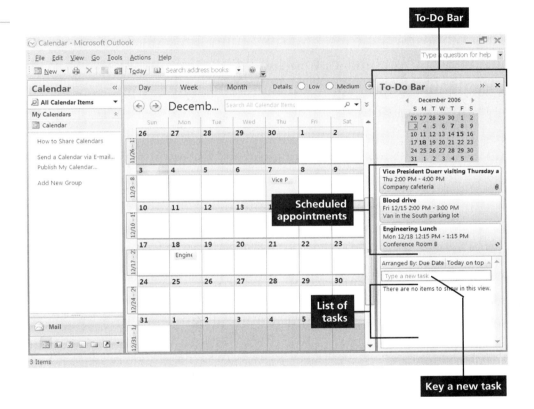

3. Click the Type a new task field, and key Lunch with Vice President Duerr. Press Enter. The task is created.

4. Click the Lunch with Vice President Duerr task. Drag it to Thursday's date on the calendar. You already have an appointment for the employee meeting from 2:00 PM to 4:00 PM for that date.

5. Double-click the Lunch with Vice President Duerr item in the calendar. An Appointment window containing the task information is displayed.

6. Click the All day event checkbox to clear the checkbox. The time fields become available.

7. Key a Start time of 12:30 PM and an End time of 1:45 PM. The Appointment window should be similar to Figure 8-7.

Figure 8-7

Creating an appointment from a task

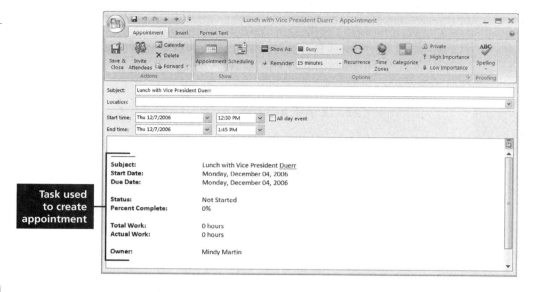

CERTIFICATION READY?
How do you create an appointment, meeting, or event from a task?
2.1.4

8. Click the Save & Close button in the Actions group on the Ribbon. The appointment created from the task is displayed on the calendar.

PAUSE. LEAVE Outlook open to use in the next exercise.

In the previous exercise, you created an appointment from a task. The task text is saved automatically in the Appointment window's memo area, storing the information with the appointment.

Marking an Appointment as Private

You can choose to mark an appointment as *private*. This feature protects the details of an activity from a casual observer, but it does not ensure privacy. Any person who has Read privileges to your calendar could access the information through a variety of methods.

MARK AN APPOINTMENT AS PRIVATE

GET READY. Before you begin these steps, be sure to launch Microsoft Outlook.

1. Click the Calendar button in the Navigation pane to display the Calendar folder. Click the Month button to display the Month view if necessary.
2. Click next Friday's date on the monthly calendar. The Blood drive is already scheduled for 2:00 PM on that date.

TROUBLESHOOTING — To ensure privacy for the details of your appointments, meetings, or events, create a separate Calendar folder that is not shared with other users.

3. On the Standard toolbar, click the New button. The Appointment window in Figure 8-1 is displayed. The date selected in the monthly calendar is already displayed in the Start time and End time fields.
4. In the Subject field, key Interview Rebecca Laszlo for receptionist.
5. In the Location field, key My office.
6. In the Start time fields, key or select a time of 4:30 PM. Key or select an End time of 5:00 PM, if necessary.
7. Click the Private button in the Options group on the Ribbon.
8. Click the Save & Close button in the Actions group on the Ribbon. The appointment is displayed on your monthly calendar.

PAUSE. LEAVE Outlook open to use in the next exercise.

CERTIFICATION READY?
How do you mark an appointment, meeting or event as private?
2.1.5

In the previous exercise, you created a one-time appointment to interview an applicant for the department receptionist. You clicked the Private button before saving the appointment. You can also open an existing appointment and click the Private button to turn on or turn off the Private feature for that appointment. Be sure to save the modified appointment after changing the Private status.

In the Day view, a lock is displayed next to a private appointment. Without permission, other users cannot open the appointment to view the details.

■ Managing Events

THE BOTTOM LINE

An *event* is an activity that lasts one or more days. In your calendar, an event is displayed as a banner at the top of the day. A *banner* is text displayed at the top of a day to indicate an event. For scheduling purposes, an event is displayed as free time. You are still available for appointments or meetings.

MANAGE EVENTS

GET READY. Before you begin these steps, be sure to launch Microsoft Outlook.

1. Click the Calendar button in the Navigation pane to display the Calendar folder. Click the Month button to display the Month view, if necessary.
2. On the Standard toolbar, click the New button. The Appointment window in Figure 8-1 is displayed.
3. In the Subject field, key Anniversary.
4. In the *Start time* field, key the date of your anniversary or a family member's anniversary.
5. Click the All day event checkbox to select the option. The time fields are dimmed.
6. Click the Private button in the Options group on the Ribbon.
7. Click the Recurrence button in the Options group on the Ribbon. The Appointment Recurrence window is displayed.
8. In the Appointment Recurrence window, click Yearly in the Recurrence pattern area. Selecting a different frequency changes the patterns available for selection on the right side in the Recurrence pattern area.
9. On the right side in the Recurrence pattern area, click the radio button to select Every [month] [date].
10. Click OK to set the recurrence pattern and return to the Appointment window. The recurrence pattern is displayed in the Appointment window.
11. In the Options group on the Ribbon, click the Reminder dropdown list. Click the 1 week option.
12. Click the Save & Close button in the Actions group on the Ribbon. The appointment is added to your calendar.
13. Click the Forward button at the top of the monthly calendar to verify that the recurring event is displayed on the correct date. Click the Back button at the top of the monthly calendar to return to the current month.

CLOSE Outlook.

CERTIFICATION READY?
How do you create a recurring appointment, meeting, or event and mark the recurring appointment, meeting, or event as private?
2.1.2 and 2.1.5

In the previous exercise, you created a private recurring event for the date of your wedding anniversary. The Appointment window is used to create an event. The methods of creating new appointments from messages or tasks that you performed in the earlier exercises in this lesson can also be used to create events.

SUMMARY SKILL MATRIX

IN THIS LESSON YOU LEARNED	MATRIX SKILL	SKILL NUMBER
To create public and private one-time and recurring appointments from scratch, a received message, or a task		
To create an appointment from scratch that will only occur once	Create a one-time appointment, meeting, or event	2.1.1
To schedule an appointment that recurs at regular intervals	Create a recurring appointment, meeting, or event	2.1.2
To create an appointment from a received message	Create an appointment, meeting, or event from an email message	2.1.3
To create an appointment from a task	Create an appointment, meeting, or event from a task	2.1.4
To mark an appointment as private, protecting the details from casual observers	Mark an appointment, meeting, or event as private	2.1.5
To use the same procedures used to manage events when working with calendar events	Create a recurring appointment, meeting, or event and Mark an appointment, meeting, or event as private	2.1.2, 2.1.5

■ Knowledge Assessment

Matching

Match the term with its definition.

a. appointment   f. free
b. banner   g. private
c. busy   h. recurring appointment
d. calendar   i. task
e. event   j. tentative

H _____ **1.** An appointment that occurs at regular intervals

E _____ **2.** An activity that lasts one or more days

A _____ **3.** A scheduled activity that does not require sending invitations to other people or resources

I _____ **4.** An activity that has to be performed

J _____ **5.** An activity is scheduled for this time period, but the activity might not occur

B _____ **6.** Text displayed at the top of a day to indicate an event

G _____ **7.** Feature that protects the details of an activity from a casual observer

C _____ **8.** An activity is scheduled for this time period

D _____ **9.** Enables you to create a schedule

F _____ **10.** No activities are scheduled for this time period

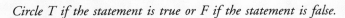

True/False

Circle T if the statement is true or F if the statement is false.

T F **1.** Use the Appointment window to schedule an event.

T **F** **2.** Appointments require invitations sent through Outlook.

T **F** **3.** By default, each appointment is one hour long.

T F **4.** You are not available for other activities when your time is displayed as busy.

T F **5.** Recurrences can be scheduled based on daily, weekly, monthly, and yearly intervals.

T F **6.** You can key text in the *Start time* and *End time* fields rather than a date.

T **F** **7.** A message is deleted automatically when it is used to create an appointment.

T **F** **8.** A task cannot be used to create an appointment unless the task is private.

T F **9.** Marking an appointment as private does not ensure that users who can view your calendar cannot view the details of the private appointment.

T F **10.** An event is displayed as a banner in your calendar.

■ Competency Assessment

Project 8-1: **Schedule Vacation**

First things first. Before you create appointments, schedule your vacation.

GET READY. Launch Outlook if it is not already running.

1. Click the Calendar button in the Navigation pane to display the Calendar folder.
2. On the Standard toolbar, click the New button. The Appointment window is displayed.
3. In the Subject field, key Vacation.
4. In the *Start time* field, key the date of the first day of your vacation.
5. In the *End time* field, key the date of the last day of your vacation.
6. Click the All day event checkbox to select the option. The time fields are dimmed.
7. Click the Save & Close button in the Actions group on the Ribbon. The appointment is added to your calendar.

   LEAVE Outlook open for the next project.

Project 8-2: **Create a One-Time Appointment**

You have been selected to create a presentation about a new product your company will sell in the coming year. You will deliver the presentation at a company dinner on Wednesday. Schedule the time to prepare the presentation.

1. Click the Calendar button in the Navigation pane to display the Calendar folder.
2. Click next Monday's date on the monthly calendar.
3. On the Standard toolbar, click the New button. The Appointment window is displayed.
4. In the Subject field, key Prepare new product presentation.
5. In the *Start time* fields, key or select the time of 9:30 AM. Key or select the End time of 2:00 PM.
6. Click the Save & Close button in the Actions group on the Ribbon. The appointment is added to the calendar.

   LEAVE Outlook open for the next project.

■ Proficiency Assessment

Project 8-3: **Schedule a Recurring Appointment**

Every week, you collect sales information to track the difference between sales goals and actual sales. Create a recurring appointment every Monday to gather the information and post the sales information for the managers to review.

1. Click the Calendar button in the Navigation pane to display the Calendar folder.
2. Click next Monday's date on the monthly calendar.
3. On the Standard toolbar, click the New button. The Appointment window is displayed.
4. In the Subject field, key Prepare Sales Report.
5. In the *Start time* fields, key or select 8:30 AM. Key or select an End time of 9:30 AM.
6. Click the Recurrence button in the Options group on the Ribbon. The Appointment Recurrence window is displayed.
7. Click OK to accept the recurrence pattern and return to the Appointment window.
8. Click the Save & Close button in the Actions group on the Ribbon. The appointment is added to the calendar.

   LEAVE Outlook open for the next project.

Project 8-4: **Create an Appointment from a Message**

A friend sent you a message about a concert in August. Create an appointment from the message.

1. If necessary, click the Mail button in the Navigation pane to display the Mail folder.
2. Click the New button in the Standard toolbar to display the Message window.
3. In the To field, key your email address. In the Subject field, key Concert! In the message area, key [Insert name of favorite musical performer] is coming to [Insert name of local concert hall]! Mark August 10 on your calendar! I already bought our tickets! Click the Send button.
4. Return to your Inbox, if necessary. Click the Send/Receive button if the message has not arrived yet.
5. Double-click the Concert message to open it.
6. Click the Move to Folder button in the Actions group on the Ribbon. In the drop-down list, click Other Folder. The *Move Item to* window is displayed.
7. In the *Move Item to* window, click Calendar, and then click OK. An Appointment window is opened.
8. Key August 10 in the *Start time* field. Key or select a Start time of 7:00 PM.
9. Key or select an End time of 11:00 PM.
10. Click the Save & Close button in the Actions group on the Ribbon.

    LEAVE Outlook open for the next project.

■ Mastery Assessment

Project 8-5: **Create an Appointment from a Task**

Last week, a coworker asked you to review a new marketing presentation. He finished the presentation yesterday. Turn the task into an appointment to review the presentation tomorrow after lunch.

1. Click the Calendar button in the Navigation pane to display the Calendar folder.
2. Display the To-Do Bar, if necessary.

3. Click the Type a new task field, and key Review presentation for Gary Schare. Press Enter. The task is created.

4. Click the Review presentation for Gary Schare task. Drag it to tomorrow's date on the calendar.

5. Double-click the Review presentation for Gary Schare item in the calendar. An Appointment window is displayed.

6. Click the All day event checkbox to clear the checkbox. The time fields become available.

7. Key or select a Start time of 3:30 PM and an End time of 5:00 PM.

8. Click the Save & Close button in the Actions group on the Ribbon. The appointment is added to the calendar.

LEAVE Outlook open for the next project.

Project 8-6: **Mark an Appointment as Private**

In Project 8-4, you created an appointment for the concert. Your taste in music might not be appreciated by everyone who views your calendar. Make the appointment private.

1. Click the Calendar button in the Navigation pane to display the Calendar folder.

2. Display August in the calendar.

3. Double-click the Concert appointment to open it.

4. Click the Private button in the Options group on the Ribbon.

5. Click the Save & Close button in the Actions group on the Ribbon. The private appointment is added to the calendar.

CLOSE Outlook.

INTERNET READY

Use the Internet to find some local events that you would like to attend. A local sports game or a concert performed by your favorite artist could be fun. Schedule the activities in your calendar.

9 Managing Meetings

LESSON SKILL MATRIX

SKILLS	MATRIX SKILL	SKILL NUMBER
Creating a Meeting		
Creating a One-Time Meeting	Create a one-time appointment, meeting, or event	2.1.1
Inviting Mandatory and Optional Attendees	Invite mandatory attendees to meetings and Invite optional attendees to meetings	2.2.1, 2.2.2
Determining When Attendees Can Meet	Determine when attendees are available to meet	2.2.3
Tracking Responses to a Meeting Request	Track responses to meeting requests	2.2.4
Modifying a Meeting		
Changing a Meeting Time	Change a meeting time	2.3.1
Proposing a New Meeting Time	Change a meeting time	2.3.1
Accepting a Proposed New Meeting Time	Change a meeting time	2.3.1
Adding and Updating a New Attendee	Add a meeting attendee and Send meeting updates only to new attendees	2.3.2, 2.3.4
Managing a Recurring Meeting		
Creating a Recurring Meeting	Create a recurring appointment, meeting, or event	2.1.2
Changing One Occurrence of a Recurring Meeting	Modify one instance of a recurring meeting	2.3.3
Scheduling A Meeting Resource	Schedule meeting resources	2.2.5
Cancelling a Meeting	Cancel a meeting	2.3.5

Gabe Mares reviewed the list of bug reports for Project Snow. The list was much longer than it should be at this stage in the software development cycle. It was obviously time to call a meeting to identify the reason for the long list of problems and determine how the problems could be resolved to meet the project deadlines.

KEY TERMS
cancel
group schedule
mandatory attendee
meeting
meeting organizer
meeting request
occurrence
optional attendee
recurring meeting
resource

SOFTWARE ORIENTATION

Microsoft Outlook's Meeting Window

The Meeting window displayed in Figure 9-1 enables you to create a meeting involving other people or resources. Scheduled meetings are displayed on your calendar.

Figure 9-1

Outlook's Meeting window

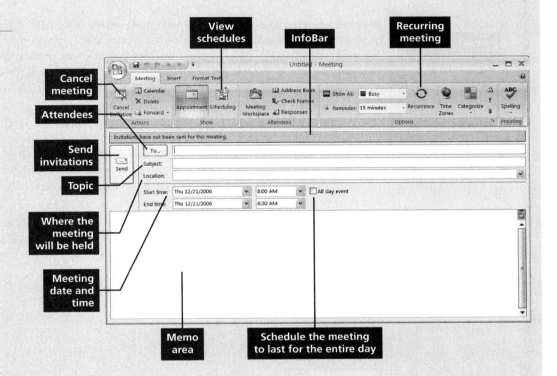

Use the Meeting window to create a meeting. Refer to Figure 9-1 as you complete the following exercises.

■ Creating a Meeting

THE BOTTOM LINE

A *meeting* is a scheduled activity that requires sending invitations to other people or resources. Basically, a meeting is an appointment that requires other attendees. Therefore, Outlook's Meeting window, shown in Figure 9-1, is very similar to the Appointment window. However, the Meeting window also includes the To field to invite attendees and the Send button to send the invitations. A meeting can occur once or at regular intervals.

→ Creating a One-Time Meeting

You can find more information on appointments in Lesson 8.

Meeting a goal often requires more than one person. Working with others to accomplish a goal usually requires meetings. Use Outlook to start planning a good meeting by selecting the right time, the right place, and the right people to accomplish the goal. A *meeting request* is an Outlook item that creates a meeting and invites attendees.

→ CREATE A ONE-TIME MEETING

You can find more information on the Calendar folder in Lesson 10.

GET READY. Before you begin these steps, be sure to launch Microsoft Outlook.

1. Click the Calendar button in the Navigation pane to display the Calendar folder. Click the Month button to display the Month view, if necessary.

2. Click the third Monday of the month on the monthly calendar. If you have already passed the third Monday of this month, select the third Monday of next month.

TROUBLESHOOTING If you completed Lesson 8, a recurring appointment is scheduled for 8:30 AM to 9:30 AM every Monday to prepare a sales report. An Engineering Lunch is scheduled for 12:15 PM to 1:15 PM on the third Monday of every month. If you did not complete Lesson 8, the busy times shown on your schedule will differ.

3. On the Standard toolbar, click the New arrow. Click Meeting Request on the drop-down menu. The Meeting window shown in Figure 9-1 is displayed. By default, the beginning of your workday, 8:00 AM in this example, is in the *Start time* field for the meeting and the time in the *End time* field is 30 minutes after the meeting starts. Because you have a recurring appointment scheduled for 8:30 AM, the InfoBar displays the message *Adjacent to another appointment on your Calendar*.

4. Click the Subject field and key Discuss Annual Convention. In the Location field, key Conference Room A.

5. Click the Scheduling button in the Show group on the Ribbon. Scheduling information is displayed, as shown in Figure 9-2.

Figure 9-2

Viewing schedules

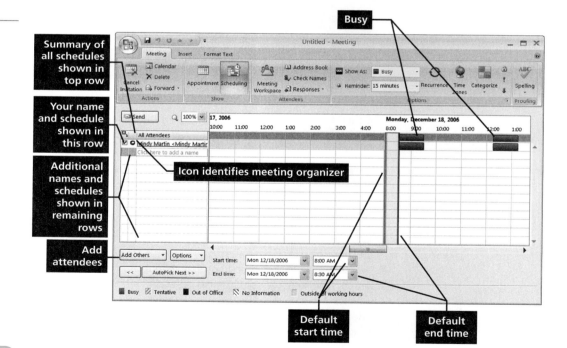

CERTIFICATION READY?
How do you create a one-time appointment, meeting, or event?
2.1.1

PAUSE. LEAVE the Meeting window open to use in the next exercise.

In the previous exercise, you started the process of creating a one-time meeting. In the next exercise, you will select the right people to make this meeting a success.

Inviting Mandatory and Optional Attendees

A **_mandatory attendee_** is a person who must attend the meeting. An **_optional attendee_** is a person who should attend the meeting, but whose presence is not required. When you select a meeting time, choose a time slot when all mandatory attendees are available.

⊕ INVITE MANDATORY AND OPTIONAL ATTENDEES

GET READY. Before you begin these steps, complete the previous exercise. The mandatory attendee used in this exercise must have an active email account and be able to respond to your meeting invitation.

 **ANOTHER WAY** If the person who will respond to your invitation is not in the address book, click the _Click here to add a name_ text in the Meeting window. Key the desired email address. Verify that the icon next to the keyed name is _Required Attendee_.

1. In the Meeting window, click the Add Others button and click Add from Address Book. The Select Attendees and Resources: Contacts window is displayed, as shown in Figure 9-3.

Figure 9-3

Select Attendees and Resources: Contacts window

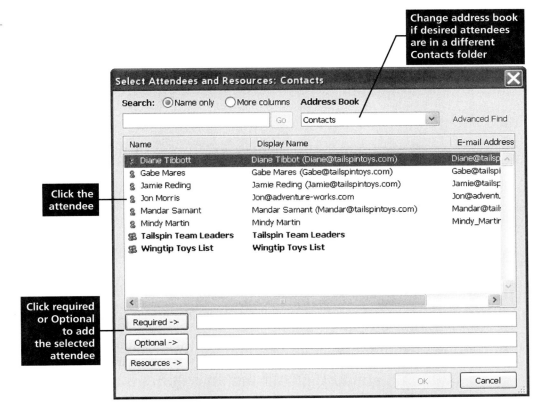

2. Click the contact information for the person who can respond to your invitation. In this example, Mindy clicks Jon Morris' contact record. Click the Required button. Jon is a mandatory attendee. Your mandatory attendee will be the real email account that can respond to your invitation.

TROUBLESHOOTING

If you invite the same real Outlook user with whom you exchanged digital IDs in Lesson 3, that user's contact record is in your Contacts folder to be used in this exercise instead of Jon Morris. If you invite a different Outlook user as your mandatory attendee, create a contact record for the new user before completing this exercise or key the new user's email address directly into the *To* field.

3. Click Gabe Mares' contact information. Click the Optional button. Gabe is an optional attendee. Click OK to return to the Meeting window. Your mandatory attendee and Gabe have been added to the list of attendees, as shown in Figure 9-4.

Figure 9-4

Attendees displayed

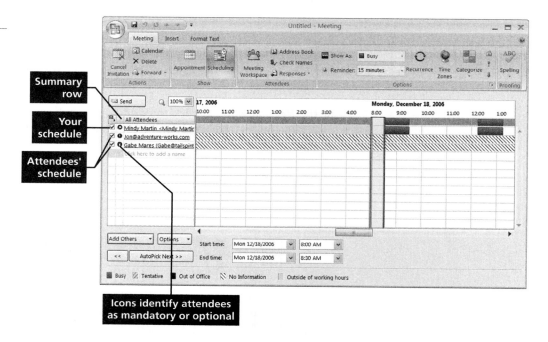

PAUSE. LEAVE the Meeting window open to use in the next exercise.

CERTIFICATION READY?
How do you invite mandatory and optional attendees to meetings?
2.2.1 and 2.2.2

In the previous exercise, you selected a mandatory attendee and an optional attendee. When planning a meeting, you should always invite at least one mandatory attendee. If a mandatory attendee is not needed to accomplish a goal at the meeting, you might not need a meeting at all. In the next exercise, you will select a time for the meeting.

Determining When Attendees Can Meet

Viewing schedules for others in your company or group can make scheduling much easier. With schedules displayed for all attendees, it is clear when all attendees are free to participate in your meeting.

⊕ DETERMINE WHEN ATTENDEES CAN MEET

GET READY. Before you begin these steps, complete the previous exercises.

You can find more information on sharing calendars in Lesson 10.

1. In the *Start time* field, key or select 10:00 AM. Notice that the green and red vertical bars indicating the start and end time for the meeting moved to enclose the 10:00 AM to 10:30 AM time slot.

2. Click the red vertical line and drag it to the right so that the bars enclose the 10:00 AM to 11:00 AM time slot. Notice that the *End time* field changed to 11:00 AM.

3. Change the *Start time* field to 8:00 AM and change the *End time* field to 9:00 AM, if necessary. The green and red vertical lines move. The meeting time overlaps your scheduled appointment.

4. Click the AutoPick Next button. Outlook examines the available calendar information and selects the first open hour. The meeting times are changed to the 9:30 AM to 10:30 AM time slot.

5. You don't want to rush your previous appointment, so click the AutoPick Next button again. The meeting times are changed to starting at 10:00 AM and ending at 11:00 AM, as shown in Figure 9-5.

Figure 9-5

Meeting time selected

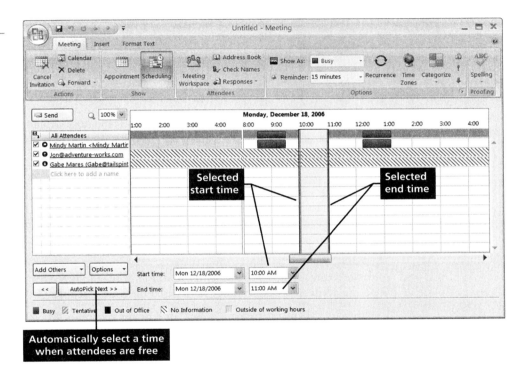

6. Click the Appointment button in the Show group on the Ribbon. The To field is automatically filled with the attendees' email addresses, and the *Start time* and *End time* fields are filled.

7. Click the message area. Key the following message. Jon, please let me know if this time is convenient for you. Gabe, I hope you can attend. Coffee and pastries will be available. Press [Enter]. Mindy

TROUBLESHOOTING

The email addresses provided in these exercises belong to unused domains owned by Microsoft. When you send a message to these addresses, you will receive an error message stating that the message could not be delivered. Delete the error messages when they arrive.

8. Compare your Meeting window to Figure 9-6. Click the Send button. Your calendar is updated, and the 10:00 AM to 11:00 AM time slot is displayed as busy.

Figure 9-6

Meeting invitation

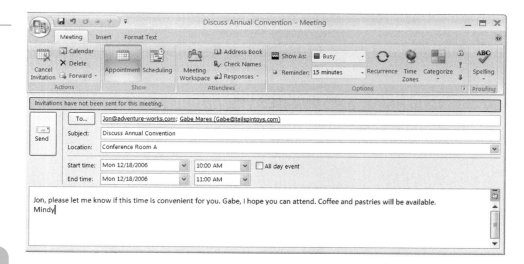

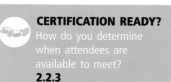

CERTIFICATION READY?
How do you determine when attendees are available to meet?
2.2.3

PAUSE. CLOSE Outlook to access the mandatory attendee's account, if necessary. If someone else is responding to the invitation, leave Outlook open to use in the next exercise.

In the previous exercise, you examined the available scheduling information for the people you want to invite to the meeting, manually selected a meeting time, and then let Outlook select a meeting time. You wrote a brief message and sent the meeting invitations. Your calendar was updated.

Ideally, you will be able to view the attendees' busy and free times before selecting a time for the meeting. In this exercise, you did not have scheduling information for the other attendees, so the available meeting times were based on your schedule.

If you use Microsoft Exchange 2000 or a newer version of Microsoft Exchange, you can view a group schedule. A *group schedule* displays scheduling information for several people. For example, you could view scheduling information for all the people in a public Contacts folder.

You used the message area to write a brief note to the attendees. However, this space can also be used to key an agenda for the meeting. You can also attach documents to the invitation before sending it. To attach documents, click the Insert tab and click the Attach File button in the Include group on the Ribbon.

Responding to a Meeting Request

By default, a meeting request arrives in your Inbox. It offers five options at the top of the message. You can accept the invitation, accept tentatively, decline, propose a new time, or view your calendar.

RESPOND TO A MEETING REQUEST

GET READY. Before you begin these steps, launch Microsoft Outlook, if necessary. Complete the previous exercises. To complete this exercise, you must have access to the email account that received the invitation for the mandatory attendee. If you do not have access to the email account, the account owner should respond to the invitation.

1. In the mandatory attendee's account, click the Mail button in the Navigation pane to display the Mail folder, if necessary.

2. If the Discuss Annual Convention message has not arrived, click the Send/Receive button.

3. Click the Discuss Annual Convention message in the message list. The message is displayed in the Preview pane, as shown in Figure 9-7.

Figure 9-7

Meeting invitation received

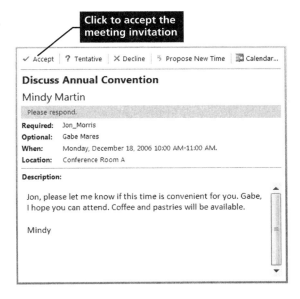

Click to accept the meeting invitation

4. Click the Accept button. A dialog box is displayed that enables you to send your response now, add a comment before sending the response, or choose to not send a response.

5. Click the Send the response now option, if necessary. Click OK. The meeting request is removed from your Inbox, and the meeting is added to your calendar.

PAUSE. CLOSE Outlook to return to your account, if necessary. If someone else responded to the invitation, leave Outlook open to use in the next exercise.

Accepting a meeting request automatically adds the meeting to your calendar, displaying the meeting time as busy. If you tentatively accept the invitation, the time is displayed as tentative in your calendar.

Tracking Responses to a Meeting Request

When an attendee responds to your meeting invitation, you receive a message. If the attendee included comments in the response, the comments are contained in the message. The meeting information stored in your calendar keeps track of the responses. Opening the Meeting window to view a summary of the responses is much more efficient than manually tracking every email you receive.

⊕ TRACK RESPONSES TO A MEETING REQUEST

GET READY. Before you begin these steps, complete the previous exercises. The mandatory attendee used in this exercise must have an active email account that received and responded to your meeting invitation.

1. In your account, click the Mail button in the Navigation pane to display the Mail folder, if necessary.

2. If the Accepted: Discuss Annual Convention message has not arrived, click the Send/Receive button.

3. Click the Accepted: Discuss Annual Convention message in the message list. The message is displayed in the Preview pane, as shown in Figure 9-8.

Figure 9-8

Message accepting the
meeting invitation

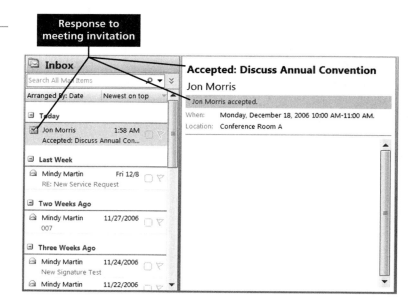

4. Click the Calendar button in the Navigation pane to display the Calendar folder. Click the Month button to display the Month view, if necessary.

5. Navigate to and double-click the Discuss Annual Convention meeting item on the calendar. The Discuss Annual Conference – Meeting window is displayed, as shown in Figure 9-9. The InfoBar contains a summary of the responses received.

Figure 9-9

Summary of responses received

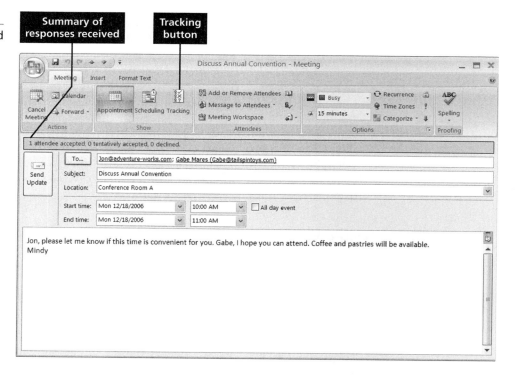

6. Click the Tracking button. Detailed tracking information is displayed, as shown in Figure 9-10. You can see at a glance which attendees have responded.

Figure 9-10

Details about responses
received

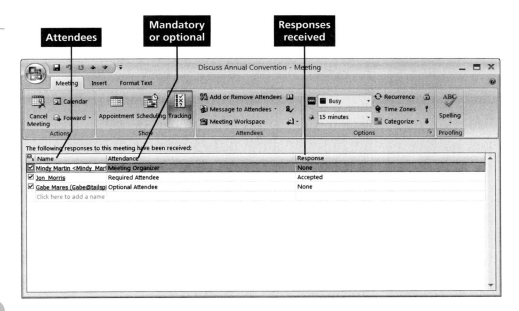

CERTIFICATION READY?
How do you track responses
to meeting requests?
2.2.4

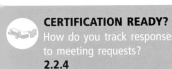

7. Close the Meeting window without saving changes.

   PAUSE. LEAVE Outlook open to use in the next exercise.

In the previous exercise, you received a response to the meeting invitations you sent earlier.
Tracking responses is a simple task, regardless of the number of attendees invited.

■ Modifying a Meeting

THE BOTTOM LINE

When you are trying to get a group of people to sit at the same table at the same time,
problems can emerge. One person will go out of town on an emergency business trip.
Another person has to attend a meeting with a higher priority. Necessary audio-visual
equipment is shipped to a trade show. The list of potential problems is endless.
Modifying a meeting and updating the attendees is a simple task in Outlook.

Changing a Meeting Time

The most common modifications to a meeting are changing the time and the location
of a meeting. In Outlook, you can modify the meeting information and then send an
update to all attendees.

⊕ CHANGE A MEETING TIME

GET READY. Before you begin these steps, complete the previous exercises. The mandatory
attendee used in this exercise must have an active email account and be able to respond to
your message.

1. In your account, click the Calendar button in the Navigation pane to display the
   Calendar folder. Click the Month button to display the Month view, if necessary.
2. Double-click the Discuss Annual Convention meeting item on the calendar. The
   Discuss Annual Conference – Meeting window is displayed, as shown in Figure 9-9.
3. Click the Start time field. Key or select 10:30 AM. Press Enter. The *End time*
   field automatically changes to 11:30 AM.

182 | Lesson 9

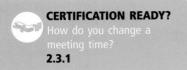

CERTIFICATION READY?
How do you change a meeting time?
2.3.1

4. Click the Send Update button below the InfoBar to send the modified information to the attendees.

PAUSE. CLOSE Outlook to access the mandatory attendee's account, if necessary. If someone else is responding to the invitation, leave Outlook open to use in the next exercise.

In the previous exercise, you modified the meeting time and sent an update to the attendees. Because this is a change to the meeting time, attendees will need to respond to the meeting invitation again.

Proposing a New Meeting Time

Meeting times are set by the ***meeting organizer***, the person who creates the meeting and sends meeting invitations. When a meeting invitation is received, the attendee can suggest a different time for the meeting that better fits the attendees' schedule.

⊖ PROPOSE A NEW MEETING TIME

GET READY. Before you begin these steps, launch Microsoft Outlook, if necessary. Complete the previous exercises. To complete this exercise, you must have access to the email account that received the invitation for the mandatory attendee. If you do not have access to the email account, the account owner should propose a new time when responding to the updated meeting invitation.

1. In the mandatory attendee's account, click the Mail button in the Navigation pane to display the Mail folder, if necessary.

2. If the Discuss Annual Convention message has not arrived, click the Send/Receive button.

3. Click the Discuss Annual Convention message in the message list. The message is displayed in the Preview pane, as shown in Figure 9-11.

Figure 9-11

Updated meeting invitation received

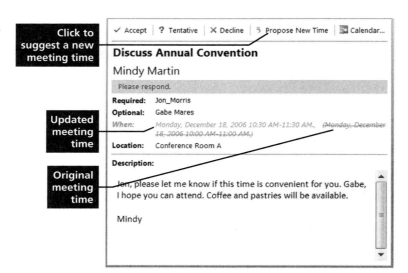

4. Click the Propose New Time button at the top of the message. The Propose New Time window is displayed, as shown in Figure 9-12.

Figure 9-12

Propose New Time window

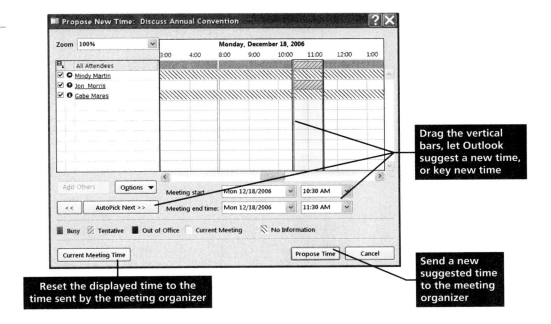

Drag the vertical bars, let Outlook suggest a new time, or key new time

Send a new suggested time to the meeting organizer

Reset the displayed time to the time sent by the meeting organizer

5. Verify that 10:30 is in the *Start time* field. Click the End time field. Key 12:00 PM. Click the Propose Time button. A Message window is displayed.

6. In the message area, key the following message. Let's add 30 minutes and conclude the meeting by offering a sampling of foods available for the convention luncheon. Press Enter. Jon

7. Compare your message to Figure 9-13 and click the Send button.

PAUSE. CLOSE Outlook to return to your account, if necessary. If someone else responded to the invitation, leave Outlook open to use in the next exercise.

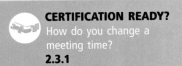

CERTIFICATION READY?
How do you change a meeting time?
2.3.1

The meeting organizer and the attendees might evaluate several different meeting times. If you share your calendar, you can prevent some message exchanges regarding meeting times by keeping your free and busy times up-to-date in your calendar. In the previous exercise, offering food samples is a good reason to extend the meeting time.

Accepting a Proposed New Meeting Time

The meeting organizer has the final word on setting the meeting time. When an attendee proposes a new meeting time, the meeting organizer must evaluate the proposed time and accept or decline the proposal.

ACCEPT A PROPOSED NEW MEETING TIME

GET READY. Before you begin these steps, complete the previous exercises. The mandatory attendee used in this exercise must have an active email account that received and responded to your meeting invitation.

Figure 9-13

New Time Proposed message

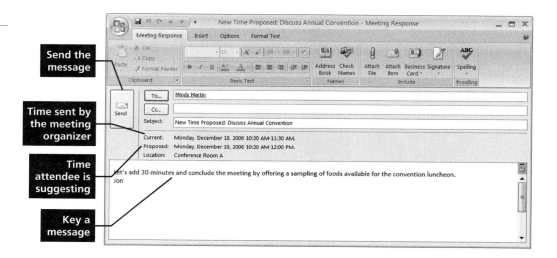

1. In your account, click the Mail button in the Navigation pane to display the Mail folder, if necessary.

2. If the New Time Proposed: Discuss Annual Convention message has not arrived, click the Send/Receive button.

3. Click the New Time Proposed: Discuss Annual Convention message in the message list. The message is displayed in the Reading pane, as shown in Figure 9-14.

Figure 9-14

Message from attendee proposing the new time

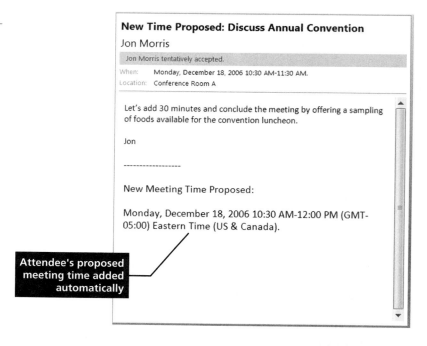

4. Click the Calendar button in the Navigation pane to display the Calendar folder. Click the Month button to display the Month view, if necessary.

5. Double-click the Discuss Annual Convention meeting item on the calendar. The Discuss Annual Conference – Meeting window is displayed, as shown in Figure 9-9. The InfoBar contains a summary of the responses received. Jon's previous acceptance has been changed to a tentative acceptance because he proposed a new time for the meeting.

6. Click the Scheduling button. Click Accept Proposal. Click Send Update.
PAUSE. LEAVE Outlook open to use in the next exercise.

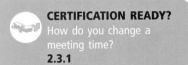

TROUBLESHOOTING

If the proposed time or the Accept Proposal button is not displayed, you can manually change the start and end time of the meeting and click Send to send the update to the attendees.

CERTIFICATION READY?
How do you change a meeting time?
2.3.1

In the previous exercise, you accepted a new meeting time proposed by an attendee. Anyone invited to the meeting can suggest a new date and time for the meeting. Only the meeting organizer can accept or decline the suggested time and change the meeting time.

When the meeting time is changed and you click the Send Update or Send button, attendees are notified of the new time. They must accept or decline the meeting again, as they did for the initial invitation.

Adding and Updating a New Attendee

When you create a meeting, you select the attendees needed to meet the meeting's objective. When the selected attendees learn about the meeting, they can suggest other individuals who should be invited to the meeting. For example, say that you created a meeting about software issues experienced by a client. You invited the project manager, the lead software developer on the team, and the service representative working with the client. The project manager suggests that you invite the trainer who has been working on-site with the client's equipment. You quickly add an attendee to invite the trainer.

⊕ **ADD AND UPDATE A NEW ATTENDEE**

GET READY. Before you begin these steps, launch Microsoft Outlook, if necessary. Complete the previous exercises.

1. In your account, click the Calendar button in the Navigation pane to display the Calendar folder.
2. Double-click the Discuss Annual Convention meeting item on the calendar. The Discuss Annual Conference – Meeting window is displayed, as shown in Figure 9-9.
3. Click the Add or Remove Attendees button in the Attendees group on the Ribbon. The Select Attendees and Resources: Contacts window is displayed, as shown in Figure 9-3. The mandatory attendee and Gabe Mares are already displayed in the fields.
4. Click the Diane Tibbott contact record and click the Optional button. Click OK to return to the Meeting window.
5. Click the Send Update button. Outlook recognizes that the list of attendees has changed and displays the Send Update to Attendees dialog box shown in Figure 9-15.

Figure 9-15

Send Update to Attendees dialog box

6. Click OK to only send the message to the added attendee. The updated meeting information is sent to Diane Tibbott.

PAUSE. LEAVE Outlook open to use in the next exercise.

CERTIFICATION READY?
How do you add a meeting attendee and send meeting updates only to new attendees?
2.3.2 and 2.3.4

In the previous exercise, you added a new attendee to the meeting and sent the updated meeting information only to Diane, the new attendee. This eliminates sending meeting information to the original attendees. In this example, the amount of information sent is minimal. However, if you had attached documents or other files, the time saved and storage space conserved for every attendee would be more obvious.

■ Managing a Recurring Meeting

THE BOTTOM LINE

A *recurring meeting* is a meeting that occurs at regular intervals. The meeting always has the same attendees, location, and purpose. The interval could be a number of days, weeks, or months. For example, status meetings commonly occur at weekly or monthly intervals.

Creating a Recurring Meeting

The process of creating a recurring meeting is very similar to creating a one-time meeting. The only difference is setting the recurrence pattern.

CREATE A RECURRING MEETING

GET READY. Before you begin these steps, be sure to launch Microsoft Outlook.

1. In your account, click the Calendar button in the Navigation pane to display the Calendar folder. Click the Month button to display the Month view, if necessary.

2. Click next Friday on the monthly calendar.

3. On the Standard toolbar, click the New arrow. Click Meeting Request on the drop-down menu. The Meeting window shown in Figure 9-1 is displayed. By default, the beginning of your workday, 8:00 AM in this example, is in the *Start time* field for the meeting and the time in the *End time* field is 30 minutes after the meeting starts.

4. Click the Subject field and key Project Status. In the Location field, key Dept Room 62.

5. Click the Scheduling button in the Show group on the Ribbon. Scheduling information is displayed.

6. Click the Add Others button and click Add from Address Book. The Select Attendees and Resources: Contacts window is displayed.

7. Press Ctrl while clicking the four Tailspin Toys employees. Click Required. Click OK to return to the Meeting window.

8. Change the *Start time* field to 9:00 AM and change the *End time* field to 10:00 AM, if necessary. The green and red vertical lines move.

9. Click the Recurrence button in the Options group on the Ribbon. The Appointment Recurrence window is displayed, as shown in Figure 9-16.

Figure 9-16

Appointment Recurrence window

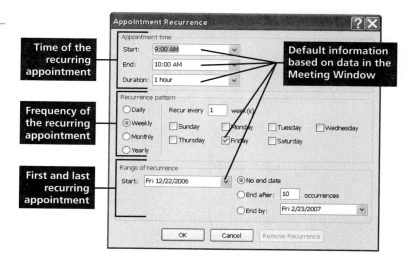

Time of the recurring appointment

Default information based on data in the Meeting Window

Frequency of the recurring appointment

First and last recurring appointment

10. Outlook presents the most likely recurrence pattern when the Appointment Recurrence window is displayed. In this case, the pattern is correct. The Project Status meeting will be held every Friday. Click OK to accept the recurrence pattern and return to the meeting window.

11. Click the Appointment button in the Show group on the Ribbon. The To field is automatically filled with the attendees' email addresses, and the recurrence pattern is displayed.

12. Compare your Meeting window to Figure 9-17. Click the Send button. Your calendar is updated, and the 9:00 AM to 10:00 AM time slot is displayed as busy for every Friday.

Figure 9-17

Meeting request for a recurring meeting

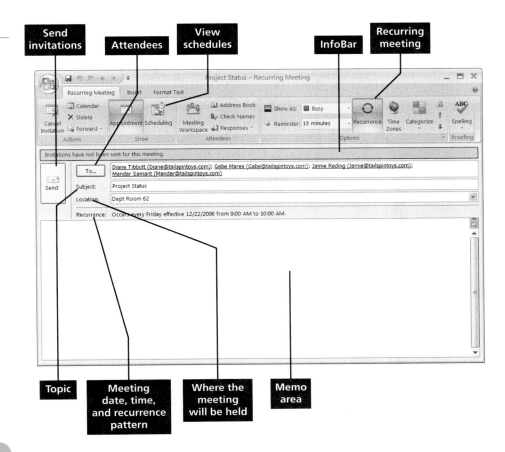

PAUSE. LEAVE Outlook open to use in the next exercise.

CERTIFICATION READY?
How do you create a recurring appointment, meeting, or event?
2.1.2

In the previous exercise, you created a recurring meeting. The attendees will meet every Friday morning to review the status of their active projects.

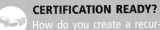

If the location of a meeting is scheduled as a resource and the room is not available for any of the recurrent meetings, you will not be able to schedule the recurrent meeting. You will learn more about scheduling resources later in this lesson.

Changing One Occurrence of a Recurring Meeting

A single meeting in a series of recurring meetings is an ***occurrence***. When a recurring meeting is held regularly for a long period of time, an occurrence will eventually conflict with some other event. You will need to change the time of a single occurrence of the meeting.

⊙ CHANGE ONE OCCURRENCE OF A RECURRING MEETING

GET READY. Before you begin these steps, complete the previous exercise to create the recurring meeting.

1. In your account, click the Calendar button in the Navigation pane to display the Calendar folder. Click the Month button to display the Month view, if necessary.

2. Double-click the second occurrence of the Project Status meeting item on the calendar. The Open Recurring Item dialog box is displayed, as shown in Figure 9-18.

Figure 9-18

Open Recurring Item dialog box

3. Click OK to open the single occurrence. The Project Status – Meeting window is displayed. The meeting information applies to the single occurrence.

4. Click the Start time field. Key or select 10:00 AM and press [Enter]. The *End time* automatically changes to 11:00 AM. Click the Send Update button. In your calendar, the single occurrence is modified to show the new time. The other occurrences are not changed.

PAUSE. LEAVE Outlook open to use in the next exercise.

CERTIFICATION READY?
How do you modify one instance of a recurring meeting?
2.3.3

In the previous exercise, you changed the time of one meeting in a series of recurring meetings. When you changed one occurrence, your calendar was updated and updates were sent to the attendees. You can change the date, time, and location of a single occurrence.

■ Scheduling a Meeting Resource

THE BOTTOM LINE

In Outlook, a ***resource*** is an item or a location that can be invited to a meeting. Resources can include cars, presentation equipment, and conference rooms. You can invite a resource to a meeting just like you invite attendees. A resource has its own mailbox and maintains its own schedule. It accepts invitations for free times and updates its calendar. It declines invitations if the requested time is already scheduled.

⊙ SCHEDULE A MEETING RESOURCE

GET READY. Before you begin these steps, be sure to launch Microsoft Outlook.

TROUBLESHOOTING   Scheduling a resource requires Microsoft Exchange and a resource with a separate mailbox.

1. Click the Calendar button in the Navigation pane to display the Calendar folder. Click the Month button to display the Month view, if necessary. Click next Thursday's date.

2. On the Standard toolbar, click the New arrow. Click Meeting Request on the dropdown menu. The Meeting window shown in Figure 9-1 is displayed.

3. Click the Subject field and key Project Presentation Review. In the Location field, key Dept Room 62.

4. Click the Scheduling button in the Show group on the Ribbon. Scheduling information is displayed.

5. Change the *Start time* field to 9:00 AM and change the *End time* field to 10:00 AM. The green and red vertical lines move.

6. Click the Add Others button and click Add from Address Book. The Select Attendees and Resources: Contacts window is displayed.

7. Click Diane Tibbott and click Required. Click OK to return to the Meeting window.

8. Click the Click here to add a name text in the Meeting window. Key AV01@tailspintoys.com. Press Enter. You are inviting a slide projector to your meeting with Diane.

9. Click the icon next to the keyed address and select Resource (Room or Equipment.) A dialog box will be displayed asking if you want to change the location to AV01. Click No.

10. Click the Appointment button in the Show group on the Ribbon.

11. Compare your Meeting window to Figure 9-19. Click the Send button. Your calendar is updated to display the meeting.

Figure 9-19

Inviting a resource to a meeting

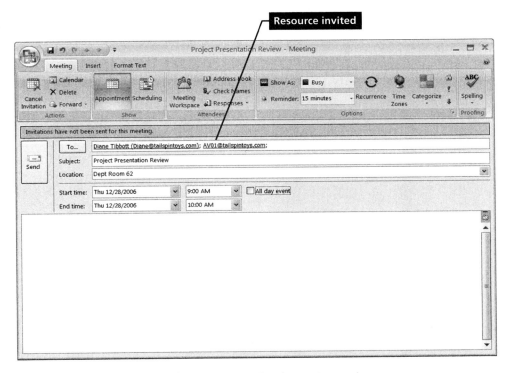

PAUSE. LEAVE Outlook open to use in the next exercise.

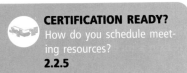

In the previous exercise, you invited AV01, a slide projector, to your meeting with Diane. In the meeting, you plan to review a presentation Diane created, so the equipment is essential to the meeting.

■ Cancelling a Meeting

THE BOTTOM LINE

Regardless of how much planning went into creating a meeting, some meetings are cancelled. When you *cancel* a meeting, it is deleted from your calendar and the attendees are notified. Reasons for cancelling a meeting are varied. For example, mandatory attendees could become unavailable or issues are resolved before the scheduled meeting occurs.

→ CANCEL A MEETING

GET READY. Before you begin these steps, complete the exercises to create the Discuss Annual Convention meeting.

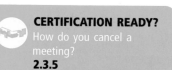 Only the meeting organizer can cancel a meeting.

1. Click the Calendar button in the Navigation pane to display the Calendar folder. Click the Month button to display the Month view, if necessary.
2. Double-click the Discuss Annual Convention meeting item on the calendar. The Discuss Annual Convention – Meeting window is displayed.
3. Click the Cancel Meeting button in the Actions group on the Ribbon.
4. Click the Memo area. Delete any existing text and key the following message. This meeting was cancelled because Jon had an emergency appendectomy earlier today. He is recovering at Mountain View Hospital and we expect him to return to the office next week. We'll reschedule the meeting after he returns. Press Enter. Mindy
5. Compare your Meeting window to Figure 9-20 and click the Send Cancellation button. The message is sent and the meeting is removed from your calendar.

Figure 9-20

Cancelling a meeting

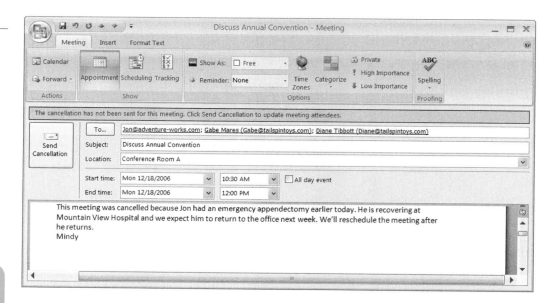

CERTIFICATION READY?
How do you cancel a meeting?
2.3.5

CLOSE Outlook.

In the previous exercise, you cancelled a meeting. A cancellation notice was sent to the attendees. If you need to track cancelled meetings or keep a record of the reason a meeting was cancelled, the cancellation notice is saved in your Sent Items folder.

In the attendee's mailbox, the cancellation notice is automatically assigned a High Importance. The attendee opens the message and clicks the Remove from Calendar button in the Respond group on the Ribbon. The attendee's calendar is updated.

SUMMARY SKILL MATRIX

IN THIS LESSON YOU LEARNED	MATRIX SKILL	SKILL NUMBER
To create a meeting		
To create a meeting that occurs once	Create a one-time appointment, meeting, or event	2.1.1
To invite attendees	Invite mandatory attendees to meetings and Invite optional attendees to meetings	2.2.1 and 2.2.2
To determine the best time for attendees to meet	Determine when attendees are available to meet	2.2.3
To track responses to a meeting request	Track responses to meeting requests	2.2.4
To modify a meeting time, location, or attendees		
To change the time of a meeting	Change a meeting time	2.3.1
To propose a new meeting time	Change a meeting time	2.3.1
To accept a new meeting time proposed by an attendee	Change a meeting time	2.3.1
To add and update a new attendee	Add a meeting attendee and Send meeting updates only to new attendees	2.3.2 and 2.3.4
To create and modify a recurring meeting		
To create a recurring meeting	Create a recurring appointment, meeting, or event	2.1.2
To change one occurrence of a recurring meeting	Modify one instance of a recurring meeting	2.3.3
To schedule meeting resources	Schedule meeting resources	2.2.5
To cancel a meeting	Cancel a meeting	2.3.5

■ Knowledge Assessment

Matching

Match the term with its definition.

a. cancel
b. group schedule
c. mandatory attendee
d. meeting
e. meeting organizer

f. meeting request
g. occurrence
h. optional attendee
i. recurring meeting
j. resource

_____ **1.** A single meeting in a series of recurring meetings

_____ **2.** An item or a location that can be invited to a meeting

_____ **3.** Displays scheduling information for several people

_____ **4.** A meeting that occurs at regular intervals

_a_
_d_
_e_
_h_
_f_
_c_

_____ 5. Delete a meeting

_____ 6. A scheduled activity that requires sending invitations to other people or resources

_____ 7. The person who creates the meeting and sends meeting invitations

_____ 8. A person who should attend the meeting, but whose presence is not required

_____ 9. Outlook item that creates the meeting and invites attendees

_____ 10. A person who must attend the meeting

True/False

Circle T if the statement is true or F if the statement is false.

T **F** 1. Outlook's Meeting window is exactly like the Appointment window.

T **F** 2. Only people or resources in your address book can be invited to a meeting.

T F 3. Every meeting should have at least one mandatory attendee.

T F 4. Your calendar is updated when you send a meeting request.

T **F** 5. When an attendee accepts a meeting request, the attendee's schedule displays the meeting time as tentative.

T F 6. Any attendee can propose a new meeting time.

T F 7. When you add an attendee, you can send updated information to only the new attendee.

T **F** 8. A recurring meeting can occur only 10 times.

T F 9. To be scheduled, a resource must have its own mailbox.

T **F** 10. Any attendee can cancel a meeting.

■ Competency Assessment

Project 9-1: Create a One-Time Meeting

It's time to launch a new project at Tailspin Toys. Gather the team leaders in a meeting to divide the duties.

GET READY. Launch Outlook if it is not already running.

1. Click the Calendar button in the Navigation pane to display the Calendar folder.

2. Click next Thursday's date.

3. On the Standard toolbar, click the New arrow. Click Meeting Request on the dropdown menu. The Meeting window is displayed.

4. Click the Subject field and key Decoder: Project Launch. In the Location field, key Dept Room 62.

5. Click the Scheduling button in the Show group on the Ribbon. Scheduling information is displayed.

6. Click the Add Others button and click Add from Address Book. The Select Attendees and Resources: Contacts window is displayed.

7. Click Jamie Reding's contact information and click the Required button. Click Mandar Samant's contact information and click the Required button. Click OK to return to the Meeting window.

8. Change the current *End time* value so the meeting is one hour long. Click the AutoPick Next button. If necessary, click the AutoPick Next button again or key 10:00 AM in the *Start time* field.

9. Click the Appointment button in the Show group on the Ribbon. The To field is automatically filled with the attendees' email addresses and the *Start time* and *End time* fields are filled.

10. Click the Send button. Your calendar is updated, and the slot is displayed as busy.

   LEAVE Outlook open for the next project.

Project 9-2: **Create a Recurring Meeting**

After the Decoder project is launched, set up a recurring meeting to monitor the project's status.

1. Click the Calendar button in the Navigation pane to display the Calendar folder.

2. Click the Thursday following the Decoder project launch.

3. On the Standard toolbar, click the New arrow. Click Meeting Request on the dropdown menu. The Meeting window is displayed.

4. Click the Subject field and key Decoder: Project Status. In the Location field, key Dept Room 62.

5. Click the Scheduling button in the Show group on the Ribbon. Scheduling information is displayed.

6. Click the Add Others button and click Add from Address Book. The Select Attendees and Resources: Contacts window is displayed.

7. Click Jamie Reding's contact information and click the Required button. Click Mandar Samant's contact information and click the Required button. Click OK to return to the Meeting window.

8. Change the *Start time* field to 10:00 AM and change the *End time* field to 11:00 AM, if necessary. The green and red vertical lines move to enclose the specified time slot.

9. Click the Recurrence button in the Options group on the Ribbon. The Appointment Recurrence window is displayed.

10. Click OK to accept the weekly recurrence pattern and return to the meeting window.

11. Click the Appointment button in the Show group on the Ribbon. The To field is automatically filled with the attendees' email addresses, and the recurrence pattern is displayed.

12. Click the Send button. Your calendar is updated and the 10:00 AM to 11:00 AM time slot is displayed as busy for every Thursday.

   LEAVE Outlook open for the next project.

■ Proficiency Assessment

Project 9-3: **Add an Attendee to a Recurring Meeting**

Diane Tibbott has been assigned to the Decoder project. Add her as an attendee to the recurring Decoder project status meeting.

1. Click the Calendar button in the Navigation pane to display the Calendar folder.

2. Double-click the first Decoder: Project Status meeting. The Open Recurring Item dialog box is displayed.

3. Click the Open the Series option and click OK.

4. Click the Scheduling button in the Show group on the Ribbon. Scheduling information is displayed.

5. Click the Add Others button and click Add from Address Book. The Select Attendees and Resources: Contacts window is displayed.

6. Click Diane Tibbott's contact information and click the Required button. Click OK to return to the Meeting window.

7. Click the Appointment button in the Show group on the Ribbon. Diane Tibbott has been added in the To field.

8. Click the Send Update button. The Send Update to Attendees dialog box is displayed.

9. Click OK. The updated meeting information is sent to Diane Tibbott.

   LEAVE Outlook open for the next project.

Project 9-4: Change the Meeting Time of a Recurring Meeting

Diane is currently assigned to the TopHat project that is coming to a close, and it takes priority over the Decoder project. To be able to participate in both meetings, Diane asked you to hold the Decoder: Project Status meeting later in the day. Change the start time of the recurring status meetings to 1:00 PM.

1. Click the Calendar button in the Navigation pane to display the Calendar folder.

2. Double-click the first Decoder: Project Status meeting. The Open Recurring Item dialog box is displayed.

3. Click the Open the Series option and click OK.

4. Click the Scheduling button in the Show group on the Ribbon. Scheduling information is displayed.

5. Click the Recurrence button in the Options group on the Ribbon. The Appointment Recurrence window is displayed.

6. Key 1:00 PM in the Start field. Verify that 2:00 PM is the time in the End field and click OK.

7. Click the Appointment button in the Show group on the Ribbon. The Recurrence pattern below the location field has been modified.

8. Click the Send Update button.

   LEAVE Outlook open for the next project.

■ Mastery Assessment

Project 9-5: Change an Occurrence of a Recurring Meeting

The TopHat project plans to camp in your meeting room for a week of intensive testing. Change the location of the first Decoder: Project Status meeting.

1. Click the Calendar button in the Navigation pane to display the Calendar folder.

2. Double-click the first Decoder: Project Status meeting. The Open Recurring Item dialog box is displayed.

3. Click OK to open this occurrence of the meeting.

4. Click the Location field. Change the location to Dept Room 50. The room is smaller and less popular as a meeting room due to a peculiar odor that has persisted since the building was purchased.

5. Click the Send Update button.

   LEAVE Outlook open for the next project.

Project 9-6: **Cancel a Meeting**

The upper management at Tailspin Toys has changed. New leadership brings new priorities. The Decoder project has been cancelled. Cancel the Decoder project launch meeting and the recurring project status meeting.

1. Click the Calendar button in the Navigation pane to display the Calendar folder.
2. Double-click the Decoder: Project Launch meeting. The Meeting window is displayed.
3. Click the Cancel Meeting button in the Actions group on the Ribbon.
4. Click the Send Cancellation button.
5. Double-click the first Decoder: Project Status meeting. The Open Recurring Item dialog box is displayed.
6. Click the Open the Series option and click OK.
7. Click the Cancel Meeting button in the Actions group on the Ribbon.
8. Click the Send Cancellation button. If a dialog box is displayed stating that the meeting request contains embedded attachments, click Yes to send the cancellation notice.

   CLOSE Outlook.

INTERNET READY

Your coworkers might not work in your office. Between telecommuting and traveling to client locations, you might find that several attendees do not attend meetings in person. Use the Internet to investigate meeting methods that can be used when all of the attendees are not in the same location.

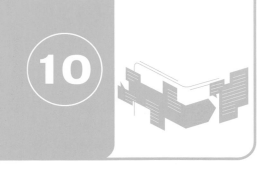

10 Advanced Calendar Management

Mindy is a co-owner of the Adventure Works resort. Mindy and her partner, Jon, work different hours so that an owner is on the premises as much as possible. Their work schedules overlap for several hours a day, and they come into the office for meetings or extra hours on busy days when necessary. Mindy has modified her Outlook calendar to reflect her unusual work schedule.

KEY TERMS
Calendar Snapshot
Greenwich Mean Time
Internet Calendar
  Subscription
overlay mode
overlay stack
side-by-side mode
time zone
work week

196

SOFTWARE ORIENTATION

Microsoft Outlook's Calendar Options Window

Customize the Outlook calendar in the Calendar Options window shown in Figure 10-1.

Figure 10-1

Outlook's Calendar Options window

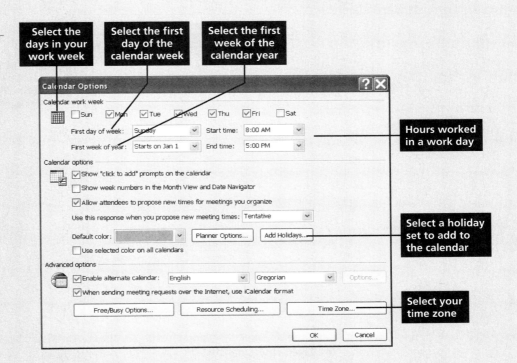

Customize the Outlook calendar to make it fit your needs or work patterns. Use the Calendar Options window to select or modify specific settings.

Customizing Your Calendar

THE BOTTOM LINE

To make your calendar more useful, you can customize it in several ways. Define your work week, display the time zones you use regularly, set your own time zone, and add holidays to the calendar.

Defining Your Work Week

Your **work week** is the hours or days you work in a calendar week. The most common work week is 8:00 AM to 5:00 PM Monday through Friday. Your work week may differ.

⊕ **DEFINE YOUR WORK WEEK**

GET READY. Before you begin these steps, be sure to launch Microsoft Outlook.

TAKE NOTE* It isn't necessary to click the Calendar button to reach the Calendar Options window, but the modifications will be displayed in the Calendar folder.

1. If necessary, click the Calendar button in the Navigation pane to display the Calendar folder.

2. Click the Tools menu, and click Options. The Options window shown in Figure 10-2 is displayed.

Figure 10-2

Options window

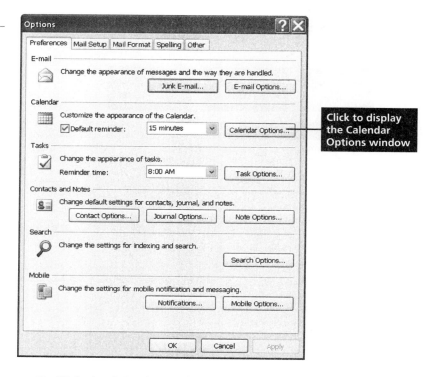

3. Click the Calendar Options button to display the Calendar Options window displayed in Figure 10-1.

4. Select the Sun checkbox to add Sunday to the work week.

5. Click the Wed checkbox to clear the checkbox, removing it from the work week.

6. Click the Start time field. Key or select 6:00 AM. Click the End time field. Key or select 3:00 PM.

7. Compare your Calendar Options window to Figure 10-3. Click OK in the Calendar Options window and the Options window to save the modified work week and return to the Calendar folder.

Figure 10-3

Modified work week

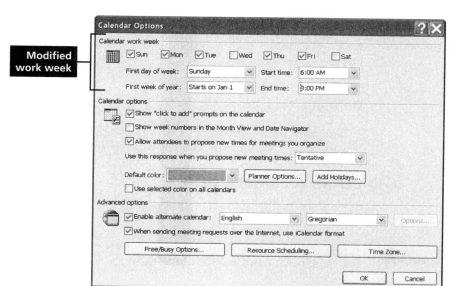

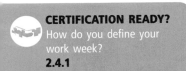

CERTIFICATION READY?
How do you define your work week?
2.4.1

8. Click the Week button, if necessary, to view the modified work week. Note that Sunday is now a workday and Wednesday and Saturday are shaded to indicate that they are not workdays.

   PAUSE. LEAVE Outlook open to use in the next exercise.

In the previous exercise, you changed the work week to reflect Mindy's work schedule. She works Sunday, Monday, Tuesday, Thursday, and Friday from 6:00 AM to 3:00 PM. She does not work Wednesday and Saturday. Outlook accommodates unusual work schedules.

Displaying Multiple Time Zones

A *time zone* is a geographic area using the same standard time. Depending on your business, family, and friends, you could communicate frequently with one or more businesses or individuals in a different time zone. To easily agree on times for meetings and phone calls, display an additional time zone on your calendar.

→ DISPLAY MULTIPLE TIME ZONES

GET READY. Before you begin these steps, be sure to launch Microsoft Outlook.

1. If necessary, click the Calendar button in the Navigation pane to display the Calendar folder.
2. Click the Tools menu, and click Options. The Options window shown in Figure 10-2 is displayed.
3. Click the Calendar Options button to display the Calendar Options window displayed in Figure 10-1.
4. Click the Time Zone button. The Time Zone window is displayed, as shown in Figure 10-4. Note that the fields in the Additional time zone area are dimmed.

Figure 10-4

Time Zone window

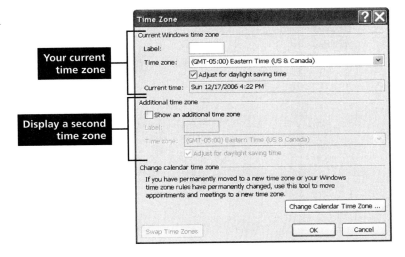

5. Click the Label field in the Current Windows time zone area. Key Current and press [Tab].
6. Click the Show an additional time zone checkbox. The fields in the Additional time zone area become available.
7. Click the Label field in the Additional time zone area. Key CA and press [Tab]. Many of the company's clients are based in California, so it is helpful to display the time in California.

If you are located in the Pacific Time Zone, select a different time zone as your second time zone.

8. In the Time zone field, select (GMT-08:00) Pacific Time (US & Canada); Tijuana. GMT refers to **Greenwich Mean Time**, the time at the Royal Observatory in Greenwich in England. Other time zones are defined by the difference between local time and GMT. Pacific Time is eight hours different from GMT.

9. Click OK in the Time Zone window. Click OK in the Calendar Options window and the Options window to return to the Calendar folder.

Additional time zones are only displayed in Day and Week views. When you schedule meetings, free and busy times for the attendees are adjusted to match your calendar because you are the meeting organizer. When invitations are sent, the meeting time in each meeting request is displayed in each attendee's local time.

10. Click the Week button to display the week, and click the Show work week option above the calendar, if necessary. Your calendar should resemble Figure 10-5. Depending on the exercises completed in other lessons, appointments and meetings will differ.

Figure 10-5

Second time zone displayed

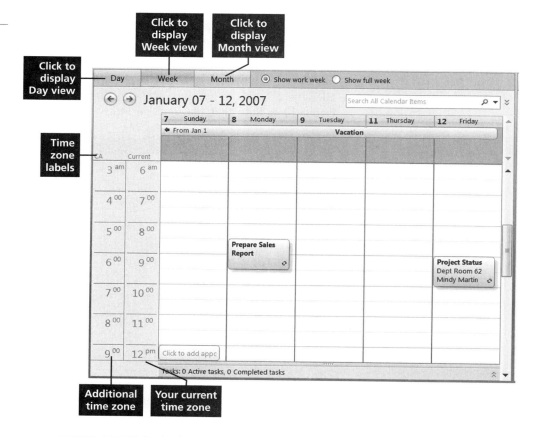

PAUSE. LEAVE Outlook open to use in the next exercise.

In the previous exercise, you displayed an additional time zone. If you frequently work with clients in other states or countries, it can be useful to display other time zones. You don't want to miss talking to an important client by calling after business hours. If you maintain a personal calendar, display your family's or friends' time zone. You won't be the favorite daughter for long if you call when it's 3:00 AM.

Changing Your Time Zone

If you move, transfer to another office, or remain onsite at a client's office for several weeks, you can change the time zone in your calendar. This will help you synchronize with the local time.

→ CHANGE YOUR TIME ZONE

GET READY. Before you begin these steps, be sure to launch Microsoft Outlook.

1. If necessary, click the Calendar button in the Navigation pane to display the Calendar folder.

2. Click the Tools menu, and click Options. The Options window shown in Figure 10-2 is displayed.

3. Click the Calendar Options button to display the Calendar Options window shown in Figure 10-1.

4. Click the Time Zone button. The Time Zone window is displayed, as shown in Figure 10-4.

5. In the Current Windows time zone area, click the Time zone field and select a time zone that differs from your current time zone by several hours.

6. Click OK in the Time Zone window. Click OK in the Calendar Options window and the Options window to return to the Calendar folder.

7. Click the Week button to display the week, if necessary. Examine your calendar. The times of any set appointments and meetings have been adjusted. It's time to return your calendar to its original time zone settings.

8. Click the Tools menu, and click Options. Click the Calendar Options button to display the Calendar Options window.

9. In the Calendar work week, click the appropriate checkboxes to match your work week. Key or select the start time and end time that matche your work schedule.

10. Click the Time Zone button to display the Time Zone window. In the Current Windows time zone area, click the Time zone field and select your current time zone. Click the Label field, select the text, and press Delete.

11. In the Additional time zone area, click the Show an additional time zone checkbox to clear the checkbox.

12. Click OK in the Time Zone window. Click OK in the Calendar Options window and the Options window to return to the Calendar folder. Your calendar should be set to display your work week.

PAUSE. LEAVE Outlook open to use in the next exercise.

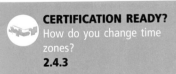

CERTIFICATION READY?
How do you change time zones?
2.4.3

In the previous exercise, you changed your time zone in your calendar. If you frequently travel and stay in a different time zone for any length of time, change the time zone to match the local time. Or, display two time zones. One time zone can match the time zone at your office and one can match the local time.

Adding Holidays to the Calendar

Holidays are classified as all-day events. In your calendar, a holiday is displayed as a banner at the top of the day. When you install Outlook, holidays are not placed on your calendar. Outlook provides standard sets of holidays based on the country. Separate sets of some religious holidays are also available. Select and add the holiday set that you use.

→ ADD HOLIDAYS TO THE CALENDAR

GET READY. Before you begin these steps, be sure to launch Microsoft Outlook.

TROUBLESHOOTING Do not add the same set of holidays more than once. If you add the same holiday set again, another set of identical holiday banners will be added to your calendar.

1. If necessary, click the Calendar button in the Navigation pane to display the Calendar folder.
2. Click the Tools menu, and click Options. The Options window shown in Figure 10-2 is displayed.
3. Click the Calendar Options button to display the Calendar Options window displayed in Figure 10-1.
4. Click the Add Holidays button. The Add Holidays to Calendar window is displayed, as shown in Figure 10-6. By default, your country or region is already selected.

Figure 10-6

Add Holidays to Calendar window

5. Click the checkbox for your country, if necessary. Click OK in the Add Holidays to Calendar window. A small window is displayed while the holidays are added to your calendar. When the holidays are added, a message is displayed telling you that the holidays were added. Click OK.
6. Click OK in the Calendar Options window and the Options window to return to the Calendar folder.
7. Click the Month button to display the Month view. If necessary, click the Forward or Back button to view a month containing a holiday. Click the Forward or Back button to return to the current month.

PAUSE. LEAVE Outlook open to use in the next exercise.

CERTIFICATION READY?
How do you add predefined holidays to the calendar?
2.4.4

In the previous exercise, you added holidays based on your country. Select another standard holiday set to add another set of holidays based on a different country or religion. Do not add the same holiday set more than once.

■ Sharing Your Calendar

THE BOTTOM LINE

When you work with others, sharing your schedule makes it easier to arrange meetings, determine deadlines, and set realistic goals. Regardless of the type of email account you use, you can share your calendar with others. You can share calendar information through a company server using Microsoft Exchange or share your calendar using the Internet.

Configuring Your Free/Busy Settings

You can find more information on creating meetings in Lesson 9.

When you create a meeting request, it is helpful to know when the meeting attendees are free to attend the meeting or are busy with other tasks. For a meeting organizer to see free/busy information, the attendees must place the information where it can be accessed.

⊖ CONFIGURE YOUR FREE/BUSY SETTINGS

GET READY. Before you begin these steps, be sure to launch Microsoft Outlook. To publish your free/busy information, you must be connected to the server that will store the data.

 If your company uses Microsoft Exchange software, free/busy times are automatically shared with others on your network. This process is not needed.

TROUBLE**SHOOTING** The system administrator for the server must set up the site, create the folder, and grant permission for you to write to the folder.

1. If necessary, click the Calendar button in the Navigation pane to display the Calendar folder.
2. Click the Tools menu, and click Options. The Options window shown in Figure 10-2 is displayed.
3. Click the Calendar Options button to display the Calendar Options window displayed in Figure 10-1.
4. Click the Free/Busy Options button. The Free/Busy Options window is displayed, as shown in Figure 10-7. By default, two months of free/busy time is already selected.

Figure 10-7

Free/Busy Options window

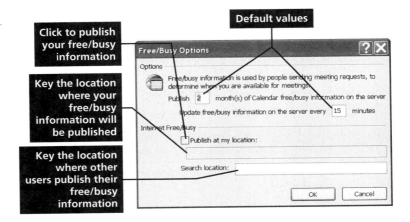

5. Select the Publish at my location checkbox. In the field below the checkbox, key the location where your free/busy information will be published. The system administrator will provide the exact location, but the keyed location should end with a .vbf extension, for example, *schedulename*.vbf.
6. Click the Search location field and key the location where other users publish their free/busy information. The system administrator will provide the exact location, but the keyed location will be similar to the location storing your information. Click OK.
7. Click OK in the Calendar Options window and the Options window to return to the Calendar folder.
   PAUSE. LEAVE Outlook open to use in the next exercise.

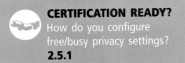

CERTIFICATION READY?
How do you configure free/busy privacy settings?
2.5.1

In the previous exercise, you used information obtained from the system administrator to publish your free/busy information and access the free/busy information published by other network users. Although your system administrator will supply the exact location, the location should resemble the following text if you use ftp to access the information.

ftp://*youruseraccount*:*yourpassword*@ftp.*servername*.com/*foldername*/*yourname*.vbf

For example, Mindy Martin keyed the following location.

ftp://Mindy_Martin:Ax75wN@ftp.adventure-works.com/scheduling/mindy.vbf

When you create or modify a contact record, you can store the location of the contact's free/busy information. Open the contact record. Click the Details button in the Show group on the Ribbon. Below the Internet Free-Busy heading, click the Address field and key the location. Click the Save & Close button on the Ribbon.

Sharing Your Calendar with Other Network Users

In the Calendar folder, the Navigation pane displays links that provide several ways to share your calendar with others. The displayed links are based on the type of accounts you have configured. For example, if you have an account that uses Microsoft Exchange server, the Open a Shared Calendar and the Share a Calendar links are displayed. If you use only a POP3 account, those two links will not be displayed.

⊕ SHARE YOUR CALENDAR WITH OTHER NETWORK USERS

GET READY. Before you begin these steps, be sure to launch Microsoft Outlook. This exercise requires a Microsoft Exchange account.

TROUBLESHOOTING If the Share My Calendar link is not displayed in the Navigation pane when you view the Calendar folder, you do not have a Microsoft Exchange account configured. If this is the case, you cannot complete this exercise.

1. If necessary, click the Calendar button in the Navigation pane to display the Calendar folder.
2. Click the Share My Calendar link.
3. Click the To field. Key the name of the individual who will view your calendar.
4. Click the Subject field. Key Share my calendar.
5. Click the message body. Key Share my calendar.
6. Click the Send button. A dialog box is displayed. Click OK to confirm the information.

    PAUSE. LEAVE Outlook open to use in the next exercise.

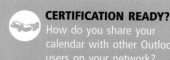

CERTIFICATION READY?
How do you share your calendar with other Outlook users on your network?
2.5.2

In the previous exercise, you granted permission for a specific individual to view your calendar. If you click the *Request permission to view recipient's Calendar* checkbox, the recipient can also grant permission for you to view the recipient's calendar.

Sending Calendar Information via Email

The Send a Calendar via E-mail link is displayed in the Navigation pane for Microsoft Exchange accounts and POP3 accounts. Click this link to send a snapshot of your calendar to anyone with an email account. A ***Calendar Snapshot*** is a picture of your calendar at a specific moment. A Calendar Snapshot cannot be updated or modified. As a new feature in Outlook 2007, you can specify the detail level displayed in the Calendars Snapshot.

⊕ SEND CALENDAR INFORMATION VIA EMAIL

GET READY. Before you begin these steps, be sure to launch Microsoft Outlook.

1. If necessary, click the Calendar button in the Navigation pane to display the Calendar folder.

2. Click the Send a Calendar via E-mail link in the Navigation pane. The Send a Calendar via E-mail window is displayed, as shown in Figure 10-8. A Message window is opened behind the Send a Calendar via E-mail window.

Figure 10-8

Send a Calendar via E-mail window

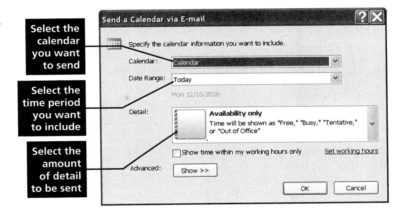

3. In the Detail field, select Limited details.

4. Click OK. If an alert box is displayed informing you that no appointments are scheduled for the date, click the Continue button. Today's calendar information is displayed in the message body and attached to the message. Outlook 2007 recipients will be able to view the attached file as an Outlook calendar.

TROUBLESHOOTING

The email addresses provided in these exercises belong to unused domains owned by Microsoft. When you send a message to these addresses, you will receive an error message stating that the message could not be delivered. Delete the error messages when they arrive.

5. In the To field, key Gabe@tailspintoys.com.

6. Compare your message to Figure 10-9. Scroll down the message body if necessary to view the data in the message. Click Send.

Figure 10-9

Sending a Calendar Snapshot

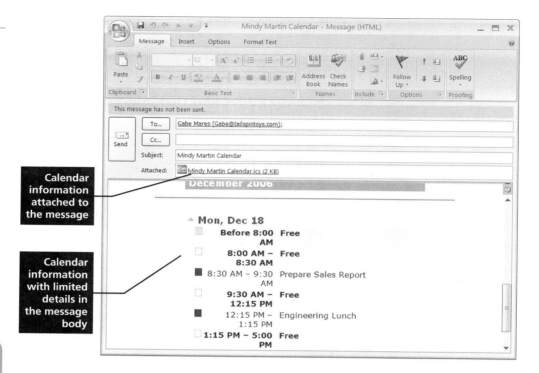

Calendar information attached to the message

Calendar information with limited details in the message body

CERTIFICATION READY?
How do you send calendar information in an email message?
2.5.3

PAUSE. LEAVE Outlook open to use in the next exercise.

In the previous exercise, you created a Calendar Snapshot and sent it to a recipient. In Outlook 2007, you can choose the level of detail to include, as shown in Table 10-1.

Table 10-1

DETAIL LEVEL	DESCRIPTION
Availability only	Time is displayed as free, busy, tentative, or out of office. This is enough information for scheduling purposes.
Limited details	The Calendar Snapshot includes availability information and the subjects of the calendar items.
Full details	The Calendar Snapshot includes availability information and all the details of the calendar items.

Publishing Calendar Information to Office Online

If you do not have a server running Microsoft Exchange or any server that can be used to share your calendar, Microsoft provides a solution. You can publish your calendar to Microsoft Office Online. You can control the amount of calendar information published and limit the number of people who can view your calendar.

⊕ PUBLISH CALENDAR INFORMATION TO OFFICE ONLINE

GET READY. Before you begin these steps, be sure to launch Microsoft Outlook.

1. If necessary, click the Calendar button in the Navigation pane to display the Calendar folder.

2. Click the Publish My Calendar link in the Navigation pane. If a dialog box is displayed informing you that you will view pages over a secure connection, click OK. The Microsoft Office Online Registration window is displayed, as shown in Figure 10-10.

Figure 10-10

Microsoft Office Online Registration window

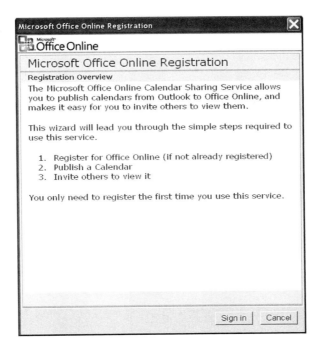

3. Click Sign in. If you have a Windows Live ID, your email address will be displayed below the Sign in to Office Online heading.

TROUBLESHOOTING

If you do not have a Windows Live ID, click the *sign up for a free account* link in the Microsoft Office Online Registration window. Follow the instructions to obtain a Windows Live ID and go back to step 1 in this exercise.

4. Click the Password field and key your password, if necessary. Click the Sign In button. A legal agreement is displayed. Key your email address in the field and click the I Accept button.

TAKE NOTE*

Use caution when you choose a display name. Other users will see this name. Be conservative if you are using Office Online as a business tool.

5. Under User Profile, click the Display Name field and key the name you want to display when you post information. Click the Next button. When your display name is accepted, click the Finish button. The Publish Calendar to Microsoft Office Online window is displayed, as shown in Figure 10-11.

Figure 10-11

Publish Calendar to Microsoft
Office Online window

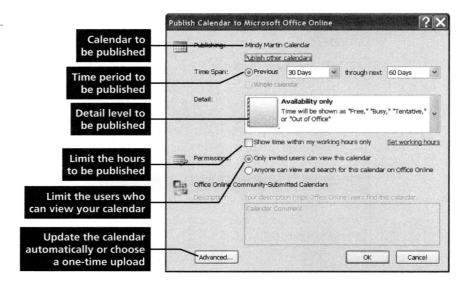

6. Click the Advanced field. The Published Calendar Settings window is displayed, as shown in Figure 10-12.

Figure 10-12

Published Calendar
Settings window

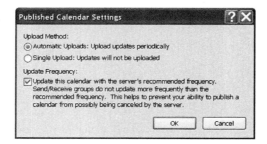

> **TAKE NOTE***
>
> If you plan to publish your calendar to Office Online to keep others aware of your schedule, you can choose to automatically upload your calendar. For this exercise, it is not necessary to keep the calendar updated.

7. Select the Single Upload: Updates will not be uploaded option. Click OK to close the Published Calendar Settings window.

8. Click OK to publish your calendar. Key your password again, if necessary. When the upload is complete, the Send a Sharing Invitation window is displayed, as shown in Figure 10-13.

Figure 10-13

Send a Sharing
Invitation window

9. Click Yes. A Share window resembling a Message window is displayed, as shown in Figure 10-14.

Figure 10-14

Share window

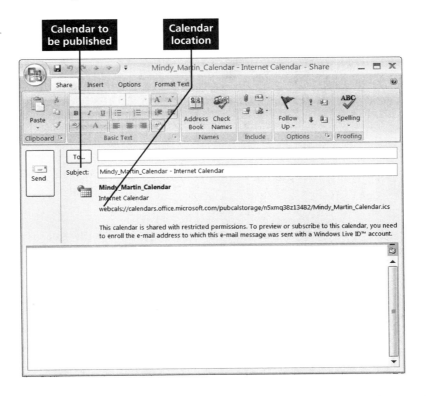

10. In the To field, key your email address. Click the Send button. The invitation is sent.

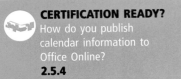 TAKE NOTE* To view your calendar, the invited individual must obtain a Windows Live ID.

PAUSE. LEAVE Outlook open to use in the next exercise.

 CERTIFICATION READY?
How do you publish calendar information to Office Online?
2.5.4

In the previous exercise, you published your calendar to Microsoft Office Online and invited another person to view your scheduling information. Office Online is an alternative location for publishing your calendar if you do not have a company server or you want to share calendar information with people who are not members of your company. In your personal life, you can use Office Online to publish a schedule for the soccer team you coach.

■ Viewing Other Users' Calendars

↓ **THE BOTTOM LINE** In the previous section, you learned several ways to share your calendar with others. Now, you will learn how to view other users' calendars. These methods are also used by others who want to view your calendar.

Viewing Another Network User's Calendar

If a person on your Microsoft Exchange network shares a calendar, you can view the user's calendar. To view the calendar the first time, the user must grant permission. After permission is granted and you access the shared calendar, a link to the shared calendar is added to the Calendar folder's Navigation pane.

→ VIEW ANOTHER NETWORK USER'S CALENDAR

GET READY. Before you begin these steps, be sure to launch Microsoft Outlook. This exercise requires a Microsoft Exchange account.

> **TROUBLESHOOTING** If you do not have a Microsoft Exchange account configured, you cannot complete this exercise.

CERTIFICATION READY?
How do you view a calendar shared by another Outlook user on your network?
2.6.1

1. If necessary, click the Calendar button in the Navigation pane to display the Calendar folder.
2. Click the Open a Shared Calendar link in the Navigation pane. The Open a Shared Calendar window is displayed.
3. Click the Name field. Key the calendar owner's name. Click OK. The shared calendar is displayed next to your calendar.

    PAUSE. LEAVE Outlook open to use in the next exercise.

In the previous exercise, you viewed a shared calendar. If you do not have permission to view the calendar, Outlook will prompt you to request permission. If you agree to request permission, a sharing request addressed to the user is displayed. Send the request to obtain permission to view the calendar.

Subscribing to an Internet Calendar

An *Internet Calendar Subscription* is a downloaded calendar that is automatically updated. When you published your calendar to Office Online in a previous exercise, you sent a message inviting another user to view your published calendar. In this exercise, you use an invitation to subscribe to an Internet calendar.

→ SUBSCRIBE TO AN INTERNET CALENDAR

GET READY. Before you begin these steps, be sure to launch Microsoft Outlook. This exercise requires Internet access. To perform this exercise, complete the previous Publish Calendar Information to Office Online exercise

1. If necessary, click the Mail button in the Navigation pane to display the Mail folder.
2. In the Inbox, double-click the Share message to open it. The message's exact subject depends on the name of the calendar you are invited to share. The message is opened, as shown in Figure 10-15.

Figure 10-15

Open Share message

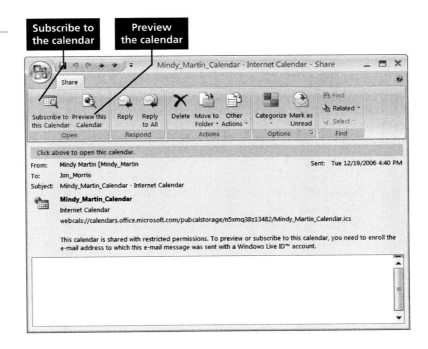

Figure 10-15

Open Share message

3. Click the Subscribe to this Calendar button in the Open group on the Ribbon. A small dialog box is displayed asking if you want to add the calendar to Outlook and subscribe to updates.

4. Click Yes. A Sign In dialog box is displayed. Key your sign in name and password. Click OK. The calendar is downloaded and displayed next to your calendar. The name of the shared calendar is added to the Navigation pane.

5. Click the Week button above the calendar, as shown in Figure 10-16.

Figure 10-16

Downloaded calendar

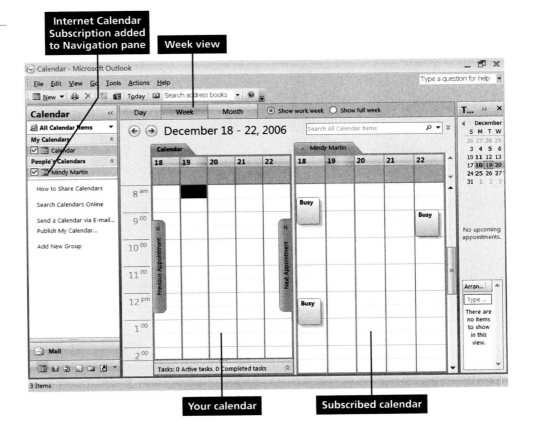

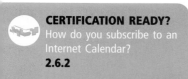

CERTIFICATION READY?
How do you subscribe to an Internet Calendar?
2.6.2

6. **CLOSE** the Share message.

   PAUSE. LEAVE Outlook open to use in the next exercise.

In the previous exercise, you received an invitation to subscribe to a calendar published at Microsoft Office Online. If you don't have an invitation, you can search Web sites that host Internet calendars, such as Microsoft Office Online.

Using Overlay Mode to View Multiple Calendars

You can view more than one calendar at a time. They could be coworkers' calendars, a separate personal calendar, or Internet Calendar Subscriptions. You can view calendars in *side-by-side mode*, displaying the calendars next to each other, as shown in Figure 10-16. Or you can use Outlook's new *overlay mode* to display calendars on top of each other. This enables you to find free time that is common to all the displayed calendars. Several calendars displayed in overlay mode are considered to be an *overlay stack*.

➔ USE OVERLAY MODE TO VIEW MULTIPLE CALENDARS

USE the calendar downloaded in the previous exercise.

1. Click the **View in Overlay Mode** toggle button on the tab next to the calendar name of the calendar on the right. The calendars will be displayed in an overlay stack, as shown in Figure 10-17.

Figure 10-17

Calendars displayed in overlay mode

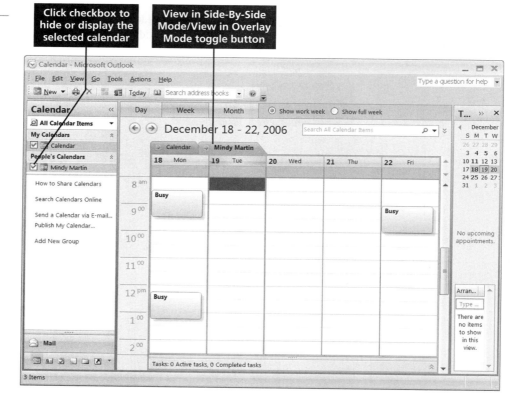

2. Click the **View in Side-By-Side Mode** toggle button on the tab next to the calendar name of the calendar on the right. The calendars will be displayed next to each other.

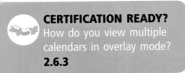

CERTIFICATION READY?
How do you view multiple calendars in overlay mode?
2.6.3

3. Click the checkbox next to the calendar's name in the Navigation pane to clear the checkbox. The second calendar is closed.

   PAUSE. LEAVE Outlook open to use in the next exercise.

In the previous exercise, you used the new overlay mode to display calendars. Use this feature when looking for common free time for several calendars. You can also use this feature to coordinate activities on several calendars.

■ Configuring Outlook to be Accessible Through the Web

THE BOTTOM LINE   Outlook Anywhere allows you to connect to your Microsoft Exchange server from outside your network. You can use a remote procedure call (RPC) to access your Microsoft Exchange account from anywhere through the Internet.

 CONFIGURE OUTLOOK TO BE ACCESSIBLE THROUGH THE WEB

GET READY. Before you begin these steps, be sure to launch Microsoft Outlook. This exercise requires a Microsoft Exchange account.

TROUBLESHOOTING   This exercise requires a Microsoft Exchange account, some setup by your system administrator, and information provided by your system administrator.

1. Click the Calendar button in the Navigation pane to display the Calendar folder, if necessary.
2. Click the Tools menu, and then click Account Settings. The Account Settings window is displayed.
3. Click More Settings. Click the Connection tab.
4. Under the Outlook Anywhere heading, select the Connect to Microsoft Exchange using HTTP checkbox.
5. Click the Exchange Proxy Settings button.
6. Key the URL provided by your system administrator to connect to your proxy server.
7. Select the Connect using SSL only checkbox, if necessary. This option increases security.
8. Select the Only connect to proxy servers that have this principal name in their certificate checkbox, if necessary. If this option is selected, key msstd: and the URL provided by your system administrator.
9. Under the Proxy authentication settings heading, select Basic Authentication or NTLM Authentication as specified by your system administrator. NTML authentication provides more security.
10. Accept the modifications you made and return to the main Outlook window.

    CLOSE Outlook.

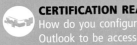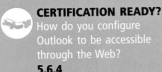

CERTIFICATION READY?
How do you configure Outlook to be accessible through the Web?
5.6.4

In the previous exercise, you configured Outlook to access your Microsoft Exchange account from anywhere through the Internet. To do so, your system must meet the following requirements:

- Your computer must use Microsoft Windows XP Service Pack 2 or better.
- The server must use Microsoft Exchange Server 2003 or Microsoft Exchange 2007 running on Microsoft Windows Server 2003.

- Your system administrator must configure the server to accept connections through HTTP.

Before starting this process, you need several pieces of information from your system administrator:

- What is the URL to connect to my proxy server for Microsoft Exchange?
- Does the server require a Secure Sockets Layer (SSL) connection?
- Should I select the option to *only connect to proxy servers that have this principal name in their certificate*? If so, what is the principal name?
- Under proxy authentication settings, should I select Basic Authentication or NTLM Authentication?

SUMMARY SKILL MATRIX

IN THIS LESSON YOU LEARNED	MATRIX SKILL	SKILL NUMBER
To make your calendar more useful by customizing your work week, time zone information, and holidays		
To define the days shown when your work week is displayed	Define your work week	2.4.1
To display the time in an additional time zone that you communicate with frequently	Display multiple time zones	2.4.2
To change your current time zone in your calendar	Change time zones	2.4.3
To display a predefined set of holidays that affect your scheduling	Add predefined holidays to the calendar	2.4.4
To share your calendar with other Outlook users through your network or the Internet		
To manage the way that your free and busy times are displayed	Configure free/busy privacy settings	2.5.1
To share your calendar with other users on a network using Microsoft Exchange	Share your calendar with other Outlook users on your network	2.5.2
To share your calendar information by sending a Calendar Snapshot in a message	Send calendar information in an email message	2.5.3
To share your calendar by publishing it to Office Online	Publish calendar information to Office Online	2.5.4
To view other users' calendars through your network or the Internet		
To view other users' calendars on a network using Microsoft Exchange	View a calendar shared by another Outlook user on your network	2.6.1
To view other users' calendars that have been published to the Internet	Subscribe to an Internet Calendar	2.6.2
To view other users' calendars in overlay or side-by-side mode	View multiple calendars in overlay mode	2.6.3
To configure Outlook to be accessible through RPC over HTTP	Configure Outlook to be accessible through the Web	5.6.4

■ Knowledge Assessment

Fill in the Blank

Complete the following sentences by writing the correct word or words in the blanks provided.

Holidays
workweek
Internet calendar subscription
timezone
overlay mode
shared Internet calendar snapshot
side-by-side
Greenwich meantime
overlay stack

1. Many people do not work on _____.
2. A common _____ is Monday through Friday.
3. A downloaded calendar that is automatically updated is a(n) _____.
4. Your _____ is based on your location.
5. _____ mode displays calendars on top of each other.
6. A(n) _____ calendar is stored on the World Wide Web.
7. To share scheduling information, send a(n) _____ in a message.
8. In _____ mode, calendars are displayed next to each other.
9. The current time at the Royal Observatory in England is _____.
10. Several calendars displayed in overlay mode are known as a(n) _____.

Multiple Choice

Circle the correct choice.

1. What is the most common work week?
   A. Sunday through Saturday
   B. Saturday and Sunday
   C. Monday through Saturday
   D. Monday through Friday

2. Which feature enables a Microsoft Exchange account user to connect to the account through the Internet?
   A. Outlook Anywhere
   B. Internet Calendar Subscription
   C. Time zones
   D. Overlay mode

3. Your time zone is determined by your distance from
   A. the North Pole.
   B. Greenwich.
   C. Boston.
   D. the Pacific Ocean.

4. In Outlook, holidays are classified as
   A. weekends.
   B. appointments.
   C. all-day events.
   D. vacations.

5. What is automatically shared with other users on a Microsoft Exchange server?
   A. Free/busy times
   B. Email
   C. Internet Calendar Subscriptions
   D. Holiday sets

D

A

 B

 C

A

B

6. Where is the best place to store the location of another person's free/busy Internet address?

   A. In your calendar

   B. In a contact record

   C. In a note

   D. In your Inbox

D

7. What does another user on your network need to view your calendar?

   A. Your email address

   B. A POP3 account

   C. Your IP address

   D. Your permission

A

8. When you share your calendar, how much detail is needed for scheduling purposes?

   A. Availability only

   B. Limited details

   C. Full details

   D. Complete calendar

D

9. What site does Microsoft offer for publishing Internet calendars?

   A. Microsoft Internet Calendars (MIC)

   B. Microsoft Fun Calendars

   C. Microsoft My Calendar

   D. Microsoft Office Online

B

10. What is an advantage of subscribing to an Internet Calendar?

   A. Internet Calendars are fun.

   B. Internet Calendars are automatically updated.

   C. Internet Calendars always contain useful information.

   D. All of the above

■ Competency Assessment

Project 10-1: Define a Work Week

Sharon Salavaria works at a trendy restaurant in downtown Boston. The restaurant is so chic that it opens at 4:00 PM, stays open for late diners, and closes at 11:00 PM. This fashionable restaurant earned a culinary award for its fine cuisine—on the four days a week that it is open. Not surprisingly, it is difficult to get a table during its limited hours. Modify your calendar to match Sharon's work week.

GET READY. Launch Outlook if it is not already running.

1. If necessary, click the Calendar button in the Navigation pane to display the Calendar folder.

2. Click the Tools menu, and click Options. The Options window is displayed.

3. Click the Calendar Options button to display the Calendar Options window.

4. Select the Sun checkbox to add Sunday to the work week.

5. Click the Thu and Fri checkboxes to clear the checkboxes, removing them from the work week. The restaurant is open Sunday through Wednesday only.

6. Click the Start time field. Key or select 3:00 PM. Click the End time field. Key or select 11:00 PM.

7. Click OK in the Calendar Options window and the Options window to save the modified work week and return to the Calendar folder.

   LEAVE Outlook open for the next project.

Project 10-2: **Change Your Time Zone**

Arthur Yasinki has been the top salesperson at his company for the last six years. His record is amazing because he lives in Florida, but his two biggest clients are located in London and San Francisco. He displays San Francisco as his current time zone and London as his additional time zone. You'll set up the additional time zone in the next project. In this project, change your current time zone to match San Francisco's time zone. If you live in the Pacific time zone, change your current time zone to the Central time zone.

1. If necessary, click the Calendar button in the Navigation pane to display the Calendar folder.
2. Click the Tools menu, and click Options. The Options window is displayed.
3. Click the Calendar Options button to display the Calendar Options window.
4. Click the Time Zone button. The Time Zone window is displayed.
5. In the Current Windows time zone area, click the Time zone field and select (GMT-08:00) Pacific Time (US & Canada); Tijuana.
6. Click OK in the Time Zone window. Click OK in the Calendar Options window and the Options window to return to the Calendar folder.

   LEAVE Outlook open for the next project.

■ Proficiency Assessment

Project 10-3: **Display Multiple Time Zones**

If you ask Arthur Yasinki for the key to his success in sales, he'll laugh and respond, "It's location, location, location." Because this phrase usually refers to brick-and-mortar stores or real estate, it might be difficult to understand his answer. When you look at his calendar, it becomes clear. Arthur spends about 200 days of every year away from home at client sites. It's no wonder that he doesn't display the time zone where he lives. In this project, add the time zone for London to your calendar display.

1. If necessary, click the Calendar button in the Navigation pane to display the Calendar folder.
2. Click the Tools menu, and click Options. The Options window is displayed.
3. Click the Calendar Options button to display the Calendar Options window.
4. Click the Time Zone button. The Time Zone window is displayed.
5. Click the Label field in the Current Windows time zone area. Key SF and press Tab.
6. Click the Show an additional time zone checkbox.
7. Click the Label field in the Additional time zone area. Key London and press Tab.
8. In the Time zone field, select (GMT) Greenwich Mean Time ; Dublin, Edinburgh, Lisbon, London.
9. Click OK in the Time Zone window. Click OK in the Calendar Options window and the Options window to return to the Calendar folder.
10. Click the Week button to display the week, if necessary.

    LEAVE Outlook open for the next project.

Project 10-4: Send Calendar Information via Email

Once a week Arthur Yasinki sends a Calendar Snapshot to the department's administrative assistant. Without access to his calendar information, the department would have a hard time finding Arthur on a map.

1. If necessary, click the Calendar button in the Navigation pane to display the Calendar folder.
2. Click the Send a Calendar via E-mail link in the Navigation pane. The Send a Calendar via E-mail window is displayed with a Message window behind it.
3. In the Date Range field, select Next 7 days.
4. In the Detail field, select Full details.
5. Click OK. The calendar information for the next seven days is displayed in the message body and attached to the message.
6. In the To field, key your email address.
7. Scroll down the message body, if necessary, to view the data in the message. Click Send.

   LEAVE Outlook open for the next project.

■ Mastery Assessment

Project 10-5: Publish Calendar Information to Office Online

Arthur Yasinki and the department's administrative assistant are trying Outlook 2007's new features. Arthur is publishing his calendar to Microsoft Office Online. The administrative assistant will subscribe to Arthur's calendar. In this project, publish your calendar to Microsoft Office Online.

1. If necessary, click the Calendar button in the Navigation pane to display the Calendar folder.
2. Click the Publish my Calendar link in the Navigation pane. The Published Calendar Settings window is displayed.
3. In the Detail field, select Limited details.
4. Click OK. Your calendar is published and the Send a Sharing Invitation window is displayed.
5. Click Yes. A Share window resembling a Message window is displayed.
6. In the To field, key your email address. Click the Send button. The invitation is sent.

   LEAVE Outlook open for the next project.

Project 10-6: Subscribe to an Internet Calendar

The department's administrative assistant is looking forward to subscribing to Arthur Yasinki's published calendar. Arthur's calendar information will be up-to-date and easy to access.

1. If necessary, click the Mail button in the Navigation pane to display the Mail folder.
2. Click the Send/Receive button if the Share message has not arrived yet. In the Inbox, double-click the Share message to open it.
3. Click the Subscribe to this Calendar button in the Open group on the Ribbon. A small dialog box is displayed asking if you want to add the calendar to Outlook and subscribe to updates.

4. Click Yes. If a Sign In dialog box is displayed, key your sign in name and password, and then click OK. The calendar is downloaded and displayed next to your calendar. The name of the shared calendar is added to the Navigation pane.

5. Click the Week button above the calendar.

6. Close the Share message.

7. Click the View in Overlay Mode button on the tab next to the calendar name of the calendar on the right. The calendars will be displayed in an overlay stack.

8. Click the checkbox next to the calendar's name in the Navigation pane to clear the checkbox. The second calendar is closed.

9. To clean up after completing these projects, configure the work week to match your schedule, set the time zone to match your schedule, verify that your calendar is not automatically uploading to Microsoft Office Online, and delete any calendar subscriptions displayed in the Navigation pane for the Calendar folder.

CLOSE Outlook.

INTERNET READY

Click the Search Calendars Online link in the Calendar folder's Navigation pane. Find a calendar you like at Microsoft's site and subscribe to the calendar.

Workplace Ready

Sharing Schedules

The number of telecommuters and freelance workers is growing all the time. New tools and technology make it easier to share information with workers in the next cubicle, the next state, or the next country.

Large corporations with remote workers can purchase standard software packages or provide customized software and security features that enable those workers to log in and access all the features of the company's network regardless of the workers' locations. Some of these features are out of reach for smaller businesses or not feasible for large corporations with only a handful of telecommuters.

That doesn't mean that smaller companies that utilize a lot of telecommuters and freelance workers do not have deadlines or that scheduling isn't necessary. Whether your employee is wearing a pinstripe suit in the board room at 8:00 AM or wearing fuzzy slippers in a home office at 11:00 PM, deadlines are critical. Consider publishing schedules to Office Online. Workers can subscribe to a master schedule that tracks progress as a project is completed.

If you publish a calendar to Office Online, consider these tips:

- Keep the calendar up-to-date. Old information doesn't help anyone.
- Send a Share message to all project members inviting them to view the calendar. They can't meet deadlines they don't know about.
- Provide the right amount of information. Too much information can be confusing. Too little information can be useless.

Circling Back

The Baldwin Museum of Science is planning a major event this summer. Ajay Manchepalli, the Director of Special Exhibits, has worked tirelessly to arrange an exhibit of Egyptian antiquities. In a small town like Sun Ridge, Wisconsin, this is a major coup. As the plan for the event develops, Ajay must schedule a whirlwind of appointments and meetings leading up to the big event.

Project 1: Modify Your Calendar

Ajay makes several calls to antiquities experts and officials in Egypt every day. He has modified his work schedule so that he is available during the day in Egypt. Change the work week to match Ajay's schedule and display Egypt's time zone so that Ajay calls during Egypt's day.

GET READY. Launch Outlook if it is not already running.

1. If necessary, click the Calendar button in the Navigation pane to display the Calendar folder.
2. Click the Tools menu, and click Options. The Options window is displayed.
3. Click the Calendar Options button to display the Calendar Options window.
4. Click the Time Zone button. The Time Zone window is displayed.
5. In the Current Windows time zone area, click the Time zone field and select (GMT-06:00) Central Time (US & Canada). Click the Label field and key Ajay.
6. Click the Show an additional time zone checkbox.
7. Click the Label field in the Additional time zone area. Key Egypt, and press Tab.
8. In the Time zone field, select (GMT + 02:00) Cairo.
9. Click OK in the Time Zone window.
10. In the Calendar Options window, click the Start time field. Key or select 2:00 AM. Click the End time field. Key or select 10:00 AM.
11. Click OK in the Calendar Options window and the Options window to return to the Calendar folder.
12. Click the Day button to display the Day view. Note that both time zones are displayed.

    LEAVE Outlook open for the next project.

Project 2: Schedule Appointments and Events

The Egypt: Sands of Mysteries exhibit is scheduled for the month of August next year. Ajay has several appointments scheduled for next week. He meets with an insurance agent on Monday, and a telephone call is already scheduled with an antiquities expert in Egypt. Add the appointments and the Sands of Mysteries exhibit to Ajay's calendar.

GET READY. Launch Outlook if it is not already running. Complete the previous project.

1. Click the Calendar button in the Navigation pane to display the Calendar folder. Click the Month button to display the Month view, if necessary.
2. Click the Forward button at the top of the monthly calendar as many times as necessary to display August of next year.
3. Click the empty area of the August 1 box.
4. On the Standard toolbar, click the New button. The Appointment window is displayed. Because you clicked August 1 in the Month view, August 1 is the date in the *Start time* and *End time* fields.
5. Click the All day event checkbox to select the option. The time fields are dimmed.

6. In the *End time* field, select August 31 of next year.

7. In the Subject field, key Egypt: Sands of Mysteries exhibit.

8. Click the Save & Close button on the Ribbon.

9. Click the Back button at the top of the monthly calendar as many times as necessary to return to the current month.

10. Click next Monday's date on the monthly calendar.

11. On the Standard toolbar, click the New button. The Appointment window is displayed.

12. In the Subject field, key Susan Metters - Insurance.

13. In the Location field, key Here. Susan will come to Ajay's office.

14. In the *Start time* field, select or key 9:00 AM. Select an *End time* of 10:00 AM.

15. Click the Save & Close button on the Ribbon.

16. Click next Wednesday's date on the monthly calendar.

17. On the Standard toolbar, click the New button. The Appointment window is displayed.

18. In the Subject field, key Professor Lorraine Nay.

19. In the Location field, key Phone. Lorraine is in Cairo, so Ajay will call her before lunch in Cairo.

20. In the *Start time* field, select or key 3:00 AM. Select an *End time* of 3:30 AM.

21. Click the Save & Close button on the Ribbon.

LEAVE Outlook open for the next project.

Project 3: **Schedule a Recurring Meeting**

Every Friday, Ajay holds a brief status meeting to update the museum director and any interested staff members. As the exhibit date approaches, this recurring meeting will be changed to one hour in length. For now, the meetings are 30 minutes long.

TROUBLESHOOTING

The email addresses provided in these exercises belong to unused domains owned by Microsoft. When you send a message to these addresses, you will receive an error message stating that the message could not be delivered. Delete the error messages when they arrive.

1. Click the Calendar button in the Navigation pane to display the Calendar folder.

2. Click next Friday on the calendar.

3. On the Standard toolbar, click the New arrow. Click Meeting Request on the drop-down menu. The Meeting window is displayed.

4. Click the Subject field and key Egypt: Sands of Mysteries Exhibit Status. In the Location field, key Director's office.

5. Click the Scheduling button in the Show group on the Ribbon. Scheduling information is displayed.

6. Click the Click here to add a name text below your name. Key Steve@baldwinmuseumofscience.com. Press Enter. Steve is the director, so click the icon next to his name to verify that he is a required attendee.

7. Click the Click here to add a name text on the next line. Key Fadi@baldwinmuseumofscience.com. Press Enter. Click the icon next to Fadi's name and select Optional Attendee.

8. Click the Click here to add a name text on the next line. Key Ryan@baldwinmuseumofscience.com. Press Enter. Click the icon next to Ryan's name and select Optional Attendee.

9. Select the *Start time* of 9:00 AM and select the *End time* of 9:30 AM, if necessary.
10. Click the Recurrence button in the Options group on the Ribbon. The Appointment Recurrence window is displayed.
11. Click OK to accept the recurrence pattern and return to the meeting window.
12. Click the Appointment button in the Show group on the Ribbon.
13. Click the Send button.
14. To clean up Outlook after completing these projects, configure the work week to match your schedule, set the time zone to match your schedule, remove the appointments, and remove the recurring meeting.

    CLOSE Outlook.

11 Managing Tasks

Developing and releasing a new product are complicated processes that can take months or years to complete. Ruth Ann Ellerbrock knows this from firsthand experience. She has managed the product development team at Trey Research for five years. In five years, her team has released only three new products. Ruth Ann and her team use the Tasks folder to track the multitude of tasks required to accomplish the goal of releasing solid, marketable new products.

KEY TERMS
assign
complete
Deferred
In Progress
owner
recurring task
task
task request
Tasks folder
to-do item

SOFTWARE ORIENTATION

Microsoft Outlook's Task Window

Create and modify your tasks in the Task window shown in Figure 11-1.

Figure 11-1

Outlook's Task window

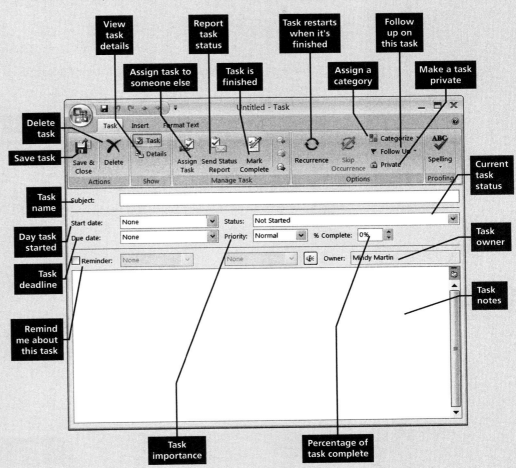

Use the Task window to create and track tasks that you are managing or performing. Keep your task information readily available in one location.

■ Creating New Tasks

THE BOTTOM LINE

Some days, it seems like everyone is telling you what to do. Keep track of everything you have to accomplish by creating tasks. A *task* is an Outlook item that can be tracked from creation to completion. Tasks are stored in the *Tasks folder*.

Creating a One-Time Task

Create a one-time task to track your progress on a task that only needs to be completed once. For example, create a task to register for a specific trade show. When you have registered for the trade show, the task is complete. You won't need to register for the trade show every week or every month.

 CREATE A ONE-TIME TASK

GET READY. Before you begin these steps, be sure to launch Microsoft Outlook.

1. If necessary, click the Tasks button in the Navigation pane to display the Tasks folder, as shown in Figure 11-2.

Figure 11-2

Tasks folder

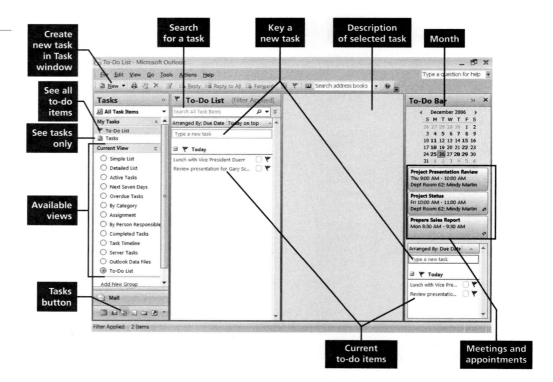

 Depending on the exercises you completed in previous lessons, you might have items displayed in the To-Do List.

2. Click the New button on the Standard toolbar. A Task window is displayed, as shown in Figure 11-1.

◆ ANOTHER WAY

In every Outlook folder, you can create a new task by selecting Task in the New drop-down menu or by pressing **Ctrl+Shift+K**.

3. In the Subject field, key Create marketing brochure.
4. In the *Due date* field, key or select the date five weeks from today.
5. In the Priority field, select Low.
6. In the task note area, key Photographer is Ann Beebe.
7. Compare your Task window to Figure 11-3. Click the Save & Close button in the Actions group on the Ribbon.

Figure 11-3

Creating a new task

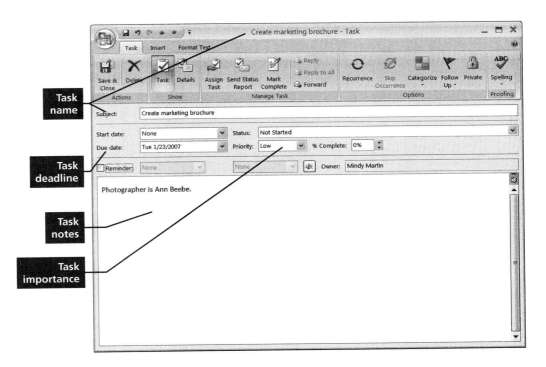

8. Compare your To-Do List to Figure 11-4. The new task is displayed below the Next Month heading because the deadline occurs next month.

Figure 11-4

New task created

New task created

PAUSE. LEAVE Outlook open to use in the next exercise.

In the previous exercise, you created a one-time task. When any task is created, it is automatically flagged for follow-up. Any Outlook item flagged for follow-up is a *to-do item*. Thus, creating a task creates a to-do item.

To-do items can include messages and contacts with a follow-up flag. To-do items are displayed on the To-Do Bar. Because to-do items are not all tasks, you can have more to-do items than tasks on your To-Do Bar.

X REF

You can find more information on completing a task later in this lesson.

Creating a Recurring Task

A *recurring task* is a task that must be completed at regular intervals. Common recurring tasks include creating a status report every week or turning in your travel receipt to the accounting department every month. When you mark a recurring task as complete, the task is automatically re-created with the next due date displayed.

CREATE A RECURRING TASK

GET READY. Before you begin these steps, be sure to launch Microsoft Outlook.

1. If necessary, click the Tasks button in the Navigation pane to display the Tasks folder.
2. Click the New button on the Standard toolbar. A Task window is displayed as shown in Figure 11-1.
3. In the Subject field, key Summarize team's progress on Vault project.
4. In the *Start date* field, select the second Monday in January of next year.
5. Click the Recurrence button in the Options group on the Ribbon. The Task Recurrence window is displayed, as shown in Figure 11-5.

Figure 11-5

Task Recurrence window

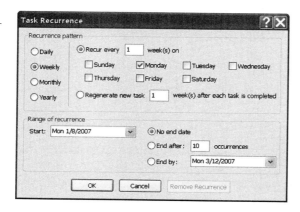

6. Click the End by radio button. In the *End by* field, key or select the second Monday in July. This ends the recurring task in six months.
7. Click OK to return to the Task window.
8. Compare your Task window to Figure 11-6. Depending on the current date, the number of days before the first deadline will differ. Click the Save & Close button in the Actions group on the Ribbon.

Figure 11-6

Creating a new recurring task

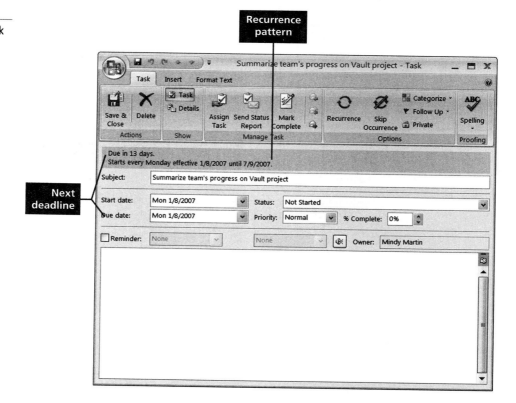

The "Due in" date message is only displayed if the deadline is 14 days or fewer in the future.

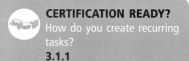

CERTIFICATION READY?
How do you create recurring tasks?
3.1.1

9. Examine your To-Do List. The new task is displayed below a heading. The heading title depends on the amount of time between today's date and the first deadline.

   PAUSE. LEAVE Outlook open to use in the next exercise.

In the previous exercise, you created a recurring task that starts in January and ends after six months. Frequently, start and end dates coincide with project deadlines.

Creating a Task from a Message

Email messages are used to convey a variety of information. Sometimes, a message contains information about tasks that must be performed. To prevent additional data entry, use the message to create a tracked task.

⊙ CREATE A TASK FROM A MESSAGE

GET READY. Before you begin these steps, be sure to launch Microsoft Outlook. This exercise requires exchanging messages with another Outlook user with an active email account who can respond to a message or who has the ability to access and use another user's Outlook profile.

1. If necessary, click the Mail button in the Navigation pane to display the Mail folder in your account.
2. Click the New button in the Standard toolbar to display a Message window.
3. Click the To field and key the recipient's email address. The recipient is the Outlook user who will create a task from this message.
4. Click the Subject field and key Travel Itinerary.
5. In the message area, key the following message.

   Hi, Press Enter. Please give a copy of your itinerary to Arlene Huff before you leave next Friday. Press Enter. Thanks, Press Enter. Mindy

6. Click the Send button to send the message.
7. In the recipient's account, click the Send/Receive button if the Travel itinerary message has not arrived.
8. Click the Travel itinerary message in the message list. Drag it to the Tasks button on the Navigation pane and drop the message on the Tasks button. A Task window containing information from the message is automatically opened, as shown in Figure 11-7.

Figure 11-7

Creating a task from
a message

9. In the Task window, click the Due date field. Key or select next Friday's date.

10. Click the Save & Close button in the Actions group on the Ribbon.

11. Click the Tasks button in the Navigation pane to display the Tasks folder. Examine your To-Do List. The new task is displayed below the Next Week heading.

PAUSE. CLOSE Outlook to return to your account if necessary. If you exchanged tasks with another user so that you received the task in your mailbox, leave Outlook open to use in the next exercise.

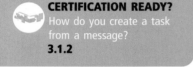

CERTIFICATION READY?
How do you create a task
from a message?
3.1.2

In the previous exercise, you created a task from a message. Using this method to create a task keeps the related message with the task.

■ Modifying and Completing a Task

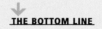
THE BOTTOM LINE

After a task is created, you will modify the task to change its status and update the amount of the task that has been completed. You can also mark a task as private, keeping the details hidden from other users. When you finish a task, mark it as complete.

Modifying a Task

Tracking the status of a task includes modifying the task's status and percentage complete. You can also modify a task's characteristics, such as its importance.

→ MODIFY A TASK

GET READY. Before you begin these steps, be sure to launch Microsoft Outlook and complete the first exercise in this lesson.

1. If necessary, click the Tasks button in the Navigation pane to display the Tasks folder.

2. Double-click the Create marketing brochure task. The task is opened in a Task window.

3. Click the Status field. Select In Progress. The **In Progress** status indicates that work on the task has started.

4. Click the % Complete field. Click the field's arrows to select 50% or key 50% in the field.

5. In the Priority field, select High.

6. Compare your Task window to Figure 11-8. Click the Save & Close button in the Actions group on the Ribbon.

Figure 11-8

Modifying a task

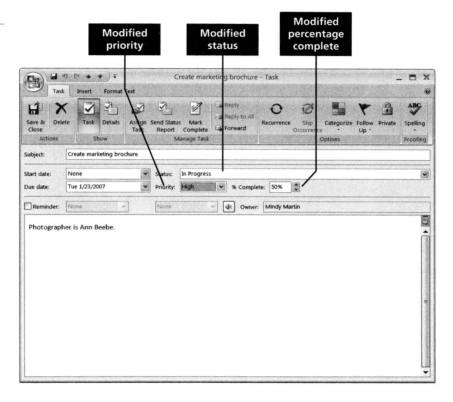

7. Double-click the Create marketing brochure task. The task is opened in a Task window.

8. Click the Status field. Select Deferred. The **Deferred** status indicates that the task has been postponed without changing the deadline or the percentage complete.

9. Click the Save & Close button in the Actions group on the Ribbon.

PAUSE. LEAVE Outlook open to use in the next exercise.

CERTIFICATION READY?
How do you set the status, priority, and percent complete of a task?
3.1.3

In the previous exercise, you modified an existing task. Shortly after changing the task's importance to High, the release date for the product described in your marketing brochure was delayed. You changed the status of the task to Deferred. You are not currently working on the task, but the task characteristics remain unchanged. The priority is still high, and it is still halfway complete.

Making a Task Private

Like appointments and meetings, you can mark a task as private. This protects the details of the task from casual observers on your network.

MAKE A TASK PRIVATE

GET READY. Before you begin these steps, be sure to launch Microsoft Outlook. Complete the previous exercise.

1. If necessary, click the Tasks button in the Navigation pane to display the Tasks folder.
2. Double-click the Create marketing brochure task. The task is opened in a Task window.
3. Click the Private button in the Options group on the Ribbon.
4. Click the Save & Close button in the Actions group on the Ribbon.

   PAUSE. LEAVE Outlook open to use in the next exercise.

CERTIFICATION READY?
How do you mark a task as private?
3.1.5

In the previous exercise, you made a task private. Because the task was deferred, you have decided to work on the marketing brochure when you have free time. With a bit of hard work, you might be able to finish the brochure before management decides to take the product off hold.

In your account, your private tasks do not look different from any other task. To see that your task is private, open the task. In a private task, the Private button in the Options group on the Ribbon is highlighted. A private task is protected from other casual observers on your network. Without permission to access your account, the details of any private task will not be visible to them.

Completing a Task

When you finish a task, mark the task as **complete**. A completed task is removed from your To-Do List. To see information about your tasks that have been marked as complete, click the Completed Tasks view in the Navigation pane.

COMPLETE A TASK

GET READY. Before you begin these steps, be sure to launch Microsoft Outlook and complete the first exercise in this lesson.

1. If necessary, click the Tasks button in the Navigation pane to display the Tasks folder.
2. Double-click the Create marketing brochure task. The task is opened in a Task window.
3. Click the Mark Complete button in the Manage Task group on the Ribbon. The Task window closes and the task is moved to the Completed Tasks list so it is no longer displayed on your To-Do List.
4. Click the Completed Tasks button in the Navigation pane to see your completed task. Click the To-Do List button in the Navigation pane to return to your normal view.

   PAUSE. LEAVE Outlook open to use in the next exercise.

CERTIFICATION READY?
How do you mark a task as complete?
3.1.4

In the previous exercise, you marked a task as complete. Completed tasks are not displayed on your To-Do List. As your list of completed tasks grows over time, the Completed Tasks view becomes a record of the tasks you have accomplished.

■ Working with Assigned Tasks

THE BOTTOM LINE In the previous section, you created, modified, and completed tasks. In this section, you will assign tasks to other Outlook users and respond to tasks assigned to you.

Assigning a Task to Someone Else

The task *owner* is the only Outlook user who can modify a task. The creator of a task is automatically the task owner. To transfer ownership of a task, you can *assign* the task to another Outlook user.

➔ ASSIGN A TASK TO SOMEONE ELSE

GET READY. Before you begin these steps, be sure to launch Microsoft Outlook.

TROUBLESHOOTING You cannot assign a task to yourself; therefore, this series of exercises requires exchanging messages with a partner using Outlook 2007. If you do not have a partner, you can use a different Outlook profile tied to a separate email account. If you need to create a profile, see Outlook's Help topics for more information.

TAKE NOTE* This exercise is performed in your account.

1. If necessary, click the Tasks button in the Navigation pane to display the Tasks folder.
2. Click the New arrow and click the Task Request option. A *task request* assigns a task to another user. The Task request window is displayed, as shown in Figure 11-9. It contains components from a Task window and a Message window.

Figure 11-9

Task request window

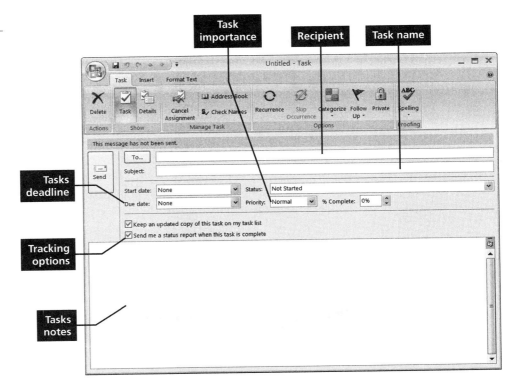

3. Click the To field and key your partner's email address. Your partner is the Outlook user who will own this task.

4. Click the Subject field and key Prepare training materials for new employees.

5. Click the Due date field. Key or select next Friday's date.

6. In the Priority field, select High.

7. In the message area, key the following message.

Hi, Press [Enter]. Please prepare training materials and a schedule for the one-day training seminar next week. Press [Enter]. Thanks, Press [Enter]. Key your name.

8. Click the Send button to send the task request. Based on the tracking options you selected, the task is displayed on your To-Do List. If necessary, click the Prepare training materials for new employees task on your To-Do List. Note that your partner is identified as the task owner, as shown in Figure 11-10.

Figure 11-10

Assigned task displayed after task request sent

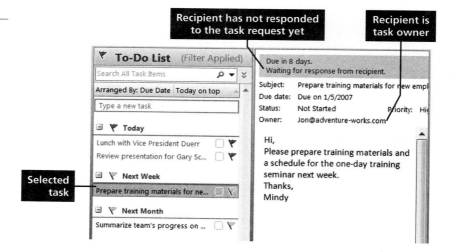

9. Click the New arrow and click the Task Request option. The Task request window is displayed.

10. Click the To field and key your partner's email address. Your partner is the Outlook user who will own this task.

11. Click the Subject field and key Greet new employees.

12. Click the Due date field. Key or select next Friday's date.

13. In the message area, key the following message.

Hi, Press [Enter]. It's a good idea to introduce ourselves to the new employees before the training session starts next Friday. Press [Enter]. Key your name.

14. Click the Send button to send the task request.

PAUSE. CLOSE Outlook to access your partner's account, if necessary. Otherwise, leave Outlook open to use in the next exercise.

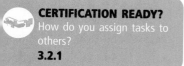

CERTIFICATION READY?
How do you assign tasks to others?
3.2.1

In the previous exercise, you sent two task requests to your partner. When you send a task request, the recipient becomes the task owner when you click the Send button. You can only recover ownership of the task if the recipient declines the task *and* you return the task to your task list.

The *Keep an updated copy of this task on my task list* option is selected by default. When the owner updates the task, it will also be updated on your task list if a connection is available.

Responding to an Assigned Task

A task request is received in your mailbox like any other message. When you receive a task request, you can accept the task, decline the task, or assign the task to another Outlook user.

⊕ RESPOND TO AN ASSIGNED TASK

GET READY. Before you begin these steps, be sure to launch Microsoft Outlook. Complete the previous exercise.

1. In your partner's account, click the Mail button in the Navigation pane to display the Mail folder, if necessary. If the task requests sent in the previous exercise have not arrived, click the Send/Receive button on the Standard toolbar.

2. In the Inbox, double-click the Task Request: Prepare training materials for new employees message to open it, as shown in Figure 11-11.

Figure 11-11

Task request received

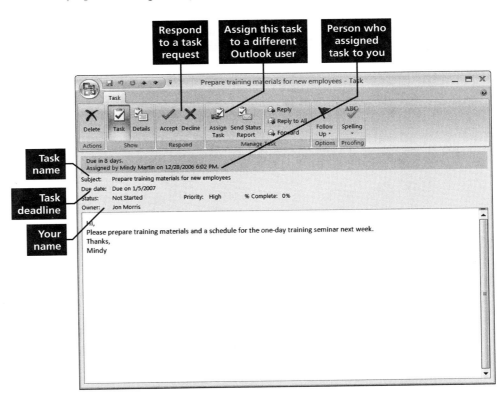

3. In the Task window, click the Accept button in the Respond group on the Ribbon. As shown in Figure 11-12, a small dialog box is displayed asking if you want to edit the message sent with the response.

Figure 11-12

Accepting Task dialog box

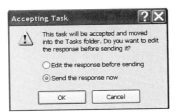

4. Click OK to send the response now. The task acceptance is sent and the task is added to your task list.

5. In the Inbox, double-click the Task Request: Greet new employees message to open it.

6. In the Task window, click the Decline button in the Respond group on the Ribbon. The small Declining Task dialog box is displayed, asking if you want to edit the message sent with the response.

7. In the Declining Task dialog box, click the Edit the response before sending option and click OK.

8. In the Task window, key I will be out of town next Friday. Click the Send button. You have declined this task, so it is not added to your task list.

   PAUSE. LEAVE Outlook open to use in the next exercise.

CERTIFICATION READY?
How do you respond to an assigned task?
3.2.2

In the previous exercise, you received two task requests. You accepted one task and declined the second. Currently, you are the owner of both tasks. When you decline a task request, you are still the owner of the task until the person who sent the original task request returns the declined task to his or her task list.

When a task you assigned to another user is declined, you will receive a Task Declined: Task Name message. Double-click the message to open it. Click the Return to Task List button in the Manage Task group on the Ribbon. Until you return the task to your task list, you are not the task owner. Even though the other user declined the task, he or she is the task owner until you reclaim ownership by returning the task to your task list. Therefore, the *Greet new employees* task in the previous exercise still belongs to your partner, even though he or she declined the task.

Reporting the Status of an Assigned Task

When you update a task assigned to you, the task copy kept on any previous owner's task list is automatically updated if the previous owner chose the tracking options when assigning the task. You can also choose to send a status report to previous task owners or interested individuals.

⊕ REPORT THE STATUS OF AN ASSIGNED TASK

GET READY. Before you begin these steps, be sure to launch Microsoft Outlook. Complete the previous exercises.

TAKE NOTE* This exercise is performed in your partner's account.

1. In your partner's account, click the Tasks button in the Navigation pane to display the Tasks folder if necessary.

2. Double-click the Prepare training materials for new employees task. The Task window is displayed.

3. Click the % Complete field. Key or select 50%.

4. Click the Send Status Report button in the Manage Task group on the Ribbon. A Message window is displayed. The person who assigned the task to you is displayed in the To field. The message content details the task's current status, as shown in Figure 11-13.

Figure 11-13

Task Status report

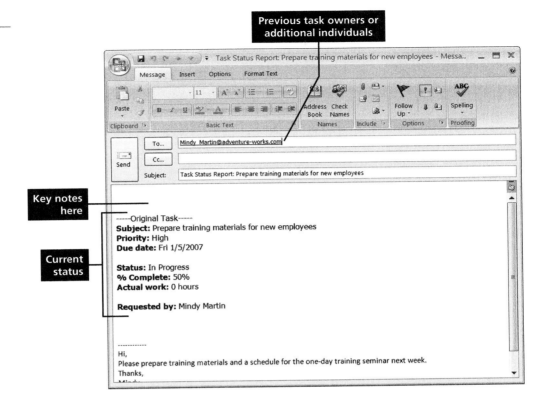

5. Click the Send button. Close the Task window.

PAUSE. CLOSE Outlook to access your account, if necessary. Otherwise, leave Outlook open to use in the next exercise.

CERTIFICATION READY?
How do you send a status report on an assigned task?
3.2.3

In the previous exercise, you sent a status report to the person who assigned the task to you. The name was filled in automatically. To see any individuals who will be automatically updated, open the task to display the Task window and click the Details button in the Show group on the Ribbon. The *Update list* field identifies individuals who are automatically updated. When you send a status report, these names will be placed automatically in the To field.

■ Searching for Tasks

THE BOTTOM LINE

Outlook's new Instant Search feature makes it simple to quickly find a task. Use Instant Search to find any text in the task item. Use text in the subject or task notes area to find a task.

SEARCH FOR TASKS

GET READY. Before you begin these steps, be sure to launch Microsoft Outlook. Instant Search must be enabled. Complete the previous exercises in this lesson.

1. In your account, click the Tasks button in the Navigation pane to display the Tasks folder if necessary. Click the To-Do List button in the Current View area on the Navigation pane, if necessary.

2. In the Instant Search box, verify that Search All Task Items is selected.

3. In the Instant Search box, key greet. As you key the search text, Outlook displays the matching task items, as shown in Figure 11-14. Note that the Task Request message in the Sent Items folder is also displayed.

Figure 11-14

Instant Search results

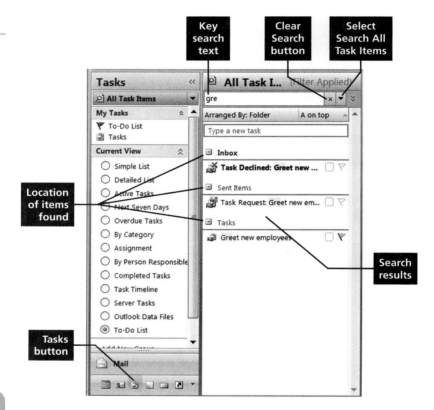

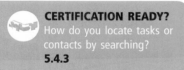

CERTIFICATION READY?
How do you locate tasks or contacts by searching?
5.4.3

4. Click the Clear Search button to clear the search criteria.
   CLOSE Outlook.

In the previous exercise, you used Outlook's new Instant Search feature to locate specific tasks. Task requests located in the Mail folders are also included in the search results.

SUMMARY SKILL MATRIX

In This Lesson You Learned	Matrix Skill	Skill Number
To create new tasks		
To create a new one-time task		
To create a new task that recurs at regular intervals	Create recurring tasks	3.1.1
To create a new task from a received message	Create a task from a message	3.1.2
To modify and complete a task		
To modify a task by changing its characteristics	Set the status, priority, and percent complete of a task	3.1.3
To protect the details of a task from other users on your network	Mark a task as private	3.1.5
To complete a task	Mark a task as complete	3.1.4
To work with assigned tasks		
To assign a task to someone else	Assign tasks to others	3.2.1
To accept or decline an assigned task	Respond to an assigned task	3.2.2
To update someone on the status of your assigned tasks	Send a status report on an assigned task	3.2.3
To use Instant Search to find tasks that meet specific criteria	Locate tasks or contacts by searching	5.4.3

■ Knowledge Assessment

Fill in the Blank?

Complete the following sentences by writing the correct word or words in the blanks provided.

1. A(n) ______________ task occurs at regular intervals.
2. Click the Tasks button to view the ______________.
3. After you start a task, the task's status is ______________.
4. The To-Do List displays tasks and ______________.
5. The task owner can ______________ the task to another Outlook user.
6. A(n) ______________ task is not displayed on your To-Do List.
7. You can track a(n) ______________ from creation to completion.
8. A(n) ______________ task is postponed.
9. Only the task ______________ can modify a task.
10. Use a(n) ______________ to assign a task to another user.

Recurring
task folder
in progress
to-do items
assign
completed
task
deferred
owner
task request

Multiple Choice

Circle the correct choice.

1. Which of the following can be a to-do item?

   A. Task

   B. Message

   C. Flagged contact

   D. All of the above

2. What is the difference between a task and a to-do item?

   A. A task takes longer to complete.

   B. To-do items are displayed on the To-Do List.

   C. Tasks can be tracked.

   D. There is no difference between a task and a to-do item.

3. What folder must be active to create a task?

   A. Tasks folder

   B. Mail folder

   C. Contacts folder

   D. Any Outlook folder

4. What is automatically created when you create a task?

   A. To-do item

   B. Deadline

   C. Task request

   D. Message

5. What happens when you complete a recurring task?

   A. The task is deleted.

   B. The task is assigned to another Outlook user.

   C. An entry is made in your calendar.

   D. The task is automatically re-created with the next due date displayed.

6. How do you protect the details of a task from casual observers on your network?

   A. Complete the task.

   B. Make the task private.

   C. Assign the task to another Outlook user.

   D. Hide the task.

7. Who owns a task you assign to another Outlook user?

   A. You

   B. You and the other Outlook user

   C. The other Outlook user

   D. No one owns the task

8. Who owns a task when you assign the task to another user and the task is declined?

   A. You

   B. You and the other Outlook user

   C. The other Outlook user

   D. No one owns the task

9. Where does a task request arrive?
   A. Tasks folder
   B. Mail folder
   C. To-Do List
   D. Task Requests folder
10. What new feature finds tasks quickly?
    A. Instant Search
    B. Search folder
    C. Sort tasks
    D. All of the above

■ Competency Assessment

Project 11-1: Create a One-Time Task

Eugene Kogan is setting up a small business to bake and sell cupcakes. He believes that "personal cakes" will be popular at children's parties, open houses, and office events. Before he can get started, Eugene needs to create a list of tasks. He is a procrastinator, so he knows that deadlines are needed to keep him focused on the business.

GET READY. Launch Outlook if it is not already running.

1. If necessary, click the Tasks button in the Navigation pane to display the Tasks folder.

2. Click the New button on the Standard toolbar. A Task window is displayed.

3. In the Subject field, key Cupcakes - Identify potential clients. In the *Due date* field, key or select the date two weeks from today. Click the Save & Close button in the Actions group on the Ribbon.

4. Click the New button on the Standard toolbar. A Task window is displayed.

5. In the Subject field, key Cupcakes - Identify competitors. In the *Due date* field, key or select the date two weeks from today. Click the Save & Close button in the Actions group on the Ribbon.

6. Click the New button on the Standard toolbar. A Task window is displayed.

7. In the Subject field, key Cupcakes - Research prices and recurring expenses. In the *Due date* field, key or select the date two weeks from today. Click the Save & Close button in the Actions group on the Ribbon.

8. Click the New button on the Standard toolbar. A Task window is displayed.

9. In the Subject field, key Cupcakes - Identify initial equipment and financial investment needed. In the *Due date* field, key or select the date four weeks from today. Click the Save & Close button in the Actions group on the Ribbon.

10. Click the New button on the Standard toolbar. A Task window is displayed.

11. In the Subject field, key Cupcakes - Identify time investment required. In the *Due date* field, key or select the date four weeks from today. Click the Save & Close button in the Actions group on the Ribbon.

12. Click the New button on the Standard toolbar. A Task window is displayed.

13. In the Subject field, key Cupcakes - Research and select marketing methods. In the *Due date* field, key or select the date four weeks from today. Click the Save & Close button in the Actions group on the Ribbon.

14. Click the New button on the Standard toolbar. A Task window is displayed.

15. In the Subject field, key Cupcakes - Write a business plan. In the *Due date* field, key or select the date six weeks from today. Click the Save & Close button in the Actions group on the Ribbon.

    LEAVE Outlook open for the next project.

Project 11-2: Modify Tasks

Eugene has made progress on making his cupcake dream come true. Update his progress on each of the tasks.

1. If necessary, click the Tasks button in the Navigation pane to display the Tasks folder.

2. Double-click the Cupcakes - Identify potential clients task. The task is opened in a Task window.

3. Click the Status field. Select In Progress.

4. Click the % Complete field. Click the field's arrows to select 50% or key 50% in the field.

5. Click the Save & Close button in the Actions group on the Ribbon.

6. Double-click the Cupcakes - Identify competitors task. The task is opened in a Task window.

7. Click the Status field. Select In Progress.

8. Click the % Complete field. Click the field's arrows to select 25% or key 25% in the field.

9. Click the Save & Close button in the Actions group on the Ribbon.

10. Double-click the Cupcakes — Research prices and recurring expenses task. The task is opened in a Task window.

11. Click the Status field. Select In Progress.

12. Click the % Complete field. Click the field's arrows to select 75% or key 75% in the field.

13. Click the Save & Close button in the Actions group on the Ribbon.

    LEAVE Outlook open for the next project.

■ Proficiency Assessment

Project 11-3: Assign a Task to Another Outlook User

Eugene has been researching his business prospects for several weeks now. He is ready to pull the information together in a business plan. However, Eugene knows that a business plan is a critical document. For example, the business plan is necessary for obtaining funds from a bank. Although Eugene has many important business skills, he decided to ask his cousin, a technical writer at Litware, Inc., to write the business plan.

TROUBLESHOOTING

You cannot assign a task to yourself; therefore, Projects 11-3 and 11-4 require exchanging messages with a partner using Outlook 2007. If you do not have a partner, you can use a different Outlook profile tied to a separate email account. If you need to create a profile, see Outlook's Help topics for more information.

1. If necessary, click the Tasks button in the Navigation pane to display the Tasks folder.
2. Double-click the Cupcakes — Write a business plan task. The task is opened in a Task window.
3. Click the Assign Task button in the Manage Task group on the Ribbon.
4. Click the To field and key the recipient's email address.
5. In the Priority field, select High.
6. In the message area, key the following message.

   Hi, Press Enter. Please let me know if you need any additional information. Press Enter. Thanks!
7. Click the Send button to send the task request.

   PAUSE. CLOSE Outlook to access your partner's account if necessary. Otherwise, leave Outlook open to use in the next exercise.

Project 11-4: Accept an Assigned Task

Eugene's cousin is helping Eugene by sorting through all of the information to create a business plan. His cousin understands the importance of creating a professional document that will give Eugene the best chance of obtaining financing from the bank.

1. In your partner's account, click the Mail button in the Navigation pane to display the Mail folder if necessary. If the task request sent in the previous project has not arrived, click the Send/Receive button on the Standard toolbar.
2. In the Inbox, double-click the Task Request: Cupcakes — Write a business plan message to open it.
3. In the Task window, click the Accept button in the Respond group on the Ribbon. A small dialog box is displayed asking if you want to edit the message sent with the response.
4. Click OK. The task acceptance is sent and the task is added to the task list.

   PAUSE. CLOSE Outlook to access your account if necessary. Otherwise, leave Outlook open to use in the next project.

■ Mastery Assessment

Project 11-5: Complete Tasks

At the end of two weeks, Eugene has completed several tasks on time. He marks these tasks as complete.

1. If necessary, click the Tasks button in the Navigation pane to display the Tasks folder.
2. Double-click the Cupcakes - Identify potential clients task. The task is opened in a Task window.
3. Click the Mark Complete button in the Manage Task group on the Ribbon. The Task window closes and the task is moved to the Completed Tasks list so it is no longer displayed on your To-Do List.
4. Double-click the Cupcakes - Identify competitors task. The task is opened in a Task window.
5. Click the Mark Complete button in the Manage Task group on the Ribbon. The Task window closes and the task is moved to the Completed Tasks list so it is no longer displayed on your To-Do List.

6. Double-click the Cupcakes — Research prices and recurring expenses task. The task is opened in a Task window.

7. Click the Mark Complete button in the Manage Task group on the Ribbon. The Task window closes and the task is moved to the Completed Tasks list so it is no longer displayed on your To-Do List.

   LEAVE Outlook open for the next project.

Project 11-6: **Find and Delete Tasks**

Eugene has been operating his cupcake business on the side for the last six months. He has decided that it's time to evaluate the possibility of quitting his day job and making cupcakes full time. Find and delete any current tasks related to the cupcake business. (This project will clean up your folders after completing all of these projects.)

1. In your account, click the Tasks button in the Navigation pane to display the Tasks folder, if necessary.

2. In the Instant Search box, verify that Search All Task Items is selected.

3. In the Instant Search box, key Cupcake. As you key the search text, Outlook displays the matching task items.

4. Select each item in the search results and click the Delete button on the Standard toolbar.

5. Click the Clear Search button to clear the search criteria.

   CLOSE Outlook.

INTERNET READY

Have you thought of starting a business? Create a task list to research your business idea. Use the Internet to research your business idea and the tasks involved.

Workplace Ready

Break It Down

Earning a degree, managing a project, and training new workers seem like unrelated activities. What do they have in common? All three activities are complicated processes that seem daunting when you look at the whole. However, each activity is made up of smaller steps. Enroll in a series of specific classes to earn a degree. Perform specific actions when you manage a project. Teach workers to follow specific steps.

Break down a large goal into smaller tasks that you can perform yourself or assign to others for completion. Start with the ultimate goal. Break it down into a list of steps to be completed. Convert the steps into tasks. Match the tasks with the people available to perform the tasks.

When you assign tasks to other people, make sure that the task owner has all the tools needed to complete the task. The task owner needs the ability and authority to perform the task. Ability includes skill and equipment. Authority ensures that the task owner can obtain any necessary information or assistance from other workers.

When you create tasks, remember these important tips.

- Break down large jobs into manageable tasks.
- Match tasks to people.
- Ensure that the task owner has the ability and authority to succeed.

12

Categories and Outlook Data Files

LESSON SKILL MATRIX

Skills	Matrix Skill	Skill Number
Working with Categories	Categorize messages, appointments, meetings, contacts, and tasks by color	5.1.1
Sorting Items by Color Category	Sort Outlook items by color category	5.1.2
Searching for Items by Category	Search Outlook items by category	5.4.4
Working with Data Files		
Creating a Data File	Create a data file	5.2.1
Selecting a Data File for a Mail Account	Add an Outlook data file to, or remove it from, a mail profile	5.2.2
Changing Data File Settings	Change data file settings	5.2.3

Bart Duncan is a sales representative for Contoso, Ltd. He sells insurance policies to businesses. He works with large corporations, small businesses, and new businesses that are struggling to grow. He categorizes his clients based on the client's number of employees. To make the client's status easily visible, Bart uses five color categories based on size. His two most important clients have separate color categories to indicate their importance in his sales activities.

SOFTWARE ORIENTATION

Microsoft Outlook's Color Categories Window

The Color Categories window displayed in Figure 12-1 enables you to create, modify, and delete color categories.

Figure 12-1

Outlook's Color Categories window

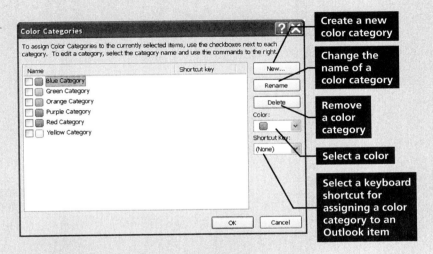

Create a new color category

Change the name of a color category

Remove a color category

Select a color

Select a keyboard shortcut for assigning a color category to an Outlook item

Use the Color Categories window to customize the new color categories for your use. Refer to Figure 12-1 as you complete the following exercises.

■ Working with Categories

THE BOTTOM LINE

A *color category* assigns a color to an Outlook item, providing a new way to visually indicate relationships among Outlook items. For example, assign a color to all Outlook items related to a specific project or a specific person. Create new color categories to increase the number of categories available for your use. Use color categories to sort or find Outlook items.

Assigning Outlook Items to Color Categories

Color categories provide a quick visual method of identifying related Outlook items. A quick glace at any Outlook window reveals the relationship between the items. For example, assign the red category to all Outlook items related to your supervisor. Your supervisor's contact record, messages exchanged with your supervisor, and meetings scheduled with your supervisor can be assigned to the same color category.

⊕ ASSIGN OUTLOOK ITEMS TO COLOR CATEGORIES

GET READY. Before you begin these steps, be sure to launch Microsoft Outlook.

1. Click the Folder List button in the Navigation pane to display the Folder List.
2. In the Instant Search box, select Search All Outlook Items, if necessary.
3. In the Instant Search box, key Tibbott. All Outlook items related to Diane Tibbott are displayed, as shown in Figure 12-2.

Figure 12-2

Search results

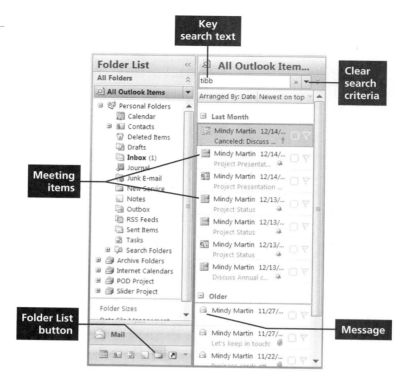

The Outlook items in the search results depend on the exercises and projects you completed in previous lessons. They could differ from the results shown here.

4. Click the first item on the list. Scroll to the end of the list. Press (Shift) and click the last item on the list. All the search results are selected.

5. Right-click one of the selected items. On the shortcut menu, point to Categorize and click the Red Category option. All the items are assigned to the Red Category. If you have not used Red Category before, a dialog box allowing you to rename the category is displayed, as shown in Figure 12-3.

Figure 12-3

Rename Category dialog box

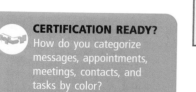

CERTIFICATION READY?

How do you categorize messages, appointments, meetings, contacts, and tasks by color?
5.1.1

You can find more information on creating rules in Lesson 5.

6. Click No in the Rename Category dialog box. You will rename the category in the next exercise.

7. Click the Clear Search button to clear the search criteria.

PAUSE. LEAVE Outlook open to use in the next exercise.

In the previous exercise, you found all the Outlook items related to a specific contact and assigned them to a category. Every Outlook item can be assigned to one or more color categories. You can also create rules to assign a color category automatically to messages you send and receive.

Modifying and Creating Color Categories

> Color categories can be created and renamed to meet your needs. Use names that identify the Outlook items assigned to the color category. Project names or an individual's name clearly identify a color category.

MODIFY AND CREATE COLOR CATEGORIES

GET READY. Before you begin these steps, complete the previous exercise.

1. Click the Mail button in the Navigation pane to display the Mail folder. Click the Inbox, if necessary. Click any message in the message list. An Outlook item must be selected to activate the Categorize button on the Standard toolbar.

2. Click the Categorize button and click the All Categories option. The Color Categories window in Figure 12-1 is displayed.

3. Click Red Category in the list of categories. Click the Rename button. The Red Category text becomes active.

4. Key Diane Tibbott and press Enter.

5. Click OK to rename the category and close the Color Categories window.

6. Click the Categorize button and click the All Categories option. The Color Categories window in Figure 12-1 is displayed.

7. Click the New button. The Add New Category window shown in Figure 12-4 is displayed.

Figure 12-4

Add New Category window

8. In the Name field, key Slider Project. In the Color field, select Dark Olive. Click OK. The new category is displayed in the Color Categories window.

9. Click OK to close the Color Categories window.

10. In the main Outlook window, click the Categorize button on the Standard toolbar to view the modified list of categories, as shown in Figure 12-5.

Figure 12-5

Modified list of available categories

11. Because a message was selected when you created the new color category, the message is assigned to the category. Right-click the selected message. Point to Categorize and select the Clear All Categories option. The category is removed from the message.

PAUSE. LEAVE Outlook open to use in the next exercise.

In the previous exercise, you renamed an existing category and created a new category. The colors offered in the Color field differ enough from each other to make the color categories distinct and easily recognizable.

You can also create categories that don't use a color. To create a colorless category, select None in the Color field in the Add New Category window.

Sorting Items by Color Category

To *sort* items, you arrange the items in a sequence based on specific criteria. After assigning Outlook items to a color category, you can use the color category as a sort criterion.

 SORT ITEMS BY COLOR CATEGORY

GET READY. Before you begin these steps, be sure to launch Microsoft Outlook.

1. If necessary, click the Mail button in the Navigation pane to display the Mail folder.
2. Click the View menu. Point to Arrange by, and click Categories. The messages in the message list are rearranged.

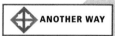

To sort items, you can click the *Arranged By: Date* text below the Instant Search box. Click *Categories* in the dropdown menu.

CERTIFICATION READY?
How do you sort Outlook
items by color category?
5.1.2

3. Scroll down to the bottom of the message list to view the categorized message if necessary. Messages without an assigned category appear at the top of the list.
4. Click the View menu. Point to Arrange by, and click Date to sort the messages by date. The messages are arranged by the default date sort.

PAUSE. LEAVE Outlook open to use in the next exercise.

In the previous exercise, you sorted messages by color category. In the Contacts folder, you can click the By Category radio button in the Navigation pane to sort contacts by category. The Tasks and Notes folders have the same By Category viewing option in the Navigation pane.

In the Calendar folder, click the View menu, point to Current View, and click By Category. Calendar items without a category are displayed first. Calendar items assigned to a color category are displayed next. The items are placed in groups based on the color categories. The order of the groups is determined alphabetically by the names of the color categories. For example, the category "Apple" will be placed before the category "Banana," regardless of the color assigned to the categories. If you added holidays to your calendar in Lesson 10, the holidays are displayed in the Holiday category.

Searching for Items by Category

Outlook's new Instant Search feature allows you to search for Outlook items that meet a variety of search criteria. In previous lessons, you keyed text used as the search criterion. You can modify the Instant Search Query Builder fields to allow you to search by category.

 You can find more information on using text as a search criterion in the Instant Search box in Lessons 3 and 7.

➔ **SEARCH FOR ITEMS BY CATEGORY**

GET READY. Before you begin these steps, complete the previous exercises in this lesson.

1. Click the Mail button in the Navigation pane to display the Calendar folder. Click the Folder List button to display the complete list of Outlook folders.

2. Click the Expand the Query Builder button next to the Instant Search box. The Query Builder is expanded, as shown in Figure 12-6.

Figure 12-6

Expanded Query Builder

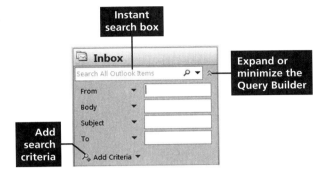

3. Click the Add Criteria arrow to display the dropdown menu. Click Categories on the dropdown menu. The Categories field is added to the Query Builder.

4. Click the Categories arrow to display the dropdown list of categories. Click the Diane Tibbott category. The search criterion is displayed in the Instant Search box, the Categories search criterion field is deleted from the Query builder, and the search results are displayed as they are located. See Figure 12-7.

Figure 12-7

Search criterion selected

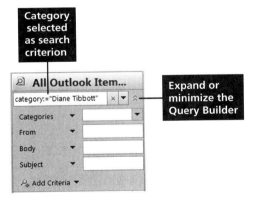

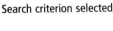

CERTIFICATION READY?
How do you search Outlook items by category?
5.4.4

5. Click the Clear Search button. The search criterion is cleared. Click the Minimize the Query Builder button to minimize the Query Builder, if necessary.

PAUSE. LEAVE Outlook open to use in the next exercise.

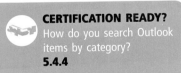

You can find more information on Search Folders in Lesson 7.

In the previous exercise, you added a selection criterion to the Instant Search Query Builder. Other characteristics, such as the Importance flag and sensitivity, can be used to locate Outlook items.

When searching for categorized messages, use the Categorized Mail Search Folder. It provides quick access to categorized messages without specifying search criteria.

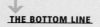

Working with Data Files

THE BOTTOM LINE

Your Outlook data is saved in an *Outlook Personal Folders file*, identified by the .pst extension. An Outlook .pst file is also known as a data file. When you backup your Outlook data or create archive files, you are creating or using Outlook Personal Folders files.

Creating a Data File

Outlook automatically creates .pst files the first time it is launched. You can create additional data files to archive items or store related information in a separate .pst file.

You can find more information on archiving Outlook items in Lesson 4.

⊕ CREATE A DATA FILE

GET READY. Before you begin these steps, be sure to launch Microsoft Outlook.

1. Click the Folder List button in the Navigation pane to display the Folder List.
2. Click the New arrow to display the dropdown list of new items you can create. Click Outlook Data File. The New Outlook Data File window is displayed, as shown in Figure 12-8.

Figure 12-8

New Outlook Data File window

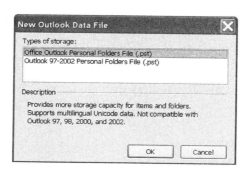

3. In the New Outlook Data File window, click OK. The Create or Open Outlook Data File window is displayed.
4. In the *File name* field, key Slider to identify the name of the .pst file. Click OK. The Create Microsoft Personal Folders window is displayed.
5. In the Create Microsoft Personal Folders window, key Slider Project in the Name field to identify the name of the folder that will be displayed in Outlook's folder list in the Navigation pane. Click OK. The Slider Project folder is displayed in the Navigation pane.
6. Click the plus sign (+) next to the Slider Project folder to display its contents, as shown in Figure 12-9.

Figure 12-9

New Outlook data file created

New data
file folder

TROUBLESHOOTING Depending on the exercises and projects you completed in previous lessons, the Outlook folders displayed in your Folder List could differ from the folders in Figure 12-9.

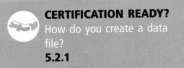

CERTIFICATION READY?
How do you create a data file?
5.2.1

PAUSE. LEAVE Outlook open to use in the next exercise.

In the previous exercise, you created a new Outlook Personal Folders file. Folders and Outlook items created or placed in the Slider Project folder are saved to the new .pst file. Optionally, when you create a new Outlook Personal Folders file, you can protect the folder with a password. This provides a convenient way to transfer Outlook data from your old computer to your new computer.

Selecting a Data File for a Mail Account

When messages are received, they are delivered to the Inbox, which is part of your default Outlook data file. If you create a new data file, you can choose to direct messages into the new data file. Normally, users will use this feature only if they send and receive messages in two or more email accounts.

TAKE NOTE* Refer to the Outlook Help to find more information about configuring Outlook to send and receive messages through a second email account.

⊕ SELECT A DATA FILE FOR A MAIL ACCOUNT

GET READY. Before you begin these steps, complete the previous exercise.

1. Click the Mail button in the Navigation pane to display the Mail folder. Click the Folder List button in the Navigation pane to display the Folder List.
2. Click the Tools menu, and click the Account Settings option. The Account Settings window is displayed. Your email account is listed. If you receive messages from more than one email account, the additional accounts will also be displayed.
3. Click your email account.

4. Click the Change Folder button near the bottom of the window. The New E-mail Delivery Location window is displayed, as shown in Figure 12-10.

Figure 12-10

New E-mail Delivery Location window

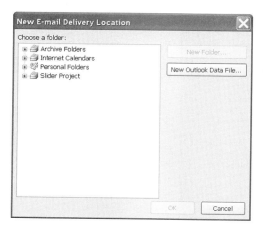

5. In the New E-mail Delivery Location window, click the Slider Project folder. Click the New Folder button. The Create Folder dialog box is displayed.

6. In the Create folder dialog box, key Inbox in the Name field and click OK.

7. In the New E-mail Delivery Location window, click the Inbox folder you just created in the Slider Project folder. Click OK. In the Account Settings window, you can see that mail will be delivered to Slider.pst.

8. Click the Change Folder button near the bottom of the window. The New E-mail Delivery Location window is displayed.

9. In the New E-mail Delivery Location window, click the plus sign (+) next to the Personal Folders folder and then click the Inbox folder in the Personal Folders folder. Click OK. This returns Outlook to your original data file settings. In the Account Settings window, you can see that mail will be delivered to the original location.

10. Click the Close button to close the Account Settings window.

PAUSE. LEAVE Outlook open to use in the next exercise.

CERTIFICATION READY?
How do you add an Outlook data file to, or remove it from, a mail profile?
5.2.2

In the previous exercise, you selected a new data file for an email account. All arriving messages will be delivered to the new data file.

Changing Data File Settings

After creating a data file, you can modify some of its characteristics. Characteristics include the data file's name, size, and password protection.

⊕ CHANGE DATA FILE SETTINGS

GET READY. Before you begin these steps, complete the previous exercise.

1. If necessary, click the Mail button in the Navigation pane to display the Mail folder.

 **ANOTHER WAY**
You can also access a data file's characteristics through the menu. Click the File menu and click the Data File Management option to display the Account Settings window. In the Account Settings window, click the data file's name and click the Settings button.

2. Right-click the Personal Folders folder in the Navigation pane. Click Properties for "Personal Folders" on the shortcut menu. The Outlook Today — [Personal Folders] Properties window is displayed, as shown in Figure 12-11.

Figure 12-11

Outlook Today — [Personal Folders] Properties window

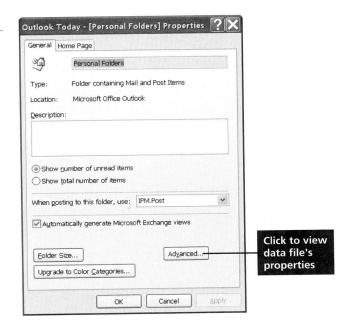

Click to view data file's properties

3. Click the Advanced button. The Personal Folders window is displayed. The name of the data file is already selected in the Name field. If you changed the name of your data file or selected a different data file, the name of this window will reflect the name of the data file.

4. Key Original Data File, replacing the existing data file name.

5. Click the Change Password button to display the Change Password window. To change the password, you would key the old password and key the new password twice. Instead, click the Cancel button to close the Change Password window.

6. Click the Compact Now button. A small alert window informs you that the data file is compacting.

7. Click the Cancel button to close the Personal Folders window. Click the Cancel button to close the Outlook Today — [Personal Folders] Properties window. CLOSE Outlook.

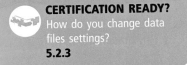

CERTIFICATION READY?
How do you change data files settings?
5.2.3

In the previous exercise, you accessed the data file settings. To *compact* your data file, a process that reduces the size of the data file, you clicked the Compact Now button. Compacting your data file is always a good idea to save space. Renaming the data file is not necessary unless you use more than one data file.

A password can be used to protect the information stored in the data file. However, you are solely responsible for remembering your password. Microsoft and your network administrator will not be able to help you access the data file if your password is lost or forgotten.

SUMMARY SKILL MATRIX

IN THIS LESSON YOU LEARNED	MATRIX SKILL	SKILL NUMBER
To work with categories by creating categories, modifying existing categories, and assigning Outlook items to categories	Categorize messages, appointments, meetings, contacts, and tasks by color	5.1.1
To sort items by color category	Sort Outlook items by color category	5.1.2
To search for items by category	Search Outlook items by category	5.4.4
To work with data files		
To create a data file	Create a data file	5.2.1
To select a data file for a mail account	Add an Outlook data file to, or remove it from, a mail profile	5.2.2
To change data file settings	Change data file settings	5.2.3

■ Knowledge Assessment

Matching

Match the term with its definition.

a. archive
b. color category
c. compact
d. criteria
e. Instant Search

f. Outlook Personal Folders file
g. rule
h. search
i. search folder
j. sort

_____ **1.** Color assigned to an Outlook item, providing a way to visually indicate relationships among Outlook items

_____ **2.** Defines an action that happens automatically when messages are received or sent

_____ **3.** A virtual folder that searches your email folders to locate items that meet the saved search criteria

_____ **4.** Try to find items that meet specific criteria

_____ **5.** Characteristics used to select items

_____ **6.** Search function that displays items as they are found

_____ **7.** Process that reduces the size of a data file

_____ **8.** Arrange items in a sequence based on specific criteria

_____ **9.** Store messages in a separate folder to reduce the number of messages in the folders you use most often

_____ **10.** File containing stored Outlook data

True/False

Circle T if the statement is true or F if the statement is false.

T F **1.** You can create new color categories.

T F **2.** A color category indicates a relationship among Outlook items.

T F **3.** Rules can't be used to assign color categories.

T F **4.** A color category must use a color.

T F **5.** You can use color categories to sort Outlook items.

T F **6.** When sorted, items without a color category are displayed below items with a color category.

T F **7.** Use Outlook's Instant Search feature to create a Search Folder.

T F **8.** Outlook automatically creates data files the first time it is launched.

T F **9.** Archived Outlook items are stored in data files.

T F **10.** Outlook data files can be protected by a password.

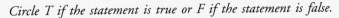

■ Competency Assessment

Project 12-1: Assign an Outlook Item to a Color Category

Terry Crayton at Trey Research is starting a new project. She will be working closely with Charles Fitzgerald. She decides to assign a color category to their correspondence.

GET READY. Launch Outlook if it is not already running.

> **TROUBLESHOOTING**
>
> The email addresses provided in these exercises belong to unused domains owned by Microsoft. When you send a message to these addresses, you will receive an error message stating that the message could not be delivered. Delete the error messages when they arrive.

1. Click the Mail button in the Navigation pane to display the Mail folder, if necessary.
2. On the Standard toolbar, click the New button. The Message window is displayed.
3. In the To field, key Charles@treyresearch.net.
4. In the Subject field, key Project Team.
5. In the message area, key the following message.

   Hi Charles, Press Enter twice. I look forward to working with you on the new project. The product sounds like an interesting challenge. Press Enter twice. Terry

6. Click the Send button.
7. Click the Sent Items folder in the Navigation pane.
8. Click the Project Team message in the message list.
9. Click the Categorize button on the Standard toolbar. Click Green Category in the dropdown list. If you have not used Green Category before, a dialog box allowing you to rename the category is displayed.
10. Click No in the Rename Category dialog box.

    LEAVE Outlook open for the next project.

Project 12-2: **Modify a Color Category**

The new project that Terry Crayton and Charles Fitzgerald are leading has been named. Change the name of Green Category to POD Project.

1. Click the Mail button in the Navigation pane to display the Mail folder, if necessary.
2. Click the Sent Items folder in the Navigation pane.
3. Click the Project Team message in the message list.
4. Click the Categorize button on the Standard toolbar. Click All Categories in the dropdown list. The Color Categories window is displayed.
5. Click Green Category in the list of categories. Click the Rename button. The Green Category text becomes active.
6. Key POD Project and press Enter.
7. Click OK to rename the category and close the Color Categories window.

   LEAVE Outlook open for the next project.

■ Proficiency Assessment

Project 12-3: **Sort Items by Color Category**

A week later, Terry Crayton needs to find the message she sent to Charles. Because only one message has been sent, sorting the sent messages is the simplest way to find the message.

1. Click the Mail button in the Navigation pane to display the Mail folder if necessary.
2. Click the Sent Items folder in the Navigation pane.
3. Click the View menu. Point to Arrange by, and click Categories. The messages in the message list are rearranged.
4. Scroll down the list of messages to view the message in the POD Project category.
5. Click the View menu. Point to Arrange by, and click Date to sort the messages by date.

   LEAVE Outlook open for the next project.

Project 12-4: **Search Items by Category**

Several weeks later, the POD project is in full swing. Terry has added new contacts, and dozens of messages have been exchanged with POD Project team members. Searching is the easiest way to view all Outlook items associated with the project.

1. Click the Mail button in the Navigation pane to display the Calendar folder. Click the Folder List button to display the complete list of Outlook folders.
2. Click the Expand the Query Builder button next to the Instant Search box. The Query Builder is expanded.
3. If the Categories field is not displayed on the expanded Query Builder, click the Add Criteria arrow to display the dropdown menu. Click Categories on the dropdown menu. The Categories field is added to the Query Builder.
4. Click the Categories arrow to display the dropdown list of categories. Click the POD Project category. The search criterion is displayed in the Instant Search box, and the search results are displayed as they are located.
5. Click the Clear Search button. The search criterion is cleared. Click the Minimize the Query Builder button to minimize the Query Builder, if necessary.

   LEAVE Outlook open for the next project.

■ Mastery Assessment

Project 12-5: Create a Data File

Terry has been assigned to the POD project exclusively. She creates a new data file that she will use until the project is complete.

1. Click the Folder List button in the Navigation pane to display the Folder List, if necessary.
2. Click the New arrow to display the dropdown list of new items you can create. Click Outlook Data File. The New Outlook Data File window is displayed.
3. In the New Outlook Data File window, click OK. The Create or Open Outlook Data File window is displayed.
4. In the *File name* field, key POD to identify the name of the .pst file. Click OK. The Create Microsoft Personal Folders window is displayed.
5. In the Create Microsoft Personal Folders window, key POD Project in the Name field to identify the name of the folder that will be displayed in Outlook's folder list in the Navigation pane. Click OK. The POD Project folder is displayed in the Navigation pane.

   LEAVE Outlook open for the next project.

Project 12-6: Select a Data File for a Mail Account

After creating the new data file, Terry has to add the data file to her mail account.

1. Click the Mail button in the Navigation pane to display the Mail folder. Click the Folder List button in the Navigation pane to display the Folder List.
2. Click the Tools menu and click the Account Settings option. The Account Settings window is displayed. Your email account is listed.
3. Click your email account.
4. Click the Change Folder button near the bottom of the window. The New E-mail Delivery Location window is displayed.
5. In the New E-mail Delivery Location window click the POD Project folder. Click the New Folder button. The Create Folder dialog box is displayed.
6. In the Create folder dialog box, key Inbox in the Folder Name field and click OK.
7. In the New E-mail Delivery Location window click the Inbox folder you just created in the Slider Project folder. Click OK. In the Account Settings window, you can see that mail will be delivered to POD.pst.
8. Before finishing these projects, you will change the data file to your default data file. Click the Change Folder button near the bottom of the window. The New E-mail Delivery Location window is displayed.
9. In the New E-mail Delivery Location window, expand the Personal Folders folder and click the Inbox folder. Click OK. This returns your original data file settings. In the Account Settings window, you can see that mail will be delivered to the original location.
10. Click the Close button to close the Account Settings window.

    CLOSE Outlook.

INTERNET READY

If you subscribe to an email provider such as Earthlink or Roadrunner, your account comes with several mailboxes. Many people use one mailbox for business correspondence, one mailbox for personal correspondence, and one mailbox for shopping or other activities. Access your account on the Internet to configure a mailbox, add a data file in Outlook, and associate the mailbox with the data file in Outlook.

↻ Circling Back

Benjamin Martin is a corporate travel agent with Margie's Travel. Next month, the executives at Fourth Coffee are meeting in Orlando for a workshop. Ben must arrange travel for 15 executives from three different locations, make hotel reservations, and reserve vehicles for the 15 workshop participants.

⊙ Project 1: Create Tasks

To make the project more manageable, Ben creates tasks. He bases the tasks on the participants' home city. All participants will be booked on Blue Yonder Airlines.

GET READY. Launch Outlook if it is not already running.

1. If necessary, click the Tasks button in the Navigation pane to display the Tasks folder.
2. Click the New button on the Standard toolbar. A Task window is displayed.
3. In the Subject field, key Fourth Coffee - Make five reservations to Orlando from Chicago.
4. In the *Due date* field, key or select the date for next Friday.
5. In the Priority field, select High.
6. In the task note area, key the following list of names. These executives are travelling from Chicago to Orlando.
   Michael Allen
   Stephanie Conroy
   Bob Gage
   Roger Lengel
   Deborah Poe
7. Click the Save & Close button in the Actions group on the Ribbon.
8. Click the New button on the Standard toolbar. A Task window is displayed.
9. In the Subject field, key Fourth Coffee - Make five reservations to Orlando from Las Vegas.
10. In the *Due date* field, key or select the date for next Friday.
11. In the Priority field, select High.
12. In the task note area, key the following list of names. These executives are travelling from Las Vegas to Orlando.
    Grant Culbertson
    Brian Groth
    Jenny Lysaker
    Laura Norman
    Kevin Verboort
13. Click the Save & Close button in the Actions group on the Ribbon.
    LEAVE Outlook open for the next project.

Project 2: **Assign a Task**

Rachel Valdez has offered to help make the arrangements. Assign Rachel the task of making reservations from Seattle to Orlando.

GET READY. Launch Outlook if it is not already running.

The email addresses provided in these exercises belong to unused domains owned by Microsoft. When you send a message to these addresses, you will receive an error message stating that the message could not be delivered. Delete the error messages when they arrive.

1. If necessary, click the Tasks button in the Navigation pane to display the Tasks folder.
2. Click the New arrow and click the Task Request option.
3. Click the To field and key Rachel@margiestravel.com.
4. In the Subject field, key Fourth Coffee - Make five reservations to Orlando from Seattle.
5. In the *Due date* field, key or select the date for next Friday.
6. In the Priority field, select High.
7. In the task note area, key the following list of names. These executives are travelling from Seattle to Orlando.

   Terry Adams

   Kari Hension

   Tamara Johnston

   Paula Nartker

   Benjamin C. Willett
8. Click the Send button to send the task request.

   LEAVE Outlook open for the next project.

Project 3: **Assign Fourth Coffee Items to a Color Category**

Ben frequently handles large travel projects for Fourth Coffee. He decided to create a color category that matches the color category used for Fourth Coffee in his physical file cabinets.

GET READY. Launch Outlook if it is not already running.

1. If necessary, click the Tasks button in the Navigation pane to display the Tasks folder.
2. Click one of the Fourth Coffee tasks.
3. Click the Categorize button and click the All Categories option. The Color Categories window is displayed.
4. Click Orange Category in the list of categories. Click the Rename button. The Orange Category text becomes active.
5. Key Fourth Coffee and press Enter.
6. Click OK to rename the category. Close the Color Categories window.
7. Click the first Fourth Coffee task. Press Ctrl and click the other two Fourth Coffee tasks.
8. Click the Categorize button on the Standard toolbar. Click the Fourth Coffee category in the dropdown list.

   CLOSE Outlook.

Appendix A
Microsoft Certified Application Specialist (MCAS) Skills

Matrix Skill	Skill Number	Lesson Number
Send messages to multiple recipients	1.1.1	2
Reply to a message	1.1.2	2
Resend a message	1.1.3	2
Forward a message	1.1.4	2
Create and modify a personal signature	1.2.1	2
Create internal and external Out of Office Messages	1.2.2	2
Attach files and items to a message	1.3.1	2
Preview a message attachment in Outlook	1.3.2	2
Save attachments to a specific location	1.3.3	2
Open a message attachment	1.3.4	2
Set message sensitivity level	1.4.1	3
Set mail importance level	1.4.2	3
Digitally sign a message	1.5.1	3
Restrict permissions to a message	1.5.2	3
Encrypt a message	1.5.3	3
Add or remove a flag for follow up	1.6.1	3
Delay delivery of a message	1.6.2	3
Request read or delivery receipts	1.6.3	3
Create email polls using standard or custom voting buttons	1.6.4	3
Request that replies be sent to a specific email address	1.6.5	3
Show, hide, or move the Reading pane	1.7.1	1
Automatically preview messages	1.7.2	2
Create a one-time appointment, meeting, or event	2.1.1	8, 9
Create a recurring appointment, meeting, or event	2.1.2	8, 9
Create an appointment, meeting, or event from an email message	2.1.3	8, 9
Create an appointment, meeting, or event from a task	2.1.4	8
Mark an appointment, meeting, or event as private	2.1.5	8
Invite mandatory attendees to meetings	2.2.1	9
Invite optional attendees to meetings	2.2.2	9
Determine when attendees are available to meet	2.2.3	9
Track responses to meeting requests	2.2.4	9
Schedule meeting resources	2.2.5	9
Change a meeting time	2.3.1	9
Add a meeting attendee	2.3.2	9
Modify one instance of a recurring meeting	2.3.3	9
Send meeting updates only to new attendees	2.3.4	9
Cancel a meeting	2.3.5	9

continued

262

Matrix Skill	Skill Number	Lesson Number
Define your work week	2.4.1	10
Display multiple time zones	2.4.2	10
Change time zones	2.4.3	10
Add predefined holidays to the calendar	2.4.4	10
Configure free/busy privacy settings	2.5.1	10
Share your calendar with other Outlook users on your network	2.5.2	10
Send calendar information in an email message	2.5.3	10
Publish calendar information to Office Online	2.5.4	10
View a calendar shared by another Outlook user on your network	2.6.1	10
Subscribe to an Internet Calendar	2.6.2	10
View multiple calendars in overlay mode	2.6.3	10
Create recurring tasks	3.1.1	11
Create a task from a message	3.1.2	11
Set the status, priority, and percent complete of a task	3.1.3	11
Mark a task as complete	3.1.4	11
Mark a task as private	3.1.5	11
Assign tasks to others	3.2.1	11
Respond to an assigned task	3.2.2	11
Send a status report on an assigned task	3.2.3	11
Create a contact from a blank contact	4.1.1	6
Create a contact from a message header	4.1.2	6
Create a contact from an electronic business card	4.1.3	7
Save a contact received as a contact record	4.1.4	6
Modify contact information	4.1.5	6
Edit an electronic business card	4.2.1	7
Send an electronic business card to others	4.2.2	7
Use an electronic business card as an automatic signature in messages	4.2.3	7
Create and modify distribution lists	4.3	6
Create a secondary address book for personal contacts	4.4.1	7
Import a secondary address book from a file	4.4.2	7
Categorize messages, appointments, meetings, contacts, and tasks by color	5.1.1	5, 12
Sort Outlook items by color category	5.1.2	12
Create a data file	5.2.1	12
Add an Outlook data file to, or remove it from, a mail profile	5.2.2	12
Change data file settings	5.2.3	12
Create and move mail folders	5.3.1	4
Move mail between folders	5.3.2	4
Specify where a copy of a sent message is saved	5.3.3	2
Empty the Deleted Mail and Sent Items folders	5.3.4	4
Manage junk email messages	5.3.5	3
Search all email folders in a single search	5.4.1	3
Locate all items related to a specific person by searching	5.4.2	7

continued

Matrix Skill	Skill Number	Lesson Number
Locate tasks or contacts by searching	5.4.3	7, 11
Search Outlook items by category	5.4.4	12
Create a custom Search Folder	5.4.5	7
Create a rule to move email messages	5.5.1	5
Create a rule to categorize email	5.5.2	5
Create a rule to forward email	5.5.3	5
Create a rule to delete email	5.5.4	5
Show, hide, or minimize the To Do Bar	5.6.1	1
Customize the To Do Bar	5.6.2	1
Select the default format for messages	5.6.3	3
Configure Outlook to be accessible through the Web	5.6.4	10

TO USE MICROSOFT OFFICE PROFESSIONAL 2007, YOU WILL NEED:

COMPONENT	REQUIREMENT
Computer and processor	500 megahertz (MHz) processor or higher[1]
Memory	256 megabyte (MB) RAM or higher[1,2]
Hard disk	2 gigabyte (GB); a portion of this disk space will be freed after installation if the original download package is removed from the hard drive.
Drive	CD-ROM or DVD drive
Display	1024x768 or higher resolution monitor
Operating system	Microsoft Windows XP with Service Pack (SP) 2, Windows Server 2003 with SP1, or later operating system[3]
Other	Certain inking features require running Microsoft Windows XP Tablet PC Edition or later. Speech recognition functionality requires a close-talk microphone and audio output device. Information Rights Management features require access to a Windows 2003 Server with SP1 or later running Windows Rights Management Services.
	Connectivity to Microsoft Exchange Server 2000 or later is required for certain advanced functionality in Outlook 2007. Instant Search requires Microsoft Windows Desktop Search 3.0. Dynamic Calendars require server connectivity.
	Connectivity to Microsoft Windows Server 2003 with SP1 or later running Microsoft Windows SharePoint Services is required for certain advanced collaboration functionality. Microsoft Office SharePoint Server 2007 is required for certain advanced functionality. PowerPoint Slide Library requires Office SharePoint Server 2007. To share data among multiple computers, the host computer must be running Windows Server 2003 with SP1, Windows XP Professional with SP2, or later.
	Internet Explorer 6.0 or later, 32 bit browser only. Internet functionality requires Internet access (fees may apply).
Additional	Actual requirements and product functionality may vary based on your system configuration and operating system.

[1] 1 gigahertz (GHz) processor or higher and 512 MB RAM or higher recommended for **Business Contact Manager**. Business Contact Manager not available in all languages.
[2] 512 MB RAM or higher recommended for **Outlook Instant Search**. Grammar and contextual spelling in **Word** is not turned on unless the machine has 1 GB memory.
[3] Office Clean-up wizard not available on 64 bit OS.

action Determines what happens when a message meets the conditions defined in the rule.

address book Stores names and email addresses.

appointment A scheduled activity that does not require sending invitations to other people or resources.

archive Store messages in a separate folder to reduce the number of messages in the folders you use most often.

assign Transfer ownership of a task to another Outlook user.

attachment File sent as part of an email message.

attribute File characteristic such as size, subject, or sender.

AutoArchive Automatic function that archives messages.

AutoComplete Automatically completes the names of the months and days of the week.

AutoPreview Displays the first three lines of every message in the message list.

banner Text displayed at the top of a day to indicate an event.

busy An activity is scheduled for this time period. You are not available for other activities.

Calendar Snapshot A picture of your calendar at a specific moment.

cancel Delete a meeting.

Categorized Mail Standard Search Folder that displays messages that have an assigned color category.

color category Color assigned to an Outlook item, providing a way to visually indicate relationships among Outlook items.

compact Process that reduces the size of a data file.

complete A task is 100 percent finished.

condition Identifies the characteristics used to determine the messages affected by a rule.

contact Collection of information about a person or company.

Contacts folder Electronic organizer that enables you to create, view, and edit contact information.

Deferred Status indicating that a task has been postponed without changing the deadline or the percentage complete.

Deleted Items folder Deleted items are held in this folder until the folder is emptied. Emptying the folder removes the items from your computer.

delivery receipt Tells you that the message has arrived in the recipient's mailbox.

desktop shortcut An icon placed on the Windows desktop that launches an application, opens a folder, or opens a file.

digital ID Contains a private key that remains on your computer and a public key you give to your correspondents to verify that you are the message sender.

distribution list Group of individual contacts saved together as a single contact.

Drafts folder Outlook messages you write but haven't sent are stored in this folder.

duplicate contact Contact records containing the same information.

electronic business card Digital version of paper business cards. They can be sent as attachments, used as signatures, and used to create a contact record.

encryption Scrambles the text so that only the recipient with a key can decipher the message.

event An activity that lasts one or more days.

exception Identifies the characteristics used to exclude messages from being affected by the rule.

folder Common name for Outlook components.

free No activities are scheduled for this time period. You are available.

Greenwich Mean Time The time at the Royal Observatory in Greenwich in England.

group schedule Displays scheduling information for several people. Requires Microsoft Exchange 2000 or a more recent version of Microsoft Exchange.

Hypertext Markup Language (HTML) Formatting language that enables you to format text and insert items such as horizontal lines, pictures, and animated graphics.

import Bring information into a file from an external source.

In Progress Status indicating that work on the task has started.

Inbox folder By default, new messages are placed in this folder when they arrive.

InfoBar Banner containing information added automatically at the top of a message.

Internet Calendar Subscription A downloaded calendar that is automatically updated.

item A record stored in Outlook.

Junk E-Mail folder Messages identified as spam are placed in this folder when they arrive.

Large Mail A standard Search Folder that displays messages larger than 100 kilobytes.

mandatory attendee A person who must attend the meeting.

meeting A scheduled activity that requires sending invitations to other people or resources.

meeting organizer The person who creates the meeting and sends meeting invitations.

meeting request Outlook item that creates a meeting and invites attendees.

message header Text automatically added at the top of a message. The message header contains the sender's email address, the names of the servers used to send and transfer the message, the subject, the date, and other basic information about the message.

Microsoft Office Button Accesses the commands to open, save, print, and finish a document.

Navigation pane Provides access to Outlook components such as Contacts and the Calendar folder.

occurrence A single meeting in a series of recurring meetings.

optional attendee A person who should attend the meeting but whose presence is not required.

out of office You are not in the office during this time period.

Outbox folder Outgoing messages are held in this folder until you are connected to the Internet. When an Internet connection is detected, the message is sent.

Outlook Personal Folders file File containing stored Outlook data. It is identified by the .pst extension.

overlay mode Displays calendars on top of each other.

overlay stack Several calendars are displayed on top of each other.

owner Only Outlook user who can modify a task.

plain text Text without any formatting.

private Feature that protects the details of an activity from a casual observer, but it does not ensure privacy.

Quick Access Toolbar Toolbar that can be customized to contain commands from any tab.

read receipt Tells you that the message has been opened in the recipient's mailbox.

Reading pane Displays the text of a selected email message.

recurring appointment An appointment that occurs at regular intervals.

recurring meeting A meeting that occurs at regular intervals.

recurring task A task that must be completed at regular intervals.

resource An item or a location that can be invited to a meeting.

restore Make an item available for use. For example, moving an item out of the Deleted Items folder restores it for use.

retention rules Guidelines that determine the length of time correspondence must be kept.

Ribbon Contains commands organized into groups that are located on tabs.

Rich Text Format (RTF) Formatting system that uses tags to format text.

rule Defines an action that happens automatically when messages are received or sent.

ScreenTip Brief description of an item's purpose displayed when the mouse hovers on the item.

Search Folder A virtual folder that searches your email folders to locate items that meet the saved search criteria.

secondary address book The address book for an additional Contacts folder.

sensitivity Suggests how the recipient should treat the message and the type of information in the message. Sensitivity settings include normal, personal, private, and confidential.

Sent Items folder Items are automatically moved to this folder after they have been sent.

side-by-side mode Displays two or more calendars next to each other in the Calendar folder.

signature Text or images that are automatically placed at the end of outgoing messages.

sort Arrange items in a sequence based on specific criteria.

spam Unsolicited email sent to many email accounts.

spoofing Providing false information in a message header.

subject Topic of a message.

task An Outlook item that can be tracked from creation to completion.

task request Assigns a task to another user.

Tasks folder Store tasks in this folder.

template An existing rule provided by Outlook that contains specific pieces that can be customized to create new rules.

tentative An activity is scheduled for this time period, but the activity might not occur. You might be available for other activities.

time zone A geographic area using the same standard time.

To Do Bar New feature that summarizes information about appointments and tasks.

to-do item Any Outlook item flagged for follow-up.

Unread Mail Standard Search Folder that displays unread messages.

virtual folder A folder that does not contain the actual items it displays.

Wizard Consists of steps that walk you through completing a process in Microsoft Office applications.

work week The hours or days you work in a calendar week.

Index